THE GREEN GARDEN

Our attitude towards gardening has changed in recent years. Nowadays we know that we must look after our plot with some thought for the environment. This calls for such measures as using natural products when we can and not using planet-damaging ones.

In the following pages you will find organic fertilizers and organic pesticides, but this book is not just about organic gardening. The problem is that this concept covers only part of the safety needs of the living things in the garden.

Four biological groups meet in the plot at the back of the house. The first one of course, is the living garden. The soil and plants ... and until the 1960s it was the only one we really cared about. Then we came to realise that we had a second biological group there – the animal population. This wildlife had to be cared for, and with the 1980s came the realisation that our garden was also a tiny part of a much larger biological group – the environment as a whole.

And that's where we stand today, Garden friendly as ever and with a growing awareness that we must also be Animal friendly and Environment friendly. But there is also a fourth biological system in the garden and it does not have an active pressure group to campaign for its protection.

That fourth group consists of the people in the garden – you and the family. Every year several hundred thousand accidents occur in the area around the house and most need medical attention. This number is increasing but merely going organic is not the answer. These accidents are due to falls and not fertilizers, the result of shocks rather than sprays. So you must learn to be People friendly ... for your own sake. And that's what this book is about – the need to look after the garden, animals, environment ... and you.

THE FOUR FEATURES OF THE GREEN GARDEN

Garden Friendly
Improving the soil and caring for both the plants it supports and the non-living parts of the garden.
Pages 4–98

People Friendly
Avoiding harm to you and your family.
Pages 99–106

Animal Friendly
Avoiding harm to pets and wildlife.
Pages 107–124

Environment Friendly
Avoiding harm wherever possible to the environment and to the world's resources of materials in short supply.
Pages 125–127

Chapter 2

IMPROVING YOUR SOIL

It would be stupid to regard your soil as a mere anchorage for your plants – something to be dug when the surface is hard, to be watered when dry and weeded when it looks untidy, but not to be tended like a living thing.

Soil *is* a living thing, with millions of micro-organisms and small creatures in a single handful. It is an unbelievably complex part of the natural system, and it is the main factor in determining whether you will succeed as a gardener.

The day you started to garden on that plot of soil you disturbed the delicate balance between the various elements. However green you try to be, gardening upsets the Balance of Nature – a disturbing but inescapable fact. This means that the texture of the soil in bed, border or vegetable plot will be better or worse at this time next year. Which one depends on what you do before then.

Below is a plan to improve your soil. Follow it and you cannot fail to create a better crumb structure, an increase in the living population and better plant growth.

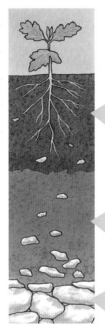

TOPSOIL is the fertile and living part of the soil. It is fertile because it contains nearly all of the humus, and it is living because it supports countless bacteria. These bacteria change various materials into plant foods. This layer varies from 5 cm in chalky soils to a metre or more in well-tended gardens. **When digging, this layer should be turned over, not buried under the subsoil.**

SUBSOIL lies under the topsoil. It can be recognised by its lighter colour, due to lack of humus. Soil structure is poor. **When digging, it should not be brought to the surface.**

BEDROCK is the mineral base below the subsoil. Usually it is the parent material of the soil above.

The 4 STEP plan to improve your soil

Soil is composed of four basic components – minerals, organic matter, air and water. The physical quality of the blend is known as the soil texture or the soil structure – but these two terms do not mean the same thing.

SOIL TEXTURE refers to the proportions of different-sized mineral particles which are present in the soil. When coarse (sand) particles predominate the texture is *light*. When minute (clay) particles are plentiful the soil is described as *heavy*. **It is not practical to change the soil texture.**

SOIL STRUCTURE refers to the way the mineral particles are joined together in the soil. They may be almost unconnected as in a very light soil with little organic matter or they may be grouped in clods, plates or crumbs in a heavy soil. A crumb structure is the ideal – such soil is described as *friable*. **It is possible to change the soil structure** by following in order the steps set out below.

STEP 1   **UNDERSTAND YOUR SOIL** Study the details of the components. See page 5.

STEP 2   **TEST YOUR SOIL** It is necessary to know whether your soil is light or heavy, acid or alkaline etc. See page 6.

STEP 3   **IMPROVE THE STRUCTURE** Each soil type calls for its own improvement routine. See page 8.

STEP 4   **ADD NUTRIENTS IF NECESSARY** Elements taken up by the plants or lost by leaching should be replaced. See page 18.

STEP 1 UNDERSTAND YOUR SOIL

MINERAL PARTICLES

The non-living skeleton of the soil which is derived from the decomposition of rocks by weathering. The fertility and size of these particles are governed by the type of parent rock.

Particle name is based on size. All **sands** have a gritty feel – **coarse sand** (0.6–2.0 mm in diameter) is distinctly gritty, **medium sand** (0.2–0.6 mm) feels like table salt and **fine sand** (0.02–0.2 mm) has a grittiness which is not easy to feel.

Silt (0.002–0.02 mm) has a silky or soapy feel.

Clay (less than 0.002 mm) feels distinctly sticky.

AIR

Air is essential for the support of plant life and desirable soil life – it is also required for the steady breakdown of organic matter which releases nutrients. Movement of air is necessary to avoid the build-up of toxic gases – this air movement takes place through the soil pores.

HUMUS

Plant and animal remains are gradually decomposed in the soil. The agents of decay are the bacteria and other microscopic organisms. They break down dead roots and underground insects as well as fallen leaves carried below the soil surface by worms. Partially decomposed organic matter with the horde of living and dead bacteria is known as **humus** to the gardener. For the scientist it has a much narrower meaning. True humus is the dark, jelly-like substance which binds mineral particles into crumbs – see page 10.

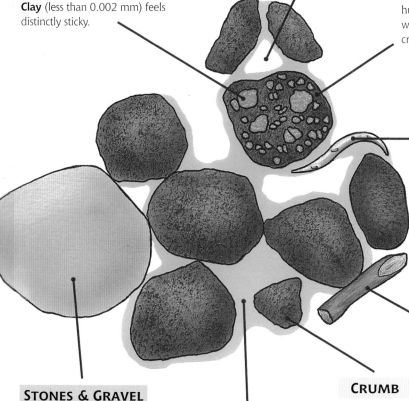

LIVING ORGANISMS

Millions of living organisms can be found in every gram of soil. Most are microscopic – bacteria, fungi, eelworms etc. Others are small but visible – insects, seeds and so on. Worms and beetles are easily seen – the largest and least welcome living thing you are likely to find is the mole.

DEAD ORGANIC MATTER

The soil is the graveyard for roots, fallen leaves, insects etc as well as the organic materials (humus makers) we add to enrich it. Dead organic matter is *not* humus until it has decomposed. It does, however, serve as the base material for high bacterial activity and humus production. With this decomposition both major nutrients and trace elements are released into the soil. Some types of dead material may take many years to decompose.

STONES & GRAVEL

These are particles larger than 2 mm in diameter. **Stones** usually refers to sizeable pieces of rock whereas **gravel** describes the smaller weathered fragments – but there is no precise distinction.

WATER-BASED SOLUTION

This is often shortened to **soil water** but it is in fact a solution containing many dissolved inorganic and organic materials. Some (e.g nitrates, phosphates and potassium salts) are plant nutrients.

CRUMB

Crumbs range from lentil- to pea-sized. The spaces between them are known as **pores**.

STEP 2 TEST YOUR SOIL

Knowing your soil type is more than a means of satisfying your idle curiosity –
the proper soil improvement programme (page 8) depends on correct identification.
The two essential tests are the walkover test and the hand test – both cost
nothing and take only a few minutes to complete. The pit test takes a little effort
and the soil kit test costs money, but both are worthwhile for the keen gardener.

The walkover test

START

Choose a day when the soil is moist and the plants are actively growing. Walk over the plot, looking carefully at the soil, weeds and plants.

Are there 30 or more large and small stones per sq metre? **YES** → **STONY SOIL**

NO

Is the soil dark brown or grey, rich in plant remains and spongy in texture? ← **YES** **PEATY SOIL**

NO

Continue with walkover test.

Afterwards carry out hand test on stone-free sample.

Continue with walkover test.

Continue with walkover test. Afterwards carry out hand test.

Are rushes and sedges present, or is the surface covered with moss and/or green slime?	**YES**	**POORLY-DRAINED SOIL**
Do the main weeds include dock, thistle, daisy, plantain or creeping buttercup? Are Rhododendron, Azalea, Heather or Camellia flourishing?	**YES**	**ACID SOIL**
Do the main weeds include clover? Are the leaves of Rhododendron, Azalea or Camellia yellow?	**YES**	**ALKALINE SOIL**
Do the main weeds include stinging nettle, sow-thistle, fat-hen, chickweed or groundsel?	**YES**	**FERTILE SOIL**

The pit test

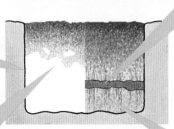

START

Choose a day when the soil is moist. Dig a pit 60 cm x 60 cm x 60 cm. This pit can be used for the drainage test (see page 17).

Is the topsoil dark, with white subsoil a few inches below the surface?

YES **CHALKY SOIL**

Is a sub-surface pan present – a hard layer with the texture and firmness of baked clay? The colour is sometimes (but not always) rusty brown.

YES

POORLY-DRAINED SOIL

YES

Are there blue or rusty brown streaks in the subsoil?

The hand test

START

Is the soil sticky on a wet day – does it cling to your footwear in large lumps under such conditions? **NO** → Pick up a handful of soil. If it is dry, moisten just enough to hold the soil together. Knead in the palm of the hand to break down lumps.

Does the soil feel or sound gritty? **YES** → **NO** Is it possible to roll the soil into a ball? **NO** → **SAND**

YES (down from START)

Pick up a handful of soil. If it is dry, moisten just enough to hold the soil together. Knead in the palm of the hand to break down lumps.

NO (from gritty) → Form the soil into a ball. Is the ball weak and easily broken and does the soil feel silky or soapy? **YES** → **SILT LOAM**

YES (roll into a ball) → Is it difficult to make a ball and get it to stick together? **YES** → **LOAMY SAND**

NO → **SANDY LOAM**

NO (from silky/soapy question) → The soil forms a strong ball. Now squeeze a small quantity with a sliding motion between finger and thumb.

SANDY CLAY

YES → The clay content is high – the soil is very sticky when wet. Is it also gritty?

NO → **CLAY**

Does the soil surface become shiny? **YES** → (to Sandy Clay path) **NO** → Is it hard to change the shape of a soil ball and can the soil be easily rolled out into threads? **YES** → **CLAY LOAM**

NO → **MEDIUM LOAM**

The soil kit test

There are several kits available for testing the nitrogen, phosphates, potash and pH content of the soil. Some involve test-tubes and indicator solutions – others are based on a probe which is inserted into the ground. These kits provide a reasonably accurate way of discovering whether your soil needs liming or not (page 17), but are less useful for determining fertilizer needs (page 18). The problem lies in the difficulty of translating the results into practical plant nutrient requirements.

STEP 3 IMPROVE THE STRUCTURE

If you are lucky you will have a medium textured (loamy) soil. It will hold water, but not too much. It will drain, but not too quickly. All you will have to do is to lay down some form of humus mulch (page 14) around the plants each year and feed if it is necessary.

Unfortunately most soils are either sandy or clayey – their drawbacks are described below. In order to create a crumb structure a combination of techniques may be required and it cannot be done overnight or in a single season – there is no magic formula.

If the ground is compacted or has not been previously cultivated it will be necessary to dig in the autumn, but as explained later it should not be an annual routine. Applying humus will be a yearly task, and adding some form of calcium may be necessary. First of all, look up your soil type below and see what you have to do.

Heavy (Clayey) Soil

Good points: Generally well supplied with plant foods which are not leached away by rain. Good water retention.

Bad points: Difficult to cultivate under most conditions. Cakes and cracks in dry weather – may waterlog in wet weather. Cold – flowers and vegetables appear later than average.

If the plot has not been cultivated before then dig thoroughly in autumn (see page 9) to expose the clods to winter frost – a generous quantity of organic matter should be incorporated at this time. Apply lime if the soil is acid or gypsum if it is not to improve the structure. Do not plant out until the soil is reasonably dry. Mulch established plants.

Medium (Loamy) Soil

Good points: Good crumb structure – possesses all the advantages, to a lesser degree, or both heavy and light soils.

Bad points: Surface capping takes place in wet weather if the silt content is high.

Try to keep it as it is, with regular dressings of humus-making materials and nutrients. Occasional applications of calcium will be necessary – dig only if the soil is compacted.

Light (Sandy) Soil

Good points: Easy to work, even when wet. Free-draining in winter. Warm – suitable for early flowers and vegetables.

Bad points: Usually short of plant foods. Frequent watering is necessary in summer or shallow-rooted plants may die. Cools down rapidly at night.

Water and food shortage are regular problems during the growing season. The structure is generally poor – lack of organic matter means that the soil is not crumbly. Digging is not the answer – the solution is to incorporate plenty of humus-making material into the top 5–10 cm in late winter or early spring. Mulching is vital to conserve moisture and reduce leaching of plant nutrients.

Chalky Soil

Good points: Best soil type for some shrubs and many alpines. Usually free-draining and warm enough for early crops.

Bad points: Sticky and soft in wet weather – often parched in summer. Nutrients may be deficient – especially trace elements. Too alkaline for many plants.

Digging must be kept shallow – add plenty of humus-making materials. Regular feeding will be necessary. Green manuring (see page 11) is a great help – so is adding topsoil if the area is small. Although the bedrock is chalk, the soil is occasionally acid.

Digging:
"Dig once if you have to – and do it properly."

Any general gardening book will list the merits of digging the vegetable plot or flower bed. The upper layer of soil is broken up and clods are exposed to the elements. Compost or manure can be incorporated and annual weeds are buried. In addition the roots of perennial weeds are exposed and can be removed. The problems with digging are sometimes not mentioned. Dig at the wrong time and you can harm the soil – dig in the wrong way and you can harm yourself. In shallow soil there is the real danger of burying the fertile top 10–15 cm and bringing up infertile clay or sand.

You should follow a no-dig programme. This consists of an initial turning over of the soil by digging if the ground has not been cultivated before or if the soil in an established plot is heavy and has been badly compacted. Follow the technique shown below. A layer of organic matter (1 bucketful per sq metre) should be spread over the surface and then forked in before you begin to dig. After that the annual treatment should be a no-dig programme using humus which will build up the fertility over the years.

1 Choose the right season – early winter for most soils and early spring for light land. Choose the right day – the ground should be moist but not waterlogged nor frozen.

2 Wear clothes that are warm – you should not be uncomfortably hot nor cold when digging. Make sure your back is fully covered and wear stout shoes.

3 Use the right equipment – a spade for general work or a fork if the soil is very heavy or stony. Carry a scraper and use it to keep the blade or prongs clean.

4 Try to keep your back straight – avoid any sudden twists from the hips and on no account strain harder than you are used to doing at home or at work.

5
Drive in the spade vertically. Press (do not kick) down on the blade. This should be at right angles to the trench.

6
The next cut should be parallel to the trench, about 15–20 cm behind the face. Do not take larger slices.

7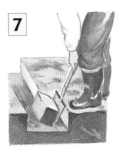
Pull steadily (do not jerk) on the handle so as to lever the soil on to the blade. Lift up the block of soil.

8
With a flick of the wrist turn the earth into the trench in front – turn the spadeful right over to bury the weeds.

9 Work for 10 minutes if you are reasonably fit but out of condition, then sit down or do a non-strenuous job until you feel rested. Work for 20 minutes between rests if you are fit and used to physical exercise. For most people 30 minutes digging is quite enough for the first day.

Large Areas

Think twice before lifting a spade if you have a large area of hard and compacted earth to turn over. A typical example is the ground left by the builders. Hire a cultivator which can work to a depth of 20 cm or call in a contractor.

Adding Humus:
"Humus is not what you think it is."

Soil bacteria hold the key to soil fertility. When alive they produce heat and transform organic materials into simple chemicals. When dead they release these nutrients plus colloidal gums. To the scientist it is these gums and not decomposing plant remains which are **humus** – the magical material which cements clay, silt and sand particles together to form soil crumbs.

Under natural conditions there is a rough balance which maintains the organic level of the soil. In a fertile soil there is a minimum of 5 per cent organic matter. Under cultivation this organic content decreases and the humus level falls. This means that you have to add **humus makers**. All are bulky organic materials which add to the humus content of the soil. When in addition these materials release plant nutrients they can be called **manures**. This means that garden compost and seaweed are manures and bark is not.

Types of Humus Maker

Raw Humus Makers

Examples: Grass clippings, fresh dung, dug-in weeds.
These organic materials contain the elements necessary to stimulate bacterial growth. Heat is produced and soil structure is improved.

Using raw humus makers is a good way of warming the earth and raising its humus content – provided you allow for the drawbacks. The rapid build-up of bacteria robs the soil of nitrogen – always add a nitrogen-rich fertilizer. Allow some time before planting, and keep the raw humus maker well away from roots.

Matured Humus Makers

Examples: Well-rotted manure, compost. These organic materials do not contain the elements necessary to stimulate bacterial growth. They have been produced from raw humus makers by composting.

The warming effect is lost but this is outweighed by the advantages. Tender roots are not damaged and the nitrogen in the soil is not locked up. Unlike the types described below these materials have more than a simple opening-up effect. The humus which was produced during the composting process promotes crumb formation when they are added to the soil.

Fibrous Materials

Examples: Peat, coir bark, sawdust. These organic materials are rich in cellulose but lack sugars and starches. There is little or no bacterial activity and so they are ineffective humus makers. Peat and coir act as sponges, improving air- and water-holding capacity. Conservationists worry about the wholesale use of peat as a general soil treatment, as supplies are limited. Peat decomposes slowly or hardly at all, but sawdust and some bark products break down more quickly. Add a nitrogen-rich fertilizer when using sawdust.

Building up the humus level

Fork in: Spread a matured humus maker over the soil in late winter/early spring and fork into the surface.

Maintaining the humus level

Mulch: Spread a layer of a matured humus maker or fibrous material over the surface in late spring when the soil is warm and moist – see page 16.

Q Humus Maker or Fertilizer – which is best?
A Neither – they are partners.

Humus Makers are bulky organic materials used in large amounts – **they improve the structure of the soil.**

Nutrients are usually present, but this plant food content is usually low, slow-acting and wrongly balanced. Fertilizers are often necessary to get the full benefit.

Fertilizers are materials containing one or more major plant nutrients – **they improve the nutrient content of the soil.**

They do not make a significant contribution to the humus content. Humus makers are generally necessary to get the full benefit. See pages 19–20 for a list of organic and mineral fertilizers.

Humus Makers

Humus maker	Nitrogen % N	Phosphates % P$_2$O$_5$	Potash % K$_2$O	Uses	Notes
Bark or Cocoa shell	$1/4$	trace	trace	Mulch	See page 15 for mulching details
Coir	$1/2$	trace	trace	Mulch	There are several peat substitutes these days – bark, cocoa shell etc. They are all fibrous or shell-based materials which break down slowly in the soil, but coir has the advantage of holding both water and air
Compost	$1 1/2$	2	$1/2$	Fork in 1 bucket per sq metre or use as a mulch	See page 15 for mulching details
Domestic waste	1	$1/2$	$1/2$	Fork in 1 bucket per sq metre	Many councils turn the waste they collect into a product for the gardener. Metal, glass, etc is removed and the organic matter is then composted before being offered for sale
Farmyard manure	$1/2$	$1/4$	$1/2$	Fork in 1 bucket per sq metre or use as a mulch	Before use, stack it under some form of roofing, cover with about 10 cm of soil and leave to decay. It is ready when the smell has disappeared and the straw is no longer recognisable
Green manure	2	$1/4$	$3/4$	Dig in summer or autumn	Green manure is a crop grown for digging in and providing humus for chalky or sandy soil. Apply a fertilizer and sow rape or mustard in April–July. Dig in 2 months after germination
Leafmould	$1/2$	$1/4$	$1/4$	Fork in 1 bucket per sq metre or use as a mulch	Collect leaves in autumn (oak and beech are the favourites) and build a heap – 15 cm layers of leaves between 2.5 cm layers of soil. Composting is slow – leave for a year
Mushroom compost	$1/2$	$1/4$	$1/2$	Fork in 1 bucket per sq metre or use as a mulch	Used to be stable manure plus soil, straw and chalk – nowadays it is composted straw. A useful material for enriching sandy soil. Do not use if you intend to grow lime haters
Peat	$3/4$	trace	trace	Use as a potting compost ingredient??	! See page 126
Poultry manure	2	$1 1/2$	1	Use as a compost ingredient	Fresh poultry manure is rich in nutrients – unfortunately it is also rich in materials which can be toxic to young roots. The best plan is to add poultry manure to the compost heap
Sawdust	$1/4$	trace	trace	Use as a compost ingredient	Cheap, but use with care. It will rob the soil of nitrogen if forked into the soil or used as a mulch. Another problem is that it may contain toxic resins. See page 13 for composting details
Seaweed	$1/4$	$1/4$	$1/2$	Dig in 1 bucket per sq metre before planting	An excellent manure maker – free for the taking if you live near the sea. Dig in without composting – both the humus and trace element content of the soil will be enriched. Wash off the salt before use
Stable manure	$3/4$	$1/4$	$1/2$	Fork in 1 bucket per sq metre or use as a mulch	Best type of manure for heavy soils. Should contain plenty of straw. Do not use it immediately. Stack it under cover for several months – see farmyard manure above
Straw	$1/2$	trace	$3/4$	Use as a compost ingredient	Straw is an active humus maker when plenty of nitrogen is present, but it is not a good idea to add it directly to the soil. It often contains weedkillers. See page 13 for composting details

Making Compost:
"No green garden can be without its compost heap."

The need for a plentiful supply of organic matter in order to improve the soil has been stressed in several parts of this book. Relying on shop-bought material is far too expensive a proposition, and picking up free animal manure at the farm or stable gate is only feasible in out-of-town areas and usually in limited quantity.

The answer is to make compost from unwanted plant material. Unfortunately the instructions in many books are based on the use of woody matter such as straw, dead leaves etc. We read about helpful lime, harmful soil, the need to turn and the value of using a nitrogen-rich activator. But in most gardens the starting point is almost entirely grass clippings from the weekly mowing of the lawn, and for grass clippings you have to use a completely different procedure. The technique on the next page was tested by Horticultural Societies all over the country.

What goes in

Successful composting takes place only when there is intense bacterial and fungal activity. Heat is generated and humus is formed. For this to take place you need a mix of materials with 30 parts of carbon to 1 part of nitrogen. As a very rough guide, waste plant material which is orange, brown or black is rich in carbon, and material which is soft and green is rich in nitrogen. If you use just grass clippings, green weeds and a few prunings then you will have a mix which contains too much nitrogen for active bacterial growth. The secret of good compost is to incorporate some carbon-rich material as outlined in the 5 step technique on page 13.

In addition to lawn clippings you can use vegetable and flower stalks, leaves, annual weeds, peat, soft hedge clippings, bracken, straw, smashed-up brassica stalks, tea leaves, peelings, household vegetable waste and egg shells. Do not use twigs, roots of perennial weeds, badly diseased plants or meat and fish waste from the kitchen.

Grass is the basic ingredient to which is added carbon-rich materials (shredded prunings, shredded paper, etc).

What comes out

Compost made from grass cuttings without some form of insulation and without a rainproof cover is a slimy green mess which has little value in the garden. Compost made by the method outlined here is quite different. The materials slowly change as a result of heat and intense bacterial activity and the compost is ready when it is crumbly and there is no unpleasant smell. It will be brown rather than green and the individual ingredients will not be easily recognisable. Compost started in the spring or summer should be ready in late autumn or the following spring. Autumn compost is for forking into the soil – spring material is excellent for mulching.

It is wise to test compost made from clippings from a weedkiller-treated lawn. Mix a sample with some seed compost and sow cress or radish seed – normal germination indicates that the garden compost is safe to use.

The materials change and the compost is ready to use when it is brown and crumbly.

The Compost Container

The Good Container

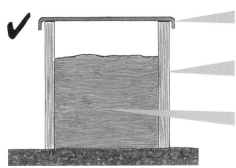

Waterproof cover Rain must be kept out of the heap. Use a rigid cover or a sheet of plastic

Thick walls Wood, breeze blocks, solid plastic and bricks are all suitable. Keeping the heat in is one of the secrets of making good compost

Large One big one always beats two small ones

The Poor Container

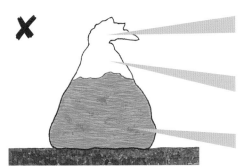

Open top Rainwater stops bacterial activity – secondary fermentation turns the compost into green, smelly sludge

Thin plastic or wire netting Vital heat is lost – it is this heat which kills weed seeds and breaks down organic matter. Put boards or bags round the sides if you can or lean it against a wall – line wire bins or plastic bags with old newspapers

Small Contents cool down too quickly

The 5 STEP Way to Make Compost

Look carefully at the features of a good container before you begin. It should be as large as practical – you cannot turn a few barrowloads of grass cuttings into true compost.

STEP 1   **Put down a layer of greenstuff** This layer should be about 25 cm deep but an exact depth is not critical. The layer should be flat and not heaped up.

STEP 2   **Sprinkle on a layer of carbon-rich material** This stage is necessary if you are making the heap with soft green material such as grass clippings. There are various carbon-rich materials you can use – wood meal made from prunings ground by a shredder is excellent and so are sawdust, straw, shredded paper and dry leaves. This layer should be about 1 cm thick. Turn into the surface of the greenstuff layer with a fork.

STEP 3   **Cover with a thin layer of soil** Forget the traditional advice to keep soil out of the compost heap. This thin soil layer provides a multitude of bacteria, mops up undesirable gases and absorbs water.

STEP 4   **Repeat steps 1–3** Continue to build up layers until all the clippings etc have been used up.

STEP 5   **Cover the top** The last step before leaving the heap is to replace the lid to keep off the rain. This step is vital. Repeat steps 1–5 next week when you have another load of grass clippings.

Mulching:

"Mulching really comes into its own in the green garden."

Details about the basic techniques of gardening appear in every textbook which sets out to show you what to do with your plot. Digging, planting, pruning, watering, weeding and so on are dealt with at length, but the virtues and practices of mulching often receive little or no attention.

All mulches reduce the growth of weeds – some stop weed growth completely and the remainder make weed control a relatively simple matter. As shown below the humus mulch bestows a host of additional benefits – improved soil structure, less need to water in summer etc. Yet most gardeners do not mulch at all, and those who do generally misunderstand and underuse the technique. Basically a mulch is a layer of material placed around plants in order to improve the soil and plant growth and/or to suppress weed growth. In this section you will learn why, where, how and when to mulch.

The Humus Mulch

Humus mulches are bulky organic materials which improve the soil, stimulate plant growth, conserve moisture and suppress the growth of annual weeds. Many materials are suitable and the usual ones are listed on the next page. Choice depends on locality, cost etc – composted manure is the best one for soil improvement, chipped bark the best for mulching, and garden compost the cheapest.

Vegetables are protected from rain splashes bouncing off the soil – a much ignored problem

Annual weed growth is suppressed – those which break through are easily removed by hand pulling and so there is no need to hoe. Vigorous perennial weeds will be able to break through – consider a weed control mulch (page 98) if they are a serious problem

A small amount of plant food is provided by some mulches such as well-rotted manure and garden compost, but this is not enough to meet the needs of most plants, so some extra feeding may be needed

Some pests and diseases are kept in check. Obviously root flies are deterred and so are moles. U.S research indicates that eelworm numbers are reduced

Soil structure is improved for a number of reasons. Humus is added, earthworm activity is increased and soil capping by rain or watering is eliminated

The soil is kept warmer than uncovered ground in winter – a definite benefit for many plants

The soil below is kept moist in summer reducing the need to water. It is also kept cooler than soil without a mulch, and research has shown that this moist and cool root zone promotes more active growth than plants in unmulched areas

14

What to use

Peat

Orthodox organic gardeners will not use peat under any circumstances for the reasons set out on page 126. There are better materials for forking in and mulching, but some green gardeners still prefer to use potting composts which contain peat rather than ones based on peat substitutes.

Bark or Cocoa shell

Bark is a better choice than peat. The chips should be 1–5 cm long. Cocoa shell is a good alternative but can be smelly when wet. Use them in the way described on page 16 – they are the most attractive mulches for use around trees and shrubs. Both will last on the surface for 2–3 years.

Well-rotted manure

Manure is less attractive than bark as a surface cover, but it is available very cheaply at the farm or stable gate and is the best soil improver of all. It must be well-rotted, and quality from an unknown source can be a problem – weed seeds may be present. Annual topping-up is necessary.

Compost

Garden compost is not only free – it gets rid of grass clippings, soft cuttings, old stems etc. It must be made properly as poor compost may be full of weed seeds – see page 13. Several brands of ready-made compost based on bark and green material are available.

Straw

Straw is easy and cheap to obtain in rural areas, and is widely used as a mulch both in grand estates and tiny allotments. It is rather unsightly, however, around the plants in a bed or border in the front garden. Two problems – weed seeds are often present and it can only be used with a nitrogen-rich fertilizer.

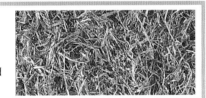

Old growing compost

Spent peat compost has the virtues and limitations of peat with the added value of having some nutrients present. Examples include the contents of used growing bags, spent tomato compost (suitable for nearly all plants) and spent mushroom compost (not for use around lime-hating plants).

Grass clippings

Short clippings from the lawn can be used as a shallow mulch – no more than 3 cm. Keep away from the crowns of the plants. Top up as necessary during early summer. Two warnings – do not use if flowering weeds were present nor if the grass has been treated with a weedkiller.

How and when to mulch

Humus mulches are insulators which help to retain the conditions occurring at the time they are put down. This means that the soil should be just right for active growth – warm and moist and not cold and dry.

The standard time for applying a humus mulch is May. Before you begin putting down organic matter it is necessary to prepare the soil surface. Remove debris and hand pull or hoe annual weeds. It is also important to get rid of perennial weeds. For the green gardener this involves digging them out to remove all the roots you can find – for the not-so-green gardener there is glyphosate to spray over the leaves. The final job is to apply a general fertilizer if necessary and rake in lightly.

The soil is moist, warm and free from weeds – it is now time to spread a 5–8 cm layer of the chosen mulching material over the ground around the stems. This covered area should extend for about 45 cm around the centre of a shrub and for 75 cm around the trunk of a moderate-sized tree. If mulching material is plentiful you can cover the whole bed or border, but with both partial and all-over cover you must make sure that the mulch does not come right up to the stems. A build-up of moist organic matter against the shoots can lead to rotting. Do not disturb this layer during the summer months. If weeds do appear pull out by hand or paint with glyphosate gel.

Some people fork in the mulch during October and then allow the soil to warm up in the spring before applying a new mulch. This is a lot of work, however, and so it is more usual to leave the mulch in place and top up as necessary in May.

Where to mulch

The humus mulch is generally used around growing plants. It is a multi-purpose layer of organic matter to protect the soil surface, cut down the need for watering and weeding and improve the soil structure. The plants which are recommended for mulching are trees, shrubs, roses and hardy perennials. Vegetables are not often given a humus mulch but are sometimes grown through a weed control mulch (page 98) and annuals are either unmulched or surrounded by a thick layer of grass clippings during the summer months. With young trees and shrubs weeds around the stems can be a serious problem, and so a circle or square of weed control mulch is placed around the stem and then covered with gravel or bark chippings. Squares of bituminous felt ('tree spats') can be bought for this purpose.

Weed Control Mulch

This type of mulch uses a plastic membrane with a covering of bark or gravel. It does not really belong here as its purpose is to control weeds rather than to increase the organic content of the soil. It is perhaps most successful when you are making a new shrub border, but it does have a place in the mixed border, vegetable plot etc. Used properly it can make most weeding a thing of the past – see page 98 for details.

Liming:
"It may be needed, but check before you start."

Tiny particles of clay group together in the presence of calcium to form crumbs which improve soil structure. **To supply calcium use either lime or gypsum** – which one depends on the acidity of the soil and the plants you grow. This improvement is short lived and these crumbs must be 'fixed' by humus.

LIME

(calcium hydroxide or calcium carbonate) This calcium source reduces acidity

Various forms are available. **Chalk** and **ground limestone** are slow-acting. **Dolomite limestone** contains magnesium – this is the recommended type. **Calcified seaweed** (coral) is the 'organic' form – long-lasting and expensive. **Hydrated lime** (slaked lime) is by far the most popular type. It is cheaper, stronger and quicker-acting than the others

Do test your soil before liming – see page 7. If an excessive amount is used, humus breaks down too quickly and some plant leaves turn yellow because of the lock-up of iron and manganese

Benefits

Improves structure of heavy soil
Calcium binds clay particles into soil crumbs

Serves as one of the plant foods
Calcium is needed in moderate amounts by plants

Frees nutrients
Elements locked up by clay particles are freed

Discourages some soil pests
Examples include club root, slugs and wireworms

Neutralises acidity
Very few plants grow well in acid soil and bacteria and earthworms decline in acid soil

GYPSUM (calcium sulphate)

This calcium source *does not* reduce acidity

Sold under various trade names – sometimes used as a gypsum/dolomite limestone mixture

It is used where heavy soil is not acid, or where the soil is acid but is used for lime-hating plants such as Rhododendrons

HOW MUCH?

LIME	
Very Acid	850 g/sq m
Acid	550 g/sq m
Neutral	275 g/sq m
Alkaline	Do not use
GYPSUM	275 g/sq m

WHEN? **Lime:** Autumn or early spring if a humus maker used. **Gypsum:** Autumn. Repeat in spring if soil structure poor.

Improving Drainage:
"Poor drainage can be a plant killer."

Faulty drainage can be a plant killer. Stagnant water around the roots starves them of air. Helpful bacterial activity is slowed down and harmful organisms flourish. **Poor drainage** is associated with heavy topsoil. Water moves very slowly, and so the answer is to improve the structure by cultural means. **Impeded drainage** is a more serious problem, as the downward movement of water is not just slowed down – it is blocked. There are three causes – non-porous rock below the soil, a sub-surface pan below the topsoil (page 6) or a high water table. See Artificial Aids below.

Cultural aids: The crumbs created by autumn digging do not last – you must build up a permanent crumb structure by applying heavy dressings of a humus maker at regular intervals. Add lime if the soil is acid – use gypsum if it is neutral or alkaline.

Artificial aids: You may be able to break up a sub-surface pan with a fork or pickaxe, but if you have a non-porous bedrock or a high water table, then there is a serious problem. Laying drains or building a soakaway is usually impractical – the easiest way is to add topsoil or create raised beds.

Drainage Test

Dig a hole 60 cm x 60 cm x 60 cm deep at the lowest part of the garden. Look inside the hole after heavy rain and see how much water is present at the bottom.

An hour after rain – no water in the hole	**Excessive drainage** If topsoil is sandy – addition of humus is essential
A few days after rain – no water in the hole	**Satisfactory drainage** No help is needed
A few days after rain – some water still present at the bottom of the hole	**Poor drainage** One or more cultural aids are needed
A few days after rain – water has seeped in from surrounding soil; hole partly filled	**Impeded drainage** An artificial aid as well as cultural aids may be needed

STEP 4 ADD NUTRIENTS IF NECESSARY

The basic difference between humus maker and fertilizer is outlined on page 10. Some devout organic gardeners refrain from using any fertilizer, relying solely on green manuring, animal manure, forked-in compost and/or surface mulching to add nutrients to the soil. They do have a point – many trees and deep-rooted shrubs live their whole lives quite happily in the garden without the use of fertilizers.

There are situations, however, where feeding is necessary. The soil may be starved of nutrients or the plants may be shallow-rooted. The fruits and flowers borne by the plants may be a drain on the soil's reserves, and for the sake of appearances the natural source of minerals (fallen leaves, decaying weeds etc) may be removed from the surface.

In these circumstances we need to add those elements which the plants use in large amounts – nitrogen, phosphorus and potash, and in some cases it is beneficial to apply them at fairly regular intervals. To do this we use a fertilizer.

There are three basic types of fertilizer – organic, mineral and chemical. The differences are outlined on the next page, and proprietary brands are often a mixture of two or all three types. Organics break down in the soil in the same way as chemicals and plant roots take up the same simple salts from both types. But the organic/mineral supporters believe there are differences – for example the organic and mineral plant foods tend to stay longer in the soil and the nitrate release is slower.

Plant nutrient	Plants most in need	Soils most in need	Signs of shortage
Nitrogen (N) the Leaf Maker	Grass • Vegetables grown for their leaves • Root-bound plants	Sandy soils • Rainy areas	Stunted growth • Small, pale green leaves • Weak stems
Phosphates (P_2O_5) the Root Maker	Young plants • Root vegetables • Fruit and seed crops	Sandy soils	Stunted growth • Small leaves with a purplish tinge • Low fruit yield
Potash (K_2O) the Flower and Fruit Maker	Fruit • Flowers • Potatoes	Sandy soils	Brown leaf edges • Low fruit yield – fruit and flowers poorly coloured Low disease resistance
Magnesium (Mg)	Roses • Tomatoes	Sandy soils • Peaty soils • K_2O-rich soils	Yellow or brown patches between the veins of older leaves • Young leaves may fall
Iron (Fe) Manganese (Mn)	Rhododendrons • Azaleas • Camellias	Chalky soils	Yellowing of young leaves
Others (Sulphur, Calcium, Boron, Zinc, Copper, Molybdenum)	Various	Various	Various – the use of humus makers, fertilizers and liming materials generally supplies sufficient amounts

Organic Fertilizers

These materials are of animal or vegetable origin. They are generally slow-acting, providing plants with a steady supply of food over a long period. Not likely to scorch leaves. Nitrogen is released by bacterial activity, so speed of action depends on soil conditions.

Mineral Fertilizers

These materials are obtained from neither plants nor animals – they are minerals mined from the earth. Some of them (e.g gypsum and chalk) provide calcium. The others supply nitrogen, phosphorus and/or potash – they may be quick- or slow-acting.

Chemical Fertilizers

These are manufactured materials and have earned the titles of 'synthetic' or 'artificial' fertilizers. They are generally quick-acting, providing plants with a boost when used as a top-dressing. Examples include sulphate of ammonia and superphosphate of lime.

Organic & Mineral Solid Feeds

Fertilizer	Nitrogen % N	Phosphates % P_2O_5	Potash % K_2O	Speed of action	Application rate	Notes
Blood meal	12	trace	trace	fq	35 g-70 g/m²	Use as a top-dressing around growing plants in spring/summer. Quick-acting under glass
Bone flour	1	20-28	0	fq	70 g-140 g/m²	Lower in nitrogen and dustier than Bone meal, but it acts more quickly
Bone meal	4	20	0	s	70 g-140 g/m²	Apply at soil preparation or planting time. Use a 'heat-treated' grade for safety
Chilian potash nitrate	15	0	10	q	35 g-70 g/m²	Use as a quick-acting top-dressing in spring/early summer – not generally available
Fish meal	6–10	6–12	1	s-fq	70 g-140 g/m²	Apply at soil preparation or planting time in winter or spring. Potash usually very low
Fish, blood & bone	3½	8	trace	fq	70 g-140 g/m²	The most popular organic compound fertilizer. Apply just before planting or around growing plants
Hoof & horn meal	14	2	0	s-fq	70 g-140 g/m²	A good source of organic nitrogen – slower than Blood meal. Apply in spring or early summer
Poultry manure (dried)	4	3	2	s-fq	70 g-275 g/m²	High rate is used at soil preparation time – low rate is for around growing plants
Rock phosphate	0	30	0	s	275 g/m²	Slow release source of phosphates – lasts for about 3 years. Good for acid soils
Rock potash	0	0	10–12	s	275 g/m²	Slow release source of potash – lasts for about 3 years. Good for light soils
Seaweed meal	3	trace	2	fq	70 g/m²	Expensive, but a good source of trace elements. Use around plants in spring or summer
Shoddy	10	trace	trace	s	550 g/m²	Waste wood and/or cotton. A poor humus maker, but provides nitrogen over a period of years
Soot	3–6	0	0	q	140 g/m²	Must be weathered before use – no longer popular & not recommended as toxins are present
Wood ash	0	trace	5–10	q	140 g-275 g/m²	Use young wood – keep in a dry place. Not recommended for chalky soils
						s = slow; fq = fairly quick; q = quick

Organic Liquid Feeds

One of the basic maxims of organic gardening is that you should 'feed the soil and not the plants'. The aim should be to create a fertile base before planting so that little or no extra feeding will be necessary, but there are times where extra nutrients may be required. Typical examples include plants where the root action may be weak or soils where trace elements may be lacking. A vegetable crop may be producing a heavy crop or the plants may be in a pot or tub which has contained the same compost for a considerable time.

Solids such as bone meal are popular, but the traditional organic gardener generally turns to a liquid feed – some can be used for spraying on the leaves as a foliar feed. A quick-acting boost is provided, but unlike solid fertilizers such as fish, blood and bone the effect will not be long-lasting.

Liquid Manure

Half fill a cloth bag with animal manure – use fresh material if possible. Sheep manure is considered the best one to use, but cow, goat and horse manure are suitable.

Tie the top of the bag with twine and then suspend it in a barrel, water butt or plastic dustbin. Add water and then tie the end of the twine to a pole so that the bag is immersed in the water.

Aim for a ratio of 1 pail of manure: 3 pails of water. Leave for about 2 weeks – the liquid manure is now ready for use.

Dilute the liquid to the colour of straw before use – do not use as a foliar feed and do not spray on to the parts of vegetables which will be eaten.

Black Jack is made by adding grass clippings to the manure.

Compost Tea

You can make this liquid feed if animal manure is not available – it once again provides a well-balanced if weak concentration of nitrogen, phosphates and potash together with a wide range of trace elements.

Using garden compost follow the steps outlined for liquid manure. Once again dilute the liquid feed to the colour of straw and use the residue in the bag for mulching or adding to the compost heap.

Comfrey Tea

The advantage of this feed is that it is higher in nutrients than the other types described here – it is a good source of potash and trace elements.

Use a container with a tap at the bottom. Cut the leaves of the plants you have grown for this purpose and place them straight away in the container. Press down and add water to the top of the leaves. Cover, and leave for about 4 weeks.

Open the tap to collect the thick black liquid. Dilute 1: 10-20 until it is the colour of straw. Can be used on food crops, but it is not recommended for acid-loving plants. Nettles can be used as an alternative to comfrey.

Liquid Seaweed

Seaweed extract can be purchased in various forms. It is a weak nitrogen/potash fertilizer with a useful trace element content. It is often claimed to be a 'bio stimulant' and over the years all sorts of benefits have been claimed – early ripening, disease resistance, root promotion, pest protection etc. Scientific tests have been inconclusive – sometimes it is highly beneficial and in other cases it has little benefit.

Chapter 3

CHOOSING THE PLANTS

The purpose of the soil in your garden is to grow plants. You may wish to be utterly conventional, with turf grasses forming a central lawn which is edged with borders and spotted with beds. These beds and borders are filled with shrubs, herbaceous perennials and bedding plants. You will almost certainly find room for some Rose bushes and a woody climber or two for the walls of the house. For many the lure of home-grown vegetables is irresistible. This standard pattern of the suburban garden is slowly changing – flowering shrubs, evergreen ground covers and small trees are becoming more popular and the classical herbaceous border is losing its appeal.

You may wish to depart from the routine pattern. There are people who devote their front gardens to alpines and bulbs – others create Rose gardens, some produce natural gardens with shrubs and wild flowers, and there is the organised chaos of the cottage garden with its herbs, annuals and old-fashioned perennials.

The range of plants you can choose from is quite staggering. The catalogue of a seed nurseryman contains many hundreds of varieties – the list of a general nurseryman is even more bewildering with all its shrubs, trees, climbers, herbaceous border plants, alpines, and so forth. A stroll around a modern garden centre is a most enjoyable experience which was denied to our ancestors, but it is also a perplexing job when the object is to pick a number of plants which will be right for the garden.

Still, you might think, the choice is up to you. It is just a matter of liking the picture in the catalogue or the specimen at the garden centre. No it isn't – there are a number of factors which must be considered if you are not going to waste a lot of time and money, and some of these factors are outside your control. Follow the step-by-step guide overleaf in order to make sure that the plants you want to grow will thrive in your garden. You need the right plant from the right supplier.

Picking the Right Plant

Step 1 Choose the Right Plant Type

"Do I want a permanent or temporary display?"
Trees and shrubs are used to form the permanent living skeleton of the garden. Hardy perennials will live in the garden for years, but die down in the winter. Annuals are for temporary display only.

"Do I want a labour-saving plant?"
Herbaceous perennials and 'hobby plants' such as Dahlias and Chrysanthemums involve a lot of work – staking, feeding, dead-heading, dividing etc. Most shrubs and trees involve little annual maintenance, but well-timed pruning may be a requirement.

"Do I want the leaves to stay on over winter?"
Choose an evergreen, but it is not always the best plant to grow. A garden filled with evergreens can look dull and unchanging – deciduous plants add an extra dimension with fresh leaves opening in the spring and changing colours in autumn.

Step 2 Choose the Right Example of this Plant Type

"What shape and size would be suitable?"
One of the commonest mistakes in gardening is to buy a plant which at maturity is far too large for the space available. Chopping back every year means that both natural beauty and floral display can be lost. Always check the expected height before buying.

"What will the growing conditions be like?"
Check if the plant has clear-cut requirements with regard to sunshine, temperature, soil texture, lime tolerance, drainage and soil moisture. Some plants are remarkably tolerant of climatic and soil conditions – others are not. Nearly all annuals need full sun, rockery perennials demand good drainage and Pieris, Rhododendron, Camellia, Calluna and Pemettya hate lime.

Step 3 Choose the Most Suitable Plant Material of this Species or Variety

"Is money the main consideration?"
Seed bought in packets or saved from your own plants is inexpensive, but it may take years to raise a shrub or herbaceous perennial by this method. Rooted cuttings taken from plants in the garden are another inexpensive source of plant material.

"Is simplicity the main consideration?"
Containers have revolutionised planting out. Just choose a container-grown specimen at any time of the year, dig a hole in the garden and pop it in. Containers are not quite that easy (page 56), but they are the most convenient and 'instant' of all plant materials.

Step 4 Buy from the Right Source of Supply

As a general rule you get what you pay for, but this does not mean that there is a 'best' supplier for all situations. A 'bargain offer' from a mail order nursery may be the right choice if you are short of money and have a large space to fill with common-or-garden shrubs, but in most cases it is preferable to see what you are buying and it is always wise to seek out a supplier with a good reputation.

PLANT TYPES

ROSES

Deciduous Shrubs and Trees of the genus Rosa, usually listed separately in the catalogues because of their importance and great popularity

A Half Standard is a Rose Tree with a 75 cm stem

A Full Standard is a Rose Tree with a 1 m stem

EVERGREEN SHRUBS & TREES

Woody plants which retain their leaves during winter

Conifers bear cones and nearly all are Evergreens

Semi-evergreens (e.g Privet) retain most of their leaves in a mild winter

A **Ground Cover** is a low-growing and spreading plant which forms a dense, leafy mat

WOODY PLANTS

Perennial plants with woody stems which survive the winter

A **Shrub** bears several woody stems at ground level

A **Tree** bears only one woody stem at ground level

A **Climber** has the ability when established to attach itself to or twine around an upright structure. Some weak-stemmed plants which require tying to stakes (e.g Climbing Roses) are included here

A **Hedge** is a continuous line of Shrubs or Trees in which the individuality of each plant is partly or wholly lost

DECIDUOUS SHRUBS & TREES

Woody plants which shed their leaves in winter

Top Fruit are Trees which produce edible fruit (e.g Apple, Pear, Peach, Plum)

Soft Fruit are Shrubs and Climbers which produce edible fruit (e.g Blackcurrant, Goose–berry). A few are Herbaceous Plants (e.g Strawberry)

VEGETABLES

Plants which are grown for their edible roots, stems or leaves. A few are grown for their fruits (e.g Tomato, Cucumber, Marrow, Capsicum)

HERBS

Plants which are grown for their medicinal value, their culinary value as garnishes or flavourings, or their cosmetic value as sweet-smelling flowers or leaves

TURF PLANTS

Low-growing carpeting plants, nearly always members of the Grass Family, which can be regularly sheared and walked upon

HERBACEOUS PLANTS

Plants with non-woody stems which generally die down in winter

BULBS

Bulbs (more correctly Bulbous Plants) produce underground fleshy organs which are offered for sale for planting indoors or outdoors. Included here are the **True Bulbs**, **Corms**, **Rhizomes** and **Tubers**

PERENNIALS

Plants which complete their life span, from seed to death, in three or more seasons

A **Hardy Perennial** (HP) will live for years in the garden – the basic plant of the herbaceous border

A **Half-hardy Perennial** (HHP) is not fully hardy and needs to spend its winter in a frost-free place (e.g Fuchsia, Geranium)

A **Greenhouse Perennial** (GP) is not suitable for outdoor cultivation

A **Rockery Perennial** (RP) is a dwarf Hardy Perennial suitable for growing in a rockery. **Alpine** is an alternative name, although some originated on the shore rather than on mountains, and some delicate True Alpines need to be grown indoors

ANNUALS

Plants which complete their life span, from seed to death, in a single season

A **Hardy Annual** (HA) is sown outdoors in spring

A **Half-hardy Annual** (HHA) cannot withstand frost, and so is raised under glass and planted outdoors when the danger of frost is past

A **Greenhouse** (or **Tender**) **Annual** (GA) is too susceptible to cold weather for outdoor cultivation, but may be planted out for a short time in summer

BIENNIALS

Plants which complete their life span, from seed to death, in two seasons

A **Hardy Biennial** (HB) is sown outdoors in summer, producing stems and leaves in the first season and flowering in the next

Some Perennials are treated as Biennials (e.g Wallflower, Daisy)

A **Bedding Plant** is an Annual or Biennial set out in quantity in autumn or spring to provide a temporary display

CHOOSING ANNUALS AND BIENNIALS

Latin name	Common name	Site & soil	Type (see page 23)	Spacing	Flowering period	Height
AGERATUM	Floss Flower	Sun or light shade – ordinary soil	HHA	20 cm	June – October	20 cm
ALTHAEA	Hollyhock	Sunny site – ordinary soil	HA or HB or HP	35 – 60 cm	July – September	1 – 3 m
ALYSSUM	Sweet Alyssum	Sunny site – well-drained soil	HA	20 cm	June – September	7 – 15 cm
AMARANTHUS	Love-lies-bleeding	Sunny site – well-drained soil	HHA	60 cm	July – October	1 m
ANTIRRHINUM	Snapdragon	Sunny site – well-drained soil	HHA	20 – 45 cm	July – October	15 cm – 1.2 m
BEGONIA	Bedding Begonia	Partial shade – humus-rich soil	HHA	12 – 35 cm	June – September	15 – 45 cm
BELLIS	Daisy	Sun or light shade – ordinary soil	HB	15 cm	March – July	7 – 15 cm
CALENDULA	Pot Marigold	Sun or light shade – poor soil	HA	30 cm	June – October	30 – 60 cm
CALLISTEPHUS	China Aster	Sunny site – well-drained soil	HHA	20 – 45 cm	August – October	20 – 75 cm
CAMPANULA	Canterbury Bell	Sunny site – well-drained soil	HB	30 cm	May – July	45 – 75 cm
CENTAUREA	Cornflower	Sun or light shade – well-drained soil	HA	20 – 30 cm	June – September	30 – 75 cm
CHEIRANTHUS	Wallflower	Sunny site – non-acid soil	HB	20 – 30 cm	March – May	20 – 60 cm
CHRYSANTHEMUM	Annual Chrysanthemum	Sunny site – non-acid soil	HA	30 cm	July – September	45 – 60 cm
CLARKIA	Clarkia	Sunny site – avoid heavy soil	HA	30 cm	July – October	45 – 60 cm
COREOPSIS	Tickseed	Sunny site – avoid heavy soil	HA	30 cm	July – September	30 – 60 cm
COSMOS	Cosmea	Sunny site – well-drained soil	HHA	45 cm	July – October	30 cm – 1 m
DAHLIA	Bedding Dahlia	Sunny site – avoid light soil	HHA	30 cm	July – November	30 – 60 cm
DELPHINIUM	Larkspur	Sun or light shade – well-drained soil	HA	45 cm	June – August	30 cm – 1.2 m
DIANTHUS	Annual Carnation	Sunny site – non-acid soil	HHA	30 cm	July – October	45 cm
DIANTHUS	Indian Pink	Sunny site – non-acid soil	HHA	15 cm	July – October	15 – 45 cm
DIANTHUS	Sweet William	Sunny site – non-acid soil	HB	20 cm	June – July	30 – 60 cm
DIGITALIS	Foxglove	Partial shade – humus-rich soil	HB	45 cm	June – August	1 – 1.5 m
DIMORPHOTHECA	Star of the Veldt	Sunny site – well-drained soil	HA	20 cm	June – August	30 cm
GODETIA	Godetia	Sunny site – well-drained soil	HA	20 – 30 cm	June – September	20 – 60 cm
GYPSOPHILA	Baby's Breath	Sunny site – non-acid soil	HA	30 cm	June – September	30 – 45 cm
HELIANTHUS	Sunflower	Sunny site – ordinary soil	HA	30 – 75 cm	July – September	60 cm – 3 m
HELICHRYSUM	Straw Flower	Sunny site – well-drained soil	HA	30 cm	July – September	30 cm – 1 m
IBERIS	Candytuft	Sunny site – well-drained soil	HA	20 cm	May – August	20 – 45 cm

Latin name	Common name	Site & soil	Type (see page 23)	Spacing	Flowering period	Height
IMPATIENS	Busy Lizzie	Sun or shade – well-drained soil	HHA	15 – 20 cm	June – October	15 – 30 cm
IPOMOEA	Morning Glory	Sunny site – well-drained soil	HHA	45 cm	July – September	1.8 – 3.5 m
LATHYRUS	Sweet Pea	Sunny site – well-drained soil	HA	15 – 30 cm	June – October	30 cm – 2.5 m
LAVATERA	Annual Mallow	Sun or light shade – ordinary soil	HA	60 cm	July – September	60 cm – 1.2 m
LOBELIA	Lobelia	Sun or light shade – ordinary soil	HHA	15 cm	June – September	10 – 20 cm
MALCOLMIA	Virginia Stock	Sun or light shade – ordinary soil	HA	10 cm	1 – 2 months after sowing	15 – 20 cm
MATTHIOLA	Brompton Stock	Sun or light shade – well-drained soil	HB	20 – 30 cm	March – May	30 – 60 cm
MATTHIOLA	Ten Week Stock	Sun or light shade – well-drained soil	HHA	20 – 30 cm	June – August	30 – 75 cm
MIMULUS	Monkey Flower	Partial shade – moist soil	HHA	20 cm	June – September	20 cm
MYOSOTIS	Forget-me-not	Light shade – well-drained soil	HB	20 cm	April – May	15 – 30 cm
NEMESIA	Nemesia	Sun or light shade – ordinary soil	HHA	15 cm	June – September	20 – 45 cm
NICOTIANA	Tobacco Plant	Sun or light shade – well-drained soil	HHA	20 – 30 cm	June – October	20 cm – 1 m
NIGELLA	Love-in-a-mist	Sun or light shade – well-drained soil	HA	20 cm	July – September	45 cm
PAPAVER	Poppy	Sun or light shade – ordinary soil	HA or HB	20 – 30 cm	May – September	15 cm – 1 m
PETUNIA	Petunia	Sunny site – ordinary soil	HHA	15 – 30 cm	June – October	15 – 45 cm
PHLOX	Annual Phlox	Sunny site – well-drained soil	HHA	20 cm	June – September	15 – 45 cm
RUDBECKIA	Rudbeckia	Sun or light shade – ordinary soil	HHA	30 – 60 cm	August – October	30 cm – 1 m
SALPIGLOSSIS	Painted Tongue	Sunny site – well-drained soil	HHA	30 cm	July – September	45 – 75 cm
SALVIA	Sage	Sunny site – ordinary soil	HA or HB or HHA	30 cm	June – October	20 – 45 cm
TAGETES	African Marigold	Sunny site – ordinary soil	HHA	30 – 45 cm	June – October	30 cm – 1 m
TAGETES	French Marigold	Sunny site ordinary soil	HHA	15 – 20 cm	June – October	15 – 30 cm
TAGETES	Tagetes	Sunny site – ordinary soil	HHA	15 – 20 cm	June – October	15 – 20 cm
TROPAEOLUM	Nasturtium	Sun or light shade – poor soil	HA	15 – 45 cm	June – October	15 cm – 1.8 m
VERBENA	Verbena	Sunny site – ordinary soil	HHA	30 cm	July – September	15 – 30 cm
VIOLA	Pansy, Viola	Sun or light shade – ordinary soil	HA or HB	20 – 30 cm	Varieties for all seasons	15 – 20 cm
VISCARIA	Viscaria	Sun or light shade – ordinary soil	HA	15 cm	June – August	15 – 30 cm
ZINNIA	Youth and Old Age	Sunny site – humus-rich soil	HHA	15 – 30 cm	July – October	15 – 75 cm

See
THE FLOWER EXPERT
*for a more complete list
together with full details
and photographs*

CHOOSING ROCKERY PERENNIALS

Latin name	Common name	Site & soil	Propagation	Notes
ACHILLEA	Alpine Yarrow	Sunny site – sandy soil	Divide clumps – spring	The Yarrow in rockeries is A. tomentosa – height 15 cm, spread 30 cm, flowers July – September. Yellow blooms are tiny
AETHIONEMA	Aethionema	Sunny site – non-acid soil	Cuttings – early summer	The popular one is A. Warley Rose – height 15 cm, spread 30 cm, flowers April – May. Colour rosy red
ALYSSUM	Alyssum	Sunny site – ordinary soil	Cuttings – early summer	A. saxatile is seen everywhere – height 20 – 30 cm, spread 45 cm, flowers April – June. Yellow flowers cover plant
ANDROSACE	Rock Jasmine	Sun or light shade – well-drained soil	Cuttings – early summer	Some are too delicate to grow outdoors. Choose A. sarmentosa chumbyi – height 10 cm, spread 60 cm, flowers April – June
ANTENNARIA	Cat's Ear	Sunny site – well-drained soil	Divide clumps – spring	A. dioica is an unspectacular ground cover – height 5 – 15 cm, spread 45 cm, flowers May – June
ARABIS	White Rock Cress	Sun or light shade – ordinary soil	Divide clumps – autumn	Very popular – height 20 cm, spread 60 cm, flowers March – April. White, pink and red varieties available
ARENARIA	Sandwort	Sun or light shade – moist soil	Divide clumps – autumn	Mat-forming plant useful for covering rocks. Small white flowers (March – July) above moss-like leaves
ARMERIA	Thrift	Sunny site – well-drained soil	Cuttings – summer	Popular – hummocks of grass-like leaves. Globular flower-heads appear in May – July – choose from white, pink or red
AUBRIETA	Rock Cress	Sunny site – well-drained soil	Divide clumps – autumn	Very popular – height 8 cm, spread 60 cm, flowers March – June. Many varieties available – pink, mauve, blue and red
CAMPANULA	Bellflower	Sun or light shade – well-drained soil	Divide clumps – spring	Several species available. One of the most popular is C. carpatica – height 25 cm, spread 30 cm, flowers June – September
CERASTIUM	Snow-in-summer	Sun or light shade – ordinary soil	Divide clumps – spring	C. tomentosum is a common sight in rockeries – height 15 cm, spread 60 cm, flowers May – July. Take care – very invasive
DIANTHUS	Rockery Pink	Sun or light shade – sandy soil	Cuttings – summer	D. deltoides is an old favourite – height 15 cm, spread 20 cm, flowers June – September. D. alpinus bears larger blooms
DODECATHEON	Shooting Star	Light shade – moist soil	Divide clumps – spring	Cyclamen-like flowers on long stalks. Usual one is D. meadia – height 45 cm, spread 30 cm, flowers June – July
DRABA	Whitlow Grass	Sunny site – well-drained soil	Sow seeds – spring	Useful for growing in crevices. Largest species is D. aizoides – height 10 cm, spread 15 cm, flowers April
DRYAS	Mountain Avens	Sunny site – non-acid soil	Cuttings – summer	Useful ground cover with blooms like small single Roses. Height 10 cm, spread 60 cm, flowers May – June
ERIGERON	Fleabane	Sunny site – sandy soil	Sow seeds – spring	Daisy-like flowers darken from white to deep pink with age. Height 20 cm, spread 60 cm, flowers June – September
ERINUS	Summer Starwort	Sun or light shade – sandy soil	Sow seeds – spring	The one you will find is E. alpinus – height 8 cm, spread 15 cm, flowers April – August. Choose from white, pink or red
GENTIANA	Gentian	Sun or light shade – well-drained soil	Divide clumps – spring or summer	Indispensable in the rockery. Many varieties available. Grow G. acaulis for large trumpet-like flowers in May and June
GERANIUM	Rock Geranium	Sunny site – well-drained soil	Divide clumps – spring	The usual one is G. cinereum – height 15 cm, spread 30 cm, flowers May – September. Pink blooms are prominently veined
GYPSOPHILA	Baby's Breath	Sunny site – well-drained soil	Cuttings – early summer	G. repens is an attractive trailing plant – height 15 cm, spread 60 cm, flowers June – August. Colour white or pink
HABERLEA	Haberlea	Partial shade – acid soil	Divide clumps – autumn	A difficult-to-grow crevice plant. Plant sideways in north-facing rockery. Lilac flowers appear in May
HELIANTHEMUM	Rock Rose	Sunny site – well-drained soil	Cuttings – summer	Usual one is a small shrub – see page 35. True alpine species are H. alpestre (height 10 cm, spread 30 cm) and H. lunulatum
HELICHRYSUM	Everlasting Flower	Sunny site – well-drained soil	Divide clumps – summer	The alpine Helichrysum is H. bellidioides – height 8 cm, spread 45 cm, flowers June – August. White is the only colour
HEPATICA	Hepatica	Sun or light shade – damp soil	Divide clumps – autumn	H. nobilis is the one you will find – height 8 cm, spread 30 cm, flowers February – April. Starry blooms – white, pink, red or blue
IBERIS	Perennial Candytuft	Sunny site – well-drained soil	Cuttings – summer	I. sempervirens is the evergreen Candytuft seen in rockeries – height 20 cm, spread 45 cm, flowers May – June. White is the only colour
LEONTOPODIUM	Edelweiss	Sunny site – well-drained soil	Sow seeds – spring	The symbol of alpine flowers, but not very attractive. Woolly leaves, furry flowers – height 15 cm, spread 20 cm, flowers June – July
LEWISIA	Lewisia	Sunny site – well-drained soil	Cuttings – early summer	Not easy to keep alive. The easiest is L. cotyledon – height 30 cm, spread 20 cm, flowers May – June. Many colours available
LINNAEA	Twin Flower	Partial shade – moist soil	Layer stems – summer	L. borealis is the basic species – height 5 cm, spread 60 cm, flowers May – July. Bell-like pink blooms
LITHOSPERMUM	Gromwell	Sunny site – humus-rich soil	Cuttings – summer	A ground cover plant with funnel-shaped blue flowers – height 15 cm, spread 60 cm, flowers June – September
LYCHNIS	Alpine Campion	Sunny site – lime-free soil	Sow seeds – spring	White or pink blooms on short stalks. A tiny plant – height 10 cm, spread 10 cm, flowers May – July

Latin name	Common name	Site & soil	Propagation	Notes
LYSIMACHIA	Creeping Jenny	Partial shade – humus-rich soil	Divide clumps – autumn	L. nummularia is an old favourite – a vigorous ground cover with yellow flowers. Height 5 cm, spread 45 cm, flowers June – July
MIMULUS	Monkey Flower	Light shade – moist soil	Divide clumps – spring	The rockery Mimulus to grow is M. primuloides – height 10 cm, spread 20 cm, flowers May – August. Trumpet-shaped yellow blooms
OXALIS	Oxalis	Sunny site – well-drained soil	Divide clumps – autumn	The most popular rockery Oxalis is O. adenophylla – height 8 cm, spread 15 cm, flowers June – July. Pink-edged white blooms
PHLOX	Dwarf Phlox	Sunny site – well-drained soil	Cuttings – summer	The Moss Phlox is an attractive carpeter – height 8 cm, spread 45 cm, flowers April – May. Pink or mauve blooms cover leaves
POLYGONUM	Rock Polygonum	Sunny site – well-drained soil	Divide clumps – autumn	P. vaccinifolium is the common rockery type – height 15 cm, spread 1 m, flowers September – December. Upright floral spikes
POTENTILLA	Rock Cinquefoil	Sunny site – ordinary soil	Divide clumps – autumn	The popular rockery Potentilla is P. nitida – height 8 cm, spread 30 cm, flowers July – September. Silvery leaves, pink blooms
PRIMULA	Rockery Primrose	Light shade – humus-rich soil	Divide clumps – after flowering	Many types available, including the old favourite Auricula. P. Wanda is popular – height 8 cm, spread 15 cm, flowers March – May
PULSATILLA	Pasque Flower	Sunny site – well-drained soil	Sow seeds – summer	Large flowers (8 cm across) followed by ferny leaves. Usual species is P. vulgaris – height 20 cm, spread 30 cm, flowers April – May
RAOULIA	Raoulia	Sunny site – sandy soil	Divide mats – autumn	A silvery mat with pale yellow minute flowers. R. australis is the best known species – height 1 cm, spread 30 cm, flowers May
SANGUINARIA	Bloodroot	Sun or light shade – humus-rich soil	Divide clumps – spring	Large flowers (45 cm across) amongst greyish leaves. Buy the double form – height 15 cm, spread 45 cm, flowers April – May
SAPONARIA	Rock Soapwort	Sunny site – well-drained soil	Cuttings – summer	S. ocymoides is a carpeting plant – height 8 cm, spread 45 cm, flowers July – September. Star-shaped blooms in pink or red
SAXIFRAGA	Saxifrage	Sun or light shade – well-drained soil	Offsets – summer	Many varieties available – usual form is a low-growing group of rosettes or mossy sheets. Flowers starry or saucer-shaped
SEDUM	Stonecrop	Sunny site – well-drained soil	Divide clumps – autumn	Many varieties available – usual form is low-growing stems, fleshy leaves and star-shaped flowers in June
SEMPERVIVUM	Houseleek	Sunny site – well-drained soil	Offsets – autumn	Ball-like rosettes of green or coloured fleshy leaves. Thick flower stems appear in July. Ideal for dry spots
SHORTIA	Shortia	Partial shade – humus-rich soil	Divide clumps – early summer	S. galacifolia is the usual one – height 15 cm, spread 30 cm, flowers April – May. Shiny, red-tinged leaves and pale pink blooms
SILENE	Moss Campion	Sunny site – well-drained soil	Cuttings – summer	Carpeting plants for planting in crevices. Narrow leaves – star-faced tubular flowers appear in summer. Do not disturb
THYMUS	Thyme	Sunny site – well-drained soil	Divide clumps – spring	T. serpyllum is the basic species – height 5 cm, spread 60 cm, flowers June – July. Starry blooms in white, pink or red

Aethionema Warley Rose

Alyssum saxatile

Campanula carpatica

Dodecatheon meadia

Gentiana acaulis

Pulsatilla vulgaris

See
THE ROCK & WATER GARDEN EXPERT
for a more complete list together with full details and photographs

The ROCK & WATER GARDEN EXPERT
Dr. D. G. Hessayon
THE WORLD'S BEST-SELLING BOOK ON ROCK & WATER GARDENS

Choosing Bulbs

Latin name	Common name	Site & soil	Planting time	Planting depth	Spacing	Flowering period	Height
ACIDANTHERA	Acidanthera	Sunny site – well-drained soil	April	10 cm	20 cm	September	1 m
ALLIUM	Flowering Garlic	Sunny site – well-drained soil	September – October	10 – 15 cm	15 – 30 cm	June – July	20 cm – 1.2 m
ANEMONE BLANDA	Daisy-flowered Windflower	Sun or light shade – well-drained soil	September	5 cm	10 cm	February – April	15 cm
ANEMONE CORONARIA	Poppy-flowered Windflower	Warm and sheltered – well-drained soil	November – April	5 cm	10 cm	February – October	15 – 20 cm
BEGONIA	Tuberous Begonia	Light shade – moist, acid soil	June	Plant sprouted tubers	30 cm	July – September	30 – 45 cm
CAMASSIA	Quamash	Sun or light shade – damp soil	September – October	10 cm	15 cm	June – July	75 cm – 1 m
CANNA	Indian Shot	Sunny site – humus-rich soil	June	5 cm	45 cm	August – October	1 – 1.2 m
CHIONODOXA	Glory of the Snow	Sun or light shade – well-drained soil	September	8 cm	10 cm	February – March	15 cm
COLCHICUM	Autumn Crocus	Sun or light shade – well-drained soil	July – August	10 cm	20 cm	September – November	15 – 20 cm
CONVALLARIA	Lily of the Valley	Partial shade – damp soil	October – March	2.5 cm	10 cm	April – May	20 cm
CRINUM	Crinum	Sunny site – well-drained soil	April – May	25 cm	45 cm	August – September	60 cm – 1 m
CROCOSMIA	Montbretia	Sunny site – well-drained soil	March	8 cm	15 cm	August – September	60 cm – 1 m
CROCUS	Crocus	Sun or light shade – well-drained soil	September – October	8 cm	10 cm	February – April	8 – 12 cm
CROCUS SPECIOSUS	Crocus	Sun or light shade – well-drained soil	July	8 cm	10 cm	August – October	8 – 12 cm
CYCLAMEN	Cyclamen	Partial shade – damp soil	July – September	5 cm	15 cm	Species for all seasons	8 – 15 cm
DAHLIA	Dahlia	Sunny site – humus-rich soil	April – May	8 cm to top of tuber	45 cm – 1 m	August – October	60 cm – 1.5 m
ERANTHIS	Winter Aconite	Sun or light shade – well-drained soil	August – September	5 cm	8 cm	January – March	8 – 10 cm
ERYTHRONIUM	Dog's-tooth Violet	Partial shade – damp soil	August – October	10 cm	10 cm	March – April	15 cm
FREESIA	Outdoor Freesia	Sunny site – light soil	April	5 cm	10 cm	August – October	30 cm
FRITILLARIA IMPERIALIS	Crown Imperial	Light shade – well-drained soil	September – November	20 cm	45 cm	April	30 cm – 1 m
FRITILLARIA MELEAGRIS	Snake's Head Fritillary	Light shade – well-drained soil	September – November	12 cm	15 cm	April	30 cm – 1 m
GALANTHUS	Snowdrop	Light shade – moist soil	September – October	10 cm	8 cm	January – March	12 – 25 cm
GALTONIA	Summer Hyacinth	Sunny site – well-drained soil	March – April	15 – 20 cm	30 cm	August – September	1 – 1.2 m
GLADIOLUS	Gladiolus	Sunny site – well-drained soil	March – May	10 – 12 cm	10 – 15 cm	July – September	30 cm – 1.2 m
GLADIOLUS COLVILLII	Species Gladiolus	Sunny site – well-drained soil	October	10 – 12 cm	10 – 15 cm	April – June	60 cm
HYACINTHUS ORIENTALIS	Dutch Hyacinth	Sun or light shade – well-drained soil	September – October	15 cm	20 cm	April – May	15 – 30 cm
HYACINTHUS O. ALBULUS	Roman Hyacinth	Sun or light shade – well-drained soil	September – October	15 cm	20 cm	March – April	15 – 30 cm
IPHEION	Spring Starflower	Sun or light shade – well-drained soil	September – October	5 cm	10 cm	April – May	15 cm
IRIS-RETICULATA group	Dwarf Iris	Sunny site – light soil	September – October	5 cm	10 cm	January – March	10 – 15 cm
IRIS-XIPHIUM group	Iris	Sunny site – light soil	September – October	10 – 15 cm	15 cm	June – July	30 – 60 cm

Latin name	Common name	Site & soil	Planting time	Planting depth	Spacing	Flowering period	Height
IXIA	Corn Lily	Sunny site – light soil	March	8 cm	10 cm	June – July	30 – 45 cm
LEUCOJUM AESTIVUM	Summer Snowflake	Sun or light shade – well-drained soil	August – September	10 cm	20 cm	April – May	60 cm
LEUCOJUM VERNUM	Spring Snowflake	Sun or light shade – well-drained soil	August – September	10 cm	10 cm	February – March	20 cm
LILIUM	Lily	Sun or light shade – well-drained soil	October	5 – 15 cm to top of bulb	15 – 45 cm	June – October	30 cm – 2.5 m
MUSCARI	Grape Hyacinth	Sunny site – well-drained soil	September – October	8 cm	10 cm	April – May	15 – 30 cm
NARCISSUS	Narcissus, Daffodil	Sun or light shade – well-drained soil	August – September	10 – 18 cm	10 – 20 cm	March – April	8 – 60 cm
NERINE	Nerine	Sunny site – well-drained soil	April – May	10 cm	15 cm	September – October	60 cm
ORNITHOGALUM	Star of Bethlehem	Sun or light shade – well-drained soil	October	5 cm	10 – 15 cm	April – May	15 – 30 cm
PUSCHKINIA	Striped Squill	Sun or light shade – well-drained soil	September – October	5 cm	8 cm	March – April	10 cm
RANUNCULUS	Turban Buttercup	Sunny site – well-drained soil	March – April	5 cm	15 cm	June – July	30 cm
SCILLA NONSCRIPTA	Bluebell	Sun or light shade – damp soil	August – September	10 cm	10 cm	April – June	20 cm
SCILLA SIBERICA	Siberian Squill	Sun or light shade – damp soil	August – September	10 cm	10 cm	March – April	15 cm
SPARAXIS	Harlequin Flower	Sunny site – well-drained soil	November	8 cm	10 cm	May – June	30 cm
TIGRIDIA	Tiger Flower	Sunny site – well-drained soil	April	10 cm	15 cm	July – September	45 cm
TRITONIA	Blazing Star	Sunny site – well-drained soil	September	5 cm	15 cm	May – June	45 cm
TULIPA	Tulip	Sunny site – well-drained soil	November – December	15 cm	12 – 20 cm	April – May	20 – 75 cm
TULIPA SPECIES	Species Tulip	Sunny site – well-drained soil	November – December	10 cm	10 – 15 cm	March – May	15 – 45 cm

Acidanthera murielae

Chionodoxa luciliae

Eranthis tubergenii

Gladiolus Red Cascade

Leucojum vernum

Tigridia pavonia

See
THE BULB EXPERT
for a more complete list
together with full details
and photographs

The **BULB EXPERT**
Dr. D. G. Hessayon

THE WORLD'S BEST-SELLING BOOK ON BULBS

CHOOSING HARDY PERENNIALS

Latin name	Common name	Site & soil	Propagation	Notes
ACANTHUS	Bear's Breeches	Sun or light shade – well-drained soil	Divide clumps – autumn	A. spinosus is the usual one – height 1.2 m, spacing 75 cm, flowers July – September. Blooms are white lipped and purple hooded
ACHILLEA	Yarrow	Sunny site – well-drained soil	Divide clumps – autumn	A. filipendulina Gold Plate bears flat-topped yellow flower-heads – height 1.4 m, spacing 60 cm, flowers June – September
AGAPANTHUS	African Lily	Sunny site – humus-rich soil	Divide clumps – spring	Large head of blue flowers above strap-like leaves. Height 75 cm, spacing 60 cm, flowers July – September. Not fully hardy
AJUGA	Bugle	Sun or light shade – ordinary soil	Divide clumps – autumn	A creeping plant – grow a variety with coloured leaves – bronze, purple, cream etc. Height 10 cm, spacing 35 cm, flowers May – August
ALCHEMILLA	Lady's Mantle	Sun or light shade – well-drained soil	Divide clumps – spring	A. mollis is an old favourite – height 45 cm, spacing 45 cm, flowers June – August. Blooms small, greenish-yellow
ALSTROEMERIA	Peruvian Lily	Sunny site – fertile soil	Sow seeds – spring	Large trumpets (5 cm across) in loose clusters. Many hybrids available – height 60 cm, spacing 45 cm, flowers June – August
ANCHUSA	Alkanet	Sunny site – well-drained soil	Divide clumps – spring	Grown for its vivid blue flowers – a straggly short-lived plant. Choose an A. azurea variety – height 45 cm – 1.5 m, flowers June – August
ANEMONE	Japanese Anemone	Sun or light shade – well-drained soil	Divide clumps – spring	Saucer-shaped blooms (5 cm across) and deeply-lobed leaves. Height 60 cm – 1.2 m, spacing 30 – 45 cm, flowers August – October
AQUILEGIA	Columbine	Partial shade – well-drained soil	Divide clumps – autumn	Old cottage-garden favourite. Choose a modern hybrid – height 45 cm – 1 m, spacing 30 – 45 cm, flowers May – June
ASTER	Michaelmas Daisy	Sunny site – well-drained soil	Divide clumps – spring	Scores of varieties available – white, red, blue, pink and mauve. Height 60 cm – 1.5 m, spacing 45 cm, flowers August – October
ASTILBE	Astilbe	Light shade – moist soil	Divide clumps – spring	Feathery plumes of tiny flowers. Many varieties of A. arendsii can be bought – height 60 cm – 1 m, spacing 45 cm, flowers June – August
BERGENIA	Large-leaved Saxifrage	Sun or light shade – well-drained soil	Divide clumps – autumn	Easy-to-grow ground cover. Fleshy leaves, Hyacinth-like flower-spikes. Height 45 cm, spacing 45 cm, flowers March – April
BRUNNERA	Perennial Forget-me-not	Partial shade – well-drained soil	Divide clumps – autumn	Easy-to-grow ground cover. Heart-shaped leaves, Myosotis-like blooms. Height 45 cm, spacing 45 cm, flowers April – June
CALTHA	Marsh Marigold	Sun or light shade – moist soil	Divide clumps – after flowering	Golden flowers (2.5 – 5 cm across) above dark green leaves. Height 30 cm, spacing 30 cm, flowers April – June
CAMPANULA	Bellflower	Sun or light shade – well-drained soil	Cuttings – spring	Blooms bell-like or star-shaped – white or blue. Several species available – height 60 cm – 1.5 m, spacing 30 – 45 cm, flowers June – August
CHRYSANTHEMUM	Chrysanthemum	Sunny site – well-drained soil	Cuttings – spring	Raised afresh each year from cuttings. Hundreds of varieties available – all colours except blue. See The Flower Expert for details
CHRYSANTHEMUM	Shasta Daisy	Sunny site – non-acid soil	Divide clumps – spring	C. maximum is the hardy Chrysanthemum. Many named varieties available – height 75 cm – 1 m, spacing 45 cm, flowers June – August
COREOPSIS	Tickseed	Sun or light shade – well-drained soil	Sow seeds – spring	Yellow Daisy-like flowers on slender stalks. C. grandiflora is the usual species – height 45 cm, spacing 45 cm, flowers June – September
CORTADERIA	Pampas Grass	Sun or light shade – well-drained soil	Buy from garden centre	Silvery plumes about 45 cm long on tall stalks. Grow a variety of C. selloana – height 1.2 – 3 m, flowers October
DELPHINIUM	Delphinium	Sunny site – well-drained soil	Divide clumps – spring	Dwarfs and giants available in white, blue, pink, mauve and purple. Height 1 – 2.5 m, spacing 45 – 75 cm, flowers June – July
DIANTHUS	Border Carnation	Sunny site – non-acid soil	Cuttings – summer	Enormous list of varieties – all sorts of colours. Height 60 cm – 1 m, spacing 45 cm, flowers July – August. Petals smooth-edged
DIANTHUS	Pinks	Sunny site – non-acid soil	Cuttings – summer	Old-fashioned and modern varieties available – smaller and daintier than Carnations. Height 30 – 45 cm, spacing 30 cm, flowers June – July
DICENTRA	Bleeding Heart	Light shade – well-drained soil	Divide clumps – autumn	Most popular Dicentra is also the largest – D. spectabilis. Height 60 cm – 1 m, spacing 45 cm, flowers May – June
DORONICUM	Leopard's Bane	Sun or light shade – well-drained soil	Divide clumps – autumn	Varieties of D. plantagineum are usually chosen – height 60 cm – 1 m, spacing 45 cm, flowers April – June. Large Daisy-like blooms
ECHINACEA	Purple Coneflower	Sunny site – well-drained soil	Divide clumps – spring	E. purpurea is the species to grow – height 1 – 1.2 m, spacing 60 cm, flowers July – October. Pink or purple petals
ECHINOPS	Globe Thistle	Sunny site – well-drained soil	Divide clumps – spring	Globular flower-heads above Thistle-like leaves. For the back of the border – height 1 – 1.5 m, spacing 60 cm, flowers July – September
ERIGERON	Fleabane	Sun or light shade – well-drained soil	Divide clumps – spring	Looks like a small Michaelmas Daisy – height 30 – 60 cm, spacing 30 cm, flowers June – August. Pink, blue and lilac available
ERYNGIUM	Sea Holly	Sunny site – well-drained soil	Divide clumps – spring	Thimble-shaped blue flowers above Thistle-like leaves. Several species available – height 45 cm – 1 m, spacing 30 – 45 cm, flowers July – September
EUPHORBIA	Spurge	Sun or light shade – well-drained soil	Cuttings – spring	Flower colour is nearly always yellow or green, but there is a bright orange one. Height 75 cm, spacing 45 cm, flowers May
FUCHSIA	Fuchsia	Sun or light shade – well-drained soil	Cuttings – summer	Hundreds of named hybrids are available – a few are hardy but most are treated as summer bedding plants. Flowers 5 – 10 cm long

Latin name	Common name	Site & soil	Propagation	Notes
GAILLARDIA	Blanket Flower	Sunny site – avoid heavy soil	Divide clumps – spring	Popular – large Daisy-like blooms (5 – 10 cm across) in yellow and red. Height 45 – 75 cm, spacing 45 cm, flowers June – September
GERANIUM	Crane's-bill	Sun or light shade – well-drained soil	Divide clumps – spring	Useful ground cover – saucer-shaped flowers in white, pink, blue or red. Height 30 – 60 cm, spacing 45 cm, flowers May – August
GEUM	Avens	Sun or light shade – well-drained soil	Divide clumps – spring	An old favourite – bright, bowl-shaped blooms on top of wiry stems. Height 30 – 60 cm, spacing 45 cm, flowers May – September
GYPSOPHILA	Baby's Breath	Sun or light shade – non-acid soil	Cuttings – summer	Tiny white or pale pink flowers form a billowy cloud above thin stems. Height 1 m, spacing 1 m, flowers June – August
HELENIUM	Sneezewort	Sun or light shade – well-drained soil	Divide clumps – autumn	Bronze-red H. autumnale Moerheim Beauty is the popular one – height 1 m, spacing 60 cm, flowers July – September. Yellow varieties available
HELLEBORUS	Christmas Rose	Partial shade – moist soil	Buy from garden centre	H. niger bears large, saucer-shaped blooms – white with golden stamens. Height 30 – 45 cm, spacing 45 cm, flowers January – March
HELLEBORUS	Lenten Rose	Partial shade – moist soil	Buy from garden centre	H. orientalis bears large, saucer-shaped blooms – white, pink or purple. Height 30 – 45 cm, spacing 45 cm, flowers February – April
HEMEROCALLIS	Day Lily	Sun or light shade – ordinary soil	Divide clumps – autumn	Large Lily-like trumpets in shades from pale yellow to rich red. Many varieties – height 1 m, spacing 60 cm, flowers June – August
HEUCHERA	Coral Flower	Sun or light shade – well-drained soil	Divide clumps – autumn	Tiny bell-shaped blooms on top of slender stems. Height 45 – 75 cm, spacing 45 cm, flowers June – August. White, pink or red
HOSTA	Plantain Lily	Partial shade – ordinary soil	Divide clumps – spring	Useful ground cover grown for its spikes of flowers and its attractive foliage. Height 45 cm – 1 m, spacing 60 cm, flowers July – August
INCARVILLEA	Chinese Trumpet Flower	Sunny site – well-drained soil	Sow seeds – spring	Large trumpets in clusters appear before the leaves. Height 30 – 60 cm, spacing 30 cm, flowers May – June. Pale or deep pink
IRIS	Iris	Sunny site – well-drained soil	Divide rhizomes – late summer	Bearded types (fleshy hairs on petals) dominate the catalogue lists. Height 20 cm – 1 m, spacing 30 cm, flowers April – June, depending on variety
KNIPHOFIA	Red Hot Poker	Sunny site – well-drained soil	Divide clumps – spring	Usual choice is a variety or hybrid of K. uvaria – height 75 cm – 1.5 m, spacing 1 m, flowers July – September. Various colour combinations
LIATRIS	Gayfeather	Sun or light shade – moist soil	Divide clumps – spring	Unusual flower-spike feature – blooms open from top downwards. Height 45 cm, spacing 45 cm, flowers August – September
LIGULARIA	Ligularia	Partial shade – moist soil	Divide clumps – autumn	Useful ground cover with large leaves and yellow or orange Daisy-like blooms. Height 1 – 1.2 m, spacing 75 cm, flowers July – September
LINUM	Perennial Flax	Sunny site – well-drained soil	Sow seeds – spring	Short-lived blooms on wiry stems – blue is the most popular colour. Height 30 – 60 cm, spacing 30 cm, flowers June – August
LUPINUS	Lupin	Sun or light shade – well-drained soil	Sow seeds – spring	Russell hybrids provide stately spires of blooms in a vast range of colours – height 1 – 1.2 m, flowers June – July
LYCHNIS	Campion	Sunny site – well-drained soil	Divide clumps – autumn	L. chalcedonica (Jerusalem Cross) is the one to grow – large heads of red blooms. Height 1 m, spacing 45 cm, flowers June – August
LYTHRUM	Purple Loosestrife	Sun or light shade – moist soil	Divide clumps – autumn	Long and narrow flower-spikes, pink or red. Basic species is L. salicaria – height 75 cm – 1.5 m, spacing 45 cm, flowers June – September
MACLEAYA	Plume Poppy	Sun or light shade – ordinary soil	Divide clumps – autumn	Space is needed for the bronzy leaves and tall plumes of pinkish flowers. Height 1.8 – 2.5 m, spacing 1 m, flowers July – August
MECONOPSIS	Meconopsis	Light shade – humus-rich soil	Sow seeds – spring	Both the blue Himalayan Poppy (1 m) and yellow Welsh Poppy (30 cm) belong here. Flowering period June – August
MONARDA	Bergamot	Sun or light shade – moist soil	Divide clumps – spring	Grow one of the named hybrids of M. didyma – height 60 cm – 1 m, spacing 60 cm, flowers June – September
NEPETA	Catmint	Sunny site – ordinary soil	Divide clumps – spring	Popular edging plant – small lavender flowers and aromatic greyish leaves. Height 30 cm – 1 m, spacing 45 cm, flowers May – September
OENOTHERA	Evening Primrose	Sunny site – well-drained soil	Divide clumps – spring	Yellow Poppy-like blooms – O. missouriensis bears the largest. Height 15 – 45 cm, spacing 30 – 45 cm, flowers July – September

Oenothera Fireworks

Hemerocallis Pink Prelude

Aquilegia McKana Hybrid

Kniphofia Royal Standard

Latin name	Common name	Site & soil	Propagation	Notes
PAEONIA	Paeony	Sunny site – well-drained soil	Buy from garden centre	Vast bowls of petals up to 18 cm across – single, double or Anemone-flowered. Height 45 cm – 1 m, spacing 45 – 60 cm, flowers April – July
PAPAVER	Oriental Poppy	Sunny site – well-drained soil	Divide clumps – spring	Bowl-shaped flowers up to 15 cm across. Many named varieties available – height 1 m, spacing 45 cm, flowers May – June
PELARGONIUM	Geranium	Sunny site – well-drained soil	Cuttings – summer	Height 30 – 60 cm, spacing 30 cm. Two basic types – Bedding Geraniums (flowers 1 – 2.5 cm) and Regal Geraniums (frilled flowers 3 – 5 cm)
PENSTEMON	Beard Tongue	Sunny site – well-drained soil	Cuttings – summer	Grow a named hybrid – height 45 – 60 cm, spacing 30 cm, flowers June – September. Red is the usual colour. Not fully hardy
PHLOX	Phlox	Sun or light shade – moist soil	Divide clumps – spring	Large trusses of flat-faced flowers. The most popular Phlox is P. paniculata – height 60 cm – 1.2 m, spacing 45 cm, flowers July – October
PHYSALIS	Chinese Lantern	Sun or light shade – ordinary soil	Divide clumps – spring	Grown for 5 cm long `lanterns' – useful for drying. Height 60 cm, spacing 1 m, fruits September – October. Gold- or flame-coloured
PLATYCODON	Balloon Flower	Sun or light shade – well-drained soil	Buy from garden centre	Unusual flower feature – buds swell into large, angular balloons before opening. Height 30 – 60 cm, spacing 30 cm, flowers June – September
POLEMONIUM	Jacob's Ladder	Sun or light shade – well-drained soil	Divide clumps – autumn	An old cottage-garden plant – choose a modern variety if space is limited. Height 30 cm – 1 m, spacing 30 cm, flowers June – August
POLYGONATUM	Solomon's Seal	Shade – ordinary soil	Divide clumps – autumn	Thrives under trees and shrubs – green-tipped white blooms in pendent clusters. Height 60 cm – 1 m, spacing 60 cm, flowers May – June
POLYGONUM	Knotweed	Sun or light shade – ordinary soil	Divide clumps – autumn	Evergreen ground cover – pokers of pink flowers. Chose a P. affine variety – height 30 cm, spacing 60 cm, flowers June – October
POTENTILLA	Cinquefoil	Sunny site – well-drained soil	Divide clumps – spring	Bright saucer-shaped flowers in reds and yellows. Several named hybrids – height 30 – 60 cm, spacing 45 cm, flowers June – September
PRIMULA	Primrose	Partial shade – humus-rich soil	Divide clumps – spring	Many species and hybrids are available – Pacific Strain of Polyanthus most popular. Height 30 cm, spacing 30 cm, flowers March – May
PYRETHRUM	Feverfew	Sunny site – well-drained soil	Divide clumps – spring	Single or double Daisy-like blooms 5 cm across – usual colours pink and red. Height 60 cm – 1 m, spacing 45 cm, flowers May – June
RUDBECKIA	Coneflower	Sun or light shade – ordinary soil	Divide clumps – spring	Dark-centred, star-shaped blooms. Popular variety is R. fulgida Goldsturm – height 60 cm, spacing 60 cm, flowers July – September
SALVIA	Perennial Sage	Sun or light shade – well-drained soil	Divide clumps – autumn	Blue – not red like the Annual Salvia. Usual species is S. superba – height 1 m, spacing 45 cm, flowers July – September
SAXIFRAGA	Saxifrage	Partial shade – humus-rich soil	Divide clumps – spring	Starry flowers above rosettes or clumps of leaves. Popular one is London Pride – height 30 cm, spacing 45 cm, flowers May – July
SCABIOSA	Scabious	Sunny site – non-acid soil	Divide clumps – spring	Flowers are frilly-edged pincushions up to 10 cm across. Basic species is S. caucasica – height 60 cm – 1 m, spacing 45 cm, flowers June – October
SEDUM	Stonecrop	Sunny site – well-drained soil	Divide clumps – spring	The popular Ice Plant is S. spectabile – height 30 – 60 cm, spacing 30 cm, flowers August – October. Flower-heads 10 – 15 cm across
SOLIDAGO	Golden Rod	Sun or light shade – well-drained soil	Divide clumps – spring	Feathery flower-heads above narrow leaves. Choose a named hybrid – height 30 cm – 2.2 m, spacing 30 – 60 cm, flowers July – September
STACHYS	Lamb's Ears	Sun or light shade – well-drained soil	Divide clumps – autumn	The popular Stachys is Lamb's Ears (S. lanata) – height 45 cm, spacing 30 cm, flowers July – August. Woolly foliage, pale purple blooms
TRADESCANTIA	Spiderwort	Sun or light shade – ordinary soil	Divide clumps – spring	Silky three-petalled blooms above sword-like leaves. The species is T. virginiana – height 45 – 60 cm, spacing 45 cm, flowers June – September
TROLLIUS	Globe Flower	Sun or light shade – moist soil	Divide clumps – autumn	Buttercup-like blooms 5 cm across. Hybrids range from pale cream to dark orange – height 45 – 75 cm, spacing 45 cm, flowers May – June
VERBASCUM	Mullein	Sunny site – well-drained soil	Root cuttings – winter	Branched flower-spikes above woolly leaves. Choose a named variety – many colours available. Height 1 – 2 m, spacing 60 cm, flowers June – August
VERONICA	Speedwell	Sun or light shade – well-drained soil	Divide clumps – autumn	Narrow spikes of blue or white blooms. Size of varieties covers a wide range – height 30 cm – 1.5 m, spacing 30 – 60 cm, flowers May – June

Rudbeckia Goldsturm

Verbascum hybridum

See
THE FLOWER EXPERT
for a more complete list
together with full details
and photographs

The FLOWER EXPERT
Dr. D. G. Hessayon

THE WORLD'S BEST-SELLING BOOK ON FLOWERS

CHOOSING CLIMBERS

Latin name	Common name	Site & soil	Deciduous (D) or Evergreen (E)	Pruning	Propagation	Notes
ACTINIDIA	Actinidia	Sunny site – ordinary soil	D	Not necessary	Cuttings – summer	A. kolomikta is the usual one – green, pink and cream leaves
ARISTOLOCHIA	Dutchman's Pipe	Sun or light shade – fertile soil	D	Not necessary	Cuttings – summer	A. macrophylla is hardy outdoors – rarely seen in Britain
CAMPSIS	Trumpet Vine	Sunny site – fertile soil	D	Cut back old stems – winter	Layer stems – summer	Self-clinging climber with red blooms. Not very hardy
CELASTRUS	Bittersweet	Sun or light shade – ordinary soil	D	Shorten stems – spring	Layer stems – summer	C. orbiculatus grown for its bright seeds and seed pods
CLEMATIS HYBRIDS	Virgin's Bower	Fussy. Sun on stems – fertile soil	D or E or semi E	Complicated. Depends on variety	Cuttings – summer	The large-flowered hybrids are the ones usually grown
CLEMATIS SPECIES	Virgin's Bower	Sunny site – fertile soil	D	Complicated. Depends on variety	Cuttings – summer	Small flowers – easier to grow than hybrids
HEDERA	Ivy	Shady site – ordinary soil	E	Not necessary	Plant rooted runners	Many colourful varieties are available – yellow, white and golden
HYDRANGEA	Climbing Hydrangea	Sun or shade – well-drained soil	D	Not necessary	Side growths – summer	H. petiolaris is a self-clinging climber
JASMINUM	Jasmine	Sunny site – ordinary soil	D	Not necessary	Cuttings – summer	J. officinale and J. o. Grandiflorum are the usual ones
LONICERA	Honeysuckle	Sun or light shade – fertile soil	D or semi E	Cut back some stems – after flowering	Cuttings – summer	Most varieties have fragrant blooms – June–August
PARTHENOCISSUS	Virginia Creeper	Sun or light shade – fertile soil	D	Remove unwanted growth – spring	Layer stems – autumn	Leaves turn red in autumn. Popular one is P. tricuspidata
PASSIFLORA	Passion Flower	Sunny site – well-drained soil	D	Remove unwanted growth – spring	Cuttings – summer	P. caerulea is the species grown – not very hardy
POLYGONUM	Russian Vine	Sun or light shade – ordinary soil	D	Remove unwanted growth – spring	Cuttings – summer	Fast-growing, twining climber. Popular one is P. baldschuanicum
SOLANUM	Perennial Nightshade	Sunny site – ordinary soil	Semi E	Remove unwanted growth – spring	Layer stems – summer	S. crispum Glasnevin is the variety to choose
VITIS	Ornamental Vine	Sun or light shade – well-drained soil	D	Remove unwanted growth – summer	Cuttings – summer	Tendril-bearing climber grown for autumn foliage colour
WISTERIA	Wistaria	Sunny site – fertile soil	D	Cut back current side growths – July	Layer stems – summer	W. sinensis is the popular one – W. floribunda Macrobotrys is more spectacular

Parthenocissus tricuspidata

Clematis jackmanii

Passiflora caerulea

Wisteria sinensis

Hedera helix Goldheart

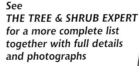
Lonicera tellmanniana

See
THE TREE & SHRUB EXPERT
for a more complete list
together with full details
and photographs

THE TREE & SHRUB EXPERT
Dr. D. G. Hessayon

THE WORLD'S BEST-SELLING BOOK ON TREES & SHRUBS

CHOOSING SHRUBS

Latin name	Common name	Site & soil	Deciduous (D) or Evergreen (E)	Pruning	Propagation	Notes
ACER	Japanese Maple	Partial shade – acid soil	D	Not necessary	Buy from garden centre	Varieties of A. palmatum grown for leaf shape and colour
ARUNDINARIA	Bamboo	Partial shade – ordinary soil	E	Not necessary	Divide clumps	Varieties range from 1–6 m tall
AUCUBA	Aucuba	Sun or shade – ordinary soil	E	Not necessary	Cuttings – summer	Popular – planted where little else will grow
BERBERIS	Barberry	Sun or light shade – ordinary soil	D or E	Not necessary	Cuttings – summer	Popular and easy – range from 60 cm – 3 m tall
BUDDLEIA	Butterfly Bush	Sunny site – well-drained soil	D or semi E	Popular varieties – cut back in March	Cuttings – autumn	Types bearing floral cones need annual pruning
BUXUS	Box	Sun or light shade – ordinary soil	E	Not necessary	Cuttings – summer	An excellent hedging or tub plant. Small glossy leaves
CALLUNA	Heather	Sunny site – acid soil	E	Lightly trim – March	Cuttings – summer	Hundreds of named varieties – 20 – 60 cm high
CAMELLIA	Camellia	Sun or light shade – acid soil	E	Not necessary	Cuttings – summer	Should be more popular – large blooms in March – May
CEANOTHUS	Californian Lilac	Sunny site – well-drained soil	D or E	D types – cut back in March	Cuttings – summer	Evergreen varieties are not fully hardy. Plant in spring
CHAENOMELES	Japonica	Sun or light shade – ordinary soil	D	Not necessary	Plant rooted suckers	Old favourite, grown for spring flowers and autumn fruits
CHIMONANTHUS	Winter Sweet	Sunny site – well-drained soil	D	Not necessary	Layer stems – summer	Fragrant flowers appear before leaves in winter
CHOISYA	Mexican Orange Blossom	Sunny site – ordinary soil	E	Not necessary	Cuttings – summer	Fragrant plant – white, starry flowers in May
CISTUS	Rock Rose	Sunny site – well-drained soil	E	Not necessary	Cuttings – summer	Succession of papery flowers throughout June and July
CORNUS	Dogwood	Sun or light shade – ordinary soil	D	Bark types – cut back in March	Cuttings – autumn	Varieties chosen for coloured bark or floral display
CORYLUS	Hazel	Sun or light shade – well-drained soil	D	Cut back old stems – March	Plant rooted suckers	Varieties chosen for twisted stems or coloured leaves
COTINUS	Smoke Bush	Sunny site – ordinary soil	D	Remove unwanted growth – spring	Plant rooted suckers	Feathery flower-heads – sold under old name Rhus cotinus
COTONEASTER	Cotoneaster	Sun or light shade – ordinary soil	D or E or semi E	Not necessary	Cuttings – summer	All shapes and sizes from ground covers to 6 m bushes
CYTISUS	Broom	Sunny site – sandy soil	D or E or semi E	Trim back – after flowering	Cuttings – summer	Flowers clothe long whippy branches in May or June
DAPHNE	Daphne	Sunny site – humus-rich soil	D or E or semi E	Not necessary	Seed or summer cuttings	Popular species is D. mezereum – purplish flowers in February
DEUTZIA	Deutzia	Sun or light shade – ordinary soil	D	Cut back – after flowering	Cuttings – autumn	White or pink flowers borne freely in June
ELAEAGNUS	Oleaster	Sun or light shade – ordinary soil	D or E	Not necessary	Plant rooted suckers	Popular variety is E. pungens Maculata – glossy, yellow-splashed leaves
ERICA	Heather	Sun or light shade – well-drained soil	E	Lightly trim – after flowering	Cuttings – summer	Varieties available for flowering at any season and for chalky soil
ESCALLONIA	Escallonia	Sun or light shade – ordinary soil	E	Cut back – autumn	Cuttings – summer	Useful as a hedge, especially in coastal areas

Berberis darwinii

Buddleia davidii

Camellia Lady Clare

Elaeagnus pungens Maculata

Latin name	Common name	Site & soil	Deciduous (D) or Evergreen (E)	Pruning	Propagation	Notes
EUONYMUS	Euonymus	Sun or light shade – ordinary soil	D or E	Not necessary	Cuttings – summer	The popular ones are the evergreens – excellent ground covers
FATSIA	Castor Oil Plant	Partial shade – ordinary soil	E	Not necessary	Cuttings – summer	Not just a house plant – grows up to 3 m outdoors
FORSYTHIA	Golden Bells	Sun or light shade – ordinary soil	D	Cut back shoots with faded blooms	Cuttings – autumn	Very popular – yellow flowers in March and April
FUCHSIA	Fuchsia	Sun or light shade – fertile soil	D	Cut back – March	Cuttings – summer	Choose a hardy variety. Pendent bells July–October
GARRYA	Silk Tassel Bush	Sun or light shade – ordinary soil	E	Not necessary	Cuttings – summer	Long and slender catkins drape bushes January – February
GENISTA	Broom	Sunny site – avoid heavy soil	D	Cut back shoots with faded blooms	Seed	Pea-like yellow flowers in June. Avoid feeding
HAMAMELIS	Witch Hazel	Sun or light shade – well-drained soil	D	Not necessary	Buy from garden centre	Fragrant flowers appear before leaves in winter
HEBE	Veronica	Sun or light shade – well-drained soil	E	Not necessary	Cuttings – summer	Small varieties, such as Autumn Glory, are completely hardy
HELIANTHEMUM	Rock Rose	Sunny site – well-drained soil	E	Cut back – after flowering	Cuttings – summer	Succession of flowers May – July. Avoid feeding
HIBISCUS	Tree Hollyhock	Sunny site – well-drained soil	D	Not necessary	Buy from garden centre	Bush grows 1.8 – 2.4 m high. Not suitable for clayey or cold sites
HYDRANGEA	Hydrangea	Partial shade – well-drained soil	D	Remove flower-heads – March	Cuttings – summer	Many Lacecap and Mophead varieties are available
HYPERICUM	St. John's Wort	Sun or shade – ordinary soil	E or semi E	Cut back – March	Cuttings – summer	Excellent yellow-flowered shrubs – usually grown as ground cover
ILEX	Holly	Sun or shade – ordinary soil	E	Trim back – spring or summer	Cuttings – autumn	Wide range of leaf and berry colours. Always buy small plants
JASMINUM	Winter Jasmine	Sun or light shade – ordinary soil	D	Cut back shoots with faded blooms	Cuttings – summer	J. nudiflorum is an old favourite – yellow flowers November – February
KALMIA	Calico Bush	Partial shade – acid soil	E	Not necessary	Cuttings – summer	Rhododendron-like bush – pink flowers in June
KERRIA	Jew's Mallow	Sun or light shade – ordinary soil	D	Cut back shoots with faded blooms	Plant rooted suckers	Popular and easy – yellow flowers in April and May
LAURUS	Bay Laurel	Sun or light shade – ordinary soil	E	Trim back – spring	Cuttings – summer	L. nobilis grows up to 6 m – leaves scorched by frost
LAVANDULA	Lavender	Sun or light shade – well-drained soil	E	Trim back – spring	Cuttings – autumn	Flowers appear in July – September – white, pink, blue or lavender
LIGUSTRUM	Privet	Sun or shade – ordinary soil	E or semi E	Trim back – May and August	Cuttings – autumn	Often regarded with contempt, but there are colourful varieties
MAGNOLIA	Magnolia	Sun or light shade – humus-rich soil	D or E	Not necessary	Layer stems – summer	Beautiful flowers (white, pink or red) on 1.2 – 6 m plants
MAHONIA	Mahonia	Partial shade – ordinary soil	E	Not necessary	Plant rooted suckers	Useful yellow-flowered shrubs – popular under trees as ground cover
PERNETTYA	Prickly Heath	Sun or light shade – acid soil	E	Trim back – summer	Plant rooted suckers	Large, porcelain-like berries throughout the winter
PHILADELPHUS	Mock Orange	Sun or light shade – ordinary soil	D	Cut back some shoots with faded blooms	Cuttings – autumn	White fragrant flowers in June and July. Wrongly called Syringa
PIERIS	Andromeda	Partial shade – acid soil	E	Not necessary	Layer stems – summer	Bright red new growth in spring. White floral sprays
POTENTILLA	Shrubby Cinquefoil	Sun or light shade – well-drained soil	D	Cut back old stems – March	Cuttings – summer	Noted for length of flowering season – May – September

Hydrangea macrophylla

Potentilla fruticosa

Euonymus alatus

Ilex aquifolium Bacciflava

Latin name	Common name	Site & soil	Deciduous (D) or Evergreen (E)	Pruning	Propagation	Notes
PRUNUS	Prunus	Sun or light shade – ordinary soil	D or E	Trim – late spring (E), late summer (D)	Cuttings (E) – summer	Evergreens include Cherry Laurel and Portugal Laurel. Useful hedging plants
PYRACANTHA	Firethorn	Sun or light shade – ordinary soil	E	Cut back unwanted stems – after flowering	Cuttings – summer	Grown for massed display of red or yellow berries in autumn
RHODODENDRON	Azalea	Partial shade – acid soil	D or E	Remove dead flowers	Layer stems – summer	Daintier than Rhododendron. Deciduous types taller than evergreens
RHODODENDRON	Rhododendron	Partial shade – acid soil	E	Remove dead flowers	Buy from garden centre	Very popular – usual height 1.2 – 2 m, usual flowering month May
RHUS	Sumach	Sunny site – ordinary soil	D	Cut stems to 30 cm – February	Plant rooted suckers	Grown for their brilliant foliage colours in autumn. Large flower spikes
RIBES	Flowering Currant	Sun or light shade – ordinary soil	D or semi E	Cut back shoots with faded blooms	Cuttings – autumn	R. sanguineum is seen everywhere. Pink or red flowers in pendent heads
ROSMARINUS	Rosemary	Sunny site – well-drained soil	E	Lightly trim – after flowering	Cuttings – summer	R. officinalis used for hedging – greyish leaves, pale blue flowers
RUBUS	Ornamental Bramble	Sun or light shade – ordinary soil	D	Bark types – cut back in March	Cuttings – summer	Varieties chosen for coloured bark or floral display
SALIX	Willow	Sun or light shade – moist soil	D	Cut back coloured bark types – March	Cuttings – autumn	Grown mainly for coloured bark – red or yellow
SANTOLINA	Lavender Cotton	Sunny site – well-drained soil	E	Trim back – after flowering	Cuttings – summer	Yellow, button-like flowers (June – August) and silvery foliage
SENECIO	Senecio	Sunny site – well-drained soil	E	Not necessary	Cuttings – summer	Yellow, Daisy-like flowers (June) and leathery foliage
SKIMMIA	Skimmia	Partial shade – acid soil	E	Not necessary	Cuttings – summer	You will need male and female plants of S. japonica for red berries
SPARTIUM	Spanish Broom	Sunny site – well-drained soil	D	Trim back last year's growth – March	Cuttings – summer	Yellow flowers, rush-like stems. Keep in check by regular pruning
SPIRAEA	Spiraea	Sun or light shade – fertile soil	D	Cut back summer-flowering types – March	Cuttings – autumn	Spring-flowering varieties white – summer-flowering ones pink or red
SYMPHORICARPOS	Snowberry	Sun or shade – ordinary soil	D	Trim back – summer	Plant rooted suckers	Rampant grower – marble-like berries in October
SYRINGA	Lilac	Sunny site – non-acid soil	D	Cut back old stems – after flowering	Buy from garden centre	Fragrant blooms in May and early June
TAMARIX	Tamarisk	Sunny site – well-drained soil	D	Cut back summer-flowering types – March	Cuttings – autumn	Spring-flowering varieties pale pink – summer-flowering ones deep pink or red
ULEX	Gorse	Sunny site – ordinary soil	E	Trim back – May	Cuttings – summer	Yellow flowers (April – May) on spiny stems. Poor on fertile sites
VIBURNUM	Viburnum	Sunny site – humus-rich soil	D or E	Not necessary	Cuttings – summer	Many varieties – year-round colour is possible by growing several types
VINCA	Periwinkle	Sun or shade – well-drained soil	E	Not necessary	Plant rooted suckers	An excellent ground cover under trees. White or blue flowers – May–September
WEIGELA	Weigela	Sun or light shade – ordinary soil	D	Cut back shoots with faded blooms	Cuttings – summer	An old favourite – arching stems bear pink or red flowers in May and June
YUCCA	Yucca	Sun or light shade – well-drained soil	E	Not necessary	Plant rooted offsets	A spectacular plant – sword-like leaves and a tall flower-head

Rhododendron Britannia

Viburnum opulus

See
THE TREE & SHRUB EXPERT
for a more complete list
together with full details
and photographs

The TREE & SHRUB EXPERT
Dr. D. G. Hessayon

THE WORLD'S BEST-SELLING BOOK ON TREES & SHRUBS

CHOOSING CONIFERS

Latin name	Common name	Notes	Species & Varieties			
			Latin name	Ultimate height	Height after 10 years	Notes
ABIES	Silver Fir	Most firs are giants – choose with care	A. balsamea Hudsonia	DWARF	30 cm	Ideal for rock gardens
			A. koreana	MEDIUM	1.8 m	Dark green foliage
ARAUCARIA	Monkey Puzzle	Once very popular – reaches 21 m in time	A. araucana	TALL	1.5 m	Branches like curved ropes
CEDRUS	Cedar	A tree for parkland rather than a suburban garden	C. atlantica Glauca	TALL	3 m	Very popular – blue-green
			C. deodara	TALL	3 m	Drooping growth habit
			C. libani	TALL	3 m	Flat-topped with age
CHAMAECYPARIS	False Cypress	The most popular evergreen trees in Britain. Scores of varieties are available, ranging from rockery dwarfs to stately trees	C. lawsoniana Allumii	MEDIUM	1.8 m	Conical – blue-grey foliage
			C. l. Ellwoodii	DWARF	1.5 m	Very popular – grey-green
			C. l. Ellwood's Gold	DWARF	1.2 m	Branchlet tips golden-yellow
			C. l. Minima Aurea	DWARF	30 cm	Compact pyramid – bright yellow
			C. l. Minima Glauca	DWARF	30 cm	Rounded – sea green foliage
			C. obtusa Nana Gracilis	DWARF	60 cm	Rounded sprays – dark foliage
			C. pisifera Boulevard	DWARF	1 m	Silver-blue feathery sprays
CRYPTOMERIA	Japanese Cedar	Slow-growing – needs acid soil	C. japonica Elegans	MEDIUM	1.8 m	Brown-green feathery sprays
CUPRESSO-CYPARIS	Leyland Cypress	The fastest growing conifer in Britain	C. leylandii	TALL	9 m	Height can be a problem
			C. l. Castlewellan	TALL	9 m	Yellow foliage in spring
CUPRESSUS	Cypress	More difficult than Chamaecyparis	C. arizonica	MEDIUM	2.2 m	Conical – blue-grey foliage
			C. macrocarpa Goldcrest	MEDIUM	2.4 m	Conical – golden foliage
GINKGO	Maidenhair Tree	Unusual – leaves are wide and deciduous	G. biloba	TALL	3 m	Pale green fan-like foliage
JUNIPERUS	Juniper	Most popular Junipers are either dwarfs or spreading ground covers. All are easy to grow, withstanding cold & poor soil conditions	J. chinensis	DWARF	1.5 m	Conical – blue-green foliage
			J. communis Compressa	DWARF	30 cm	Columnar – grey-green foliage
			J. c. Depressa Aurea	DWARF	30 cm	Spreading – golden foliage
			J. horizontalis Glauca	PROSTRATE	30 cm	2.7 m wide blue carpet
			J. media Pfitzerana	DWARF	1.2 m	Popular – wide-spreading
			J. squamata Meyeri	DWARF	1.2 m	Erect – blue-grey foliage
			J. virginiana Skyrocket	MEDIUM	1.8 m	Blue-grey narrow column
LARIX	Larch	Deciduous – too tall for average garden	L. decidua	TALL	4.5 m	Needs space and acid soil
METASEQUOIA	Dawn Redwood	Deciduous – discovered in 1941	M. glyptostroboides	TALL	4.5 m	Orange foliage in autumn
PICEA	Spruce	Most (but not all) look like Christmas Trees. Dislike dry and chalky soils	P. albertiana Conica	DWARF	60 cm	Popular rockery conifer
			P. brewerana	TALL	1.5 m	Excellent weeping conifer
			P. omorika	TALL	3 m	Best Christmas Tree
			P. pungens Koster	MEDIUM	1.8 m	Most popular Blue Spruce
PINUS	Pine	Pines are usually too tall for the average garden, but dwarf varieties are available	P. mugo Gnom	DWARF	60 cm	Globular rockery Pine
			P. nigra	TALL	3 m	Dark green foliage
			P. strobus Nana	DWARF	60 cm	Spreading – silvery foliage
			P. sylvestris	TALL	3.5 m	Familiar Scots Pine
TAXODIUM	Swamp Cypress	Deciduous – thrives in swampy soil	T. distichum	TALL	4.5 m	Large tree – ferny foliage
TAXUS	Yew	Yews are generally slow-growing. Suitable for shade	T. baccata	MEDIUM	1.8 m	Dark green tree or hedge
			T. b. Fastigiata	MEDIUM	1.5 m	Columnar Irish Yew
			T. b. Semperaurea	DWARF	60 cm	Spreading – golden foliage
THUJA	Arbor-vitae	Similar to the much more popular Chamaecyparis. Many make excellent hedges	T. occidentalis Rheingold	DWARF	1 m	Conical – bronzy foliage
			T. orientalis Aurea Nana	DWARF	60 cm	Globular – golden foliage
			T. o. Rosedalis	DWARF	60 cm	Globular – purple in autumn
			T. plicata	TALL	4.8 m	Pyramid – specimen tree
TSUGA	Hemlock	Most types too tall for gardens	T. canadensis Pendula	DWARF	60 cm	Spreading – weeping branches

See
THE EVERGREEN EXPERT
for a more complete list
together with full details
and photographs

PROSTRATE:
under 45 cm
DWARF:
45 cm–4.5 m
MEDIUM:
4.5–15 m
TALL:
Over 15 m

CHOOSING TREES

Latin name	Common name	Site & soil	Deciduous (D) or Evergreen (E)	Pruning	Notes
ACER	Maple	Sunny site – ordinary soil	D	Not necessary	Choose a variety with colourful foliage (yellow, purple or variegated) or with decorative bark
AESCULUS	Horse Chestnut	Sunny site – ordinary soil	D	Not necessary	Select a garden variety, such as A. parviflora or A. carnea Briotii
AILANTHUS	Tree of Heaven	Sun or light shade – ordinary soil	D	Cut back – spring	An exotic common name for an ordinary tree – A. altissima is the only common species
ALNUS	Alder	Sun or light shade – damp soil	D	Not necessary	Best garden variety is A. glutinosa Aurea – new foliage pale yellow
BETULA	Birch	Sun or light shade – ordinary soil	D	Remove dead wood – spring	B. pendula (Silver Birch) is the popular one – many varieties available
CARAGANA	Pea Tree	Sun or light shade – ordinary soil	D	Not necessary	Yellow, pea-like flowers. C. arborescens is the basic species. Not common
CARPINUS	Hornbeam	Sun or light shade – ordinary soil	D	Not necessary	Best garden variety is C. betulus Fastigiata – erect, columnar
CASTANEA	Sweet Chestnut	Sun or light shade – ordinary soil	D	Not necessary	Brown Chestnuts in spiny coats. Too large for the average garden
CATALPA	Indian Bean Tree	Sun or light shade – well-drained soil	D	Not necessary	Best garden variety is C. bignonioides Aurea – yellow foliage
CERCIS	Judas Tree	Sunny site – well-drained soil	D	Not necessary	Pink, pea-like flowers appear in May before the leaves
CORYLUS	Hazel	Sunny site – ordinary soil	D	Remove some old wood – spring	Choose a variety with colourful foliage (yellow or purple) or with corkscrew-like branches
CRATAEGUS	Hawthorn	Sun or light shade – ordinary soil	D	Not necessary	White, red or pink flowers in May – red or orange berries in autumn
DAVIDIA	Handkerchief Tree	Sun or light shade – fertile soil	D	Not necessary	Large white flowers in May. D. involucrata has Lime-like foliage
EUCALYPTUS	Gum Tree	Sunny site – avoid sandy soil	E	Cut back – spring	Regular pruning maintains round and waxy blue foliage
FAGUS	Beech	Sun or light shade – avoid heavy soil	D	Trim back – summer	Choose a variety of F. sylvatica. Purple, copper and yellow foliage available
FRAXINUS	Ash	Sun or light shade – ordinary soil	D	Not necessary	Choose F. excelsior Jaspidea (yellow) or F. excelsior Pendula (weeping)
GLEDITSIA	Honey Locust	Sun or light shade – well-drained soil	D	Not necessary	The one to pick is G. triacanthos Sunburst – golden foliage in spring
JUGLANS	Walnut	Sunny site – well-drained soil	D	Remove dead wood – autumn	J. regia Laciniata is the most attractive – drooping branches and deeply-cut leaves
LABURNUM	Golden Rain	Sun or light shade – ordinary soil	D	Remove dead wood – summer	Long sprays of flowers in May or June. L. watereri Vossii is the one to buy
LIQUIDAMBAR	Sweet Gum	Sun or light shade – ordinary soil	D	Not necessary	L. styraciflua is the popular one. Grown for beautiful autumn colours
LIRIODENDRON	Tulip Tree	Sunny site – ordinary soil	D	Not necessary	Choose a compact variety such as L. tulipifera Aureomarginatum
MALUS	Flowering Crab	Sunny site – well-drained soil	D	Remove dead wood – winter	White, red or pink flowers in April or May – colourful fruits in autumn
MORUS	Mulberry	Sun or light shade – ordinary soil	D	Remove dead wood – winter	M. nigra is the usual species – heart-shaped leaves and Blackberry-like fruits

Acer Brilliantissimum

Aesculus parviflora

Cercis siliquastrum

Corylus avellana Contorta

Latin name	Common name	Site & soil	Deciduous (D) or Evergreen (E)	Pruning	Notes
NOTHOFAGUS	Antarctic Beech	Sunny site – lime-free soil	D	Not necessary	N. antarctica is the one you will see – small, dark green leaves
NYSSA	Tupelo	Sun or light shade – lime-free soil	D	Not necessary	For most of the year an ordinary-looking tree – but brilliant colouring in autumn
PLATANUS	Plane	Sun or light shade – ordinary soil	D	Not necessary	Creamy patches beneath grey bark. Too large for the average garden
POPULUS	Poplar	Sun or light shade – ordinary soil	D	Remove dead wood – summer	Very quick growing – not for small gardens or close-to-house planting
PRUNUS	Ornamental Almond	Sunny site – ordinary soil	D	Remove dead wood – summer	P. dulcis is the common one – P. amygdalo-persica Pollardii the most attractive
PRUNUS	Ornamental Cherry	Sunny site – ordinary soil	D	Remove dead wood – summer	Very popular – large number of varieties available. Usual choice is a Japanese Cherry
PRUNUS	Ornamental Peach	Sunny site – ordinary soil	D	Remove dead wood – summer	Has drawbacks – short-lived and suffers from disease. P. persica Klara Meyer is the usual choice
PRUNUS	Ornamental Plum	Sunny site – ordinary soil	D	Remove dead wood – summer	P. cerasifera Nigra is a popular one – pink flowers and almost black leaves
PYRUS	Ornamental Pear	Sunny site – ordinary soil	D	Remove dead wood – winter	P. salicifolia Pendula is an attractive weeping tree – white flowers in April
QUERCUS	Oak	Sunny site – deep soil	D or E	Remove dead wood – winter	Most species are too large for ordinary gardens – evergreen Q. ilex used for hedging
ROBINIA	False Acacia	Sun or light shade – ordinary soil	D	Remove dead wood – summer	R. pseudoacacia Frisia is outstanding – layers of golden foliage all season long
SALIX	Willow	Sun or light shade – deep soil	D	Not necessary	Ordinary Weeping Willow too large for average gardens – choose instead S. caprea Pendula
SORBUS	Mountain Ash	Sun or light shade – ordinary soil	D	Not necessary	Feathery leaves – white flowers in May and red or yellow berries in autumn
SORBUS	Whitebeam	Sun or light shade – ordinary soil	D	Not necessary	Simple oval leaves – white flowers in May and red berries in autumn
TILIA	Lime	Sun or light shade – well-drained soil	D	Not necessary	Choose an aphid-resistant variety – T. petiolaris or T. euchlora
TRACHYCARPUS	Windmill Palm	Sunny site – well-drained soil	E	Remove dead leaves	The hardiest Palm for outdoors – still a gamble in most areas
ULMUS	Elm	Sun or light shade – deep soil	D	Remove dead wood when seen	Most disease-resistant is U. parvifolia (12 m, glossy leaves)

Crataegus oxyacantha Paul's Scarlet

Davidia involucrata vilmoriniana

Laburnum watereri Vossii

Prunus persica Klara Meyer

Robinia pseudoacacia Frisia

Sorbus aucuparia

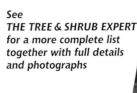
See
THE TREE & SHRUB EXPERT
for a more complete list
together with full details
and photographs

The TREE & SHRUB EXPERT
Dr. D. G. Hessayon

THE WORLD'S BEST-SELLING BOOK ON TREES & SHRUBS

CHOOSING ROSES

Part of the fun (and frustration) of this group of plants is the vast assortment from which you have to choose. Each Rose can be placed in one or other of six classes, and each class contains a bewildering array. So choice is difficult and the pitfalls can be costly – some varieties are now well past their prime and others have not yet proved their worth. Each year the members of the Royal National Rose Society vote on the best and most popular Roses – the result of the latest poll is listed on these two pages. If your search is for reliability rather than novelty, this Rose Analysis is an excellent guide.

Hybrid Tea Roses

New name: Large Flowered Roses

The most popular class – the flower stems are long and the blooms are shapely. The typical Hybrid Tea bears blooms which are medium-sized or large, with many petals forming a distinct cone. The flowers are borne singly or with several side buds.

Position	Name
1	Elina
2	Silver Jubilee
3	Royal William
4	Warm Wishes
5	Peace
6	Savoy Hotel
7 =	Paul Shirville
7 =	Double Delight
9	Nostalgia
10	Loving Memory

Floribunda Roses

New name: Cluster Flowered Roses

The Floribunda bears its flowers in clusters or trusses, and several blooms open at one time in each truss. This class is unrivalled for providing a colourful, reliable and long-lasting bedding display, but generally the flower form is inferior to that of the Hybrid Tea.

Position	Name
1	Iceberg
2	Korresia
3	Sexy Rexy
4	Irish Eyes
5	L'Aimant
6	Mountbatten
7	Queen Elizabeth
8	Amber Queen
9 =	Margaret Merril
9 =	Sunset Boulevard

Shrub Roses

A large class of bush Roses with only one feature in common – they are neither Hybrid Teas nor Floribundas. The typical Shrub is taller than a bedding Rose, and is a Species variety (related to a wild Rose), an old-fashioned hybrid or a modern Shrub Rose.

Position	Name
1	Graham Thomas
2	Sally Holmes
3	Roseraie de L'Hay
4	Gertrude Jekyll
5	Mme Isaac Pereire
6 =	Buff Beauty
6 =	Jacqueline du Pre
8 =	Nevada
8 =	Ballerina
10	Abraham Derby

Elina

Sexy Rexy

Sally Holmes

Handel

Climbers & Ramblers

A Rose which if tied to a support can be made to climb. Ramblers have long pliable stems which bear large trusses of small flowers as a single summer flush. Climbers have stiff stems which bear flowers which are larger than Rambler ones and may be repeat flowering.

Position	Name
1	Compassion
2	New Dawn
3	Penny Lane
4=	Handel
4=	Dublin Bay
6=	Golden Showers
6=	Iceberg Climbing
8	Albertine
9	Aloha
10	Gloire de Dijon

Miniature Roses

Miniatures can be used for edging beds, growing in containers or taking indoors for use as temporary pot plants. Both leaves and flowers are small, and under normal conditions the maximum height is 40 cm. Many varieties are considerably shorter.

Position	Name
1	Angela Rippon
2	Starina
3	Red Ace
4	Pour Toi
5	Baby Masquerade
6=	Irresistible
6=	Cinderella
8=	Fond Memories
8=	Orange Sunblaze
8=	Pretty Polly

See
THE ROSE EXPERT
for a more complete list together with full details and photographs

Patio Roses

A class which appeared in the 1980s and now contains many popular varieties. They were formerly grouped with the Floribundas, and are compact versions of this class. Patio Roses grow about 50 cm high and make excellent tub and edging plants.

Position	Name
1	Sweet Dream
2	Anna Ford
3	Cider Cup
4	Sweet Magic
5	Sweet Memories
6=	Pretty Polly
6=	Greenalls Glory
6=	Peter Pan
9=	Gentle Touch
9=	Summer Snow

New Roses

Fl **Floribunda**
HT **Hybrid Tea**
Cl **Climber/Rambler**
Sh **Shrub**

Every year scores of new Roses are offered for sale by growers, and these Hybrid Teas, Floribundas, Climbers and Shrubs are described in glowing terms. But not all will live up to their promise – on the right are the ones introduced since 1998 which the panel considered most reliable.

Position	Name	Class
1	Great Expectations	Fl
2	Irish Eyes	Fl
3	The Generous Gardener	Cl
4=	Champagne Moment	HT
4=	Rhapsody in Blue	Fl
6=	Crocus Rose	Sh
6=	King Mace	HT
6=	William Shakespeare 2000	Sh
9=	Buxom Beauty	HT
9=	Glorious	HT
9=	Lisa	Fl
9=	Macmillan Nurse	Sh
9=	Nostalgia	HT
9=	Twist	Cl
15=	Crown Princess Margareta	Sh
15=	For You With Love	Fl
15=	Jubilee Celebration	Sh
15=	Pride of Scotland	HT
15=	Rachel	HT
15=	Summertime	Cl

CHOOSING TOP FRUIT

There is no exact definition of top fruit. Included in this group are all the fruit-bearing woody plants which grow as trees in their natural state, but a few (e.g Quince) are shrubs. Remember that the trees will be with you for many years, so pick the site with care and prepare the soil properly.

The rootstock will largely determine the eventual height of the tree. The variety on offer may be self-sterile, and would require a suitable partner nearby to ensure pollination. Always check the details before you buy. Where space is limited buy a Family Tree – a plant grafted with several compatible varieties.

Free-standing trees (bushes and standards) are the basic form – maintenance is usually straightforward once the framework has been established. A restricted form is used where space is limited. Such forms are grown against a fence or wall and are pruned in summer.

Trunk:
Standard
2–2.5 m
Bush
60–75 cm

Trunk:
Half standard
1–1.5 m
Dwarf bush
45–60 cm

BUSH
The **bush** and **dwarf bush** have short trunks and open centres. A dwarfing rootstock is used – aim to maintain a goblet-shaped framework. For planting in a large lawn there is the **half standard** – these trees are much more difficult to look after and cropping starts later.

PYRAMID
A **pyramid** is similar to a bush but a central leader has been maintained, giving a broadly conical shape. A variation (the **spindlebush**) has the side branches trained to grow horizontally. The **dwarf pyramid** is closely planted in rows. Summer pruning is necessary.

CORDON
A **cordon** is a single-stemmed tree which is planted at 45° and tied to a permanent support system such as a fence. Dwarfing rootstocks are generally used and very vigorous varieties are usually avoided. The ultimate height is about 1.5 m and several varieties can be grown together in a restricted space.

ESPALIER
The **espalier**, like the cordon, can be grown against a wall or fence. Its advantage is that it is more decorative than the cordon, but it also takes up more space and is more difficult to maintain. Buy trees which have already been trained.

FAN
The **fan**, like the espalier, is an attractive form when planted against a wall. It requires a large space – a height of 2 m and a spread of 3 m – and careful training is essential. Note that there is no central leader. Not popular for Apples – more widely used for Cherries and Peaches.

APPLE
Apples are the most popular top fruit trees – attractive in bloom and rewarding at cropping time. Most areas of Britain are quite suitable for Apple cultivation, but some people with small gardens are put off by the thought of large standards. Standard trees are not for the average plot – these days you can buy dwarf bushes which will not reach your height in their lifetime, or you can train cordons to clothe a garden fence or wall.

If you have the skill and time, buy 1-year old maidens and train them from scratch. Otherwise buy a 3- or 4-year old tree which has already been trained.

Name	Dessert (D) or Cooking (C)	Skin colour	Season of use	Notes
BLENHEIM ORANGE	D or C	Gold, striped red	Oct-Dec	High yield
BRAMLEY'S SEEDLING	C	Green	Oct-Mar	Excellent cooker
CHARLES ROSS	D or C	Yellow, flushed red	Oct-Dec	Regular cropper
DISCOVERY	D	Bright red	Aug-Sept	Acid flesh
GEORGE CAVE	D	Yellow, marked red	Aug	Crisp flesh
GREENSLEEVES	D	Pale green	Sept-Nov	Golden Delicious type
JAMES GRIEVE	D	Yellow, speckled orange	Sept-Oct	Self-fertile

PEAR

You can choose from a large list of varieties if you can provide a warm and sheltered site – if not it would be wise to choose from Conference, Beth and Concorde. Many others in the catalogue may sound attractive, but they can be unreliable in cooler areas or in a poor season. A late frost can be disastrous.

Pears are much less popular than Apples in gardens, which means that you probably will have to provide a suitable pollination partner in your own plot. If space is limited, grow several different cordons. Or you can plant a Family Tree – the basic type carries Conference, Doyenné du Comice and Williams' Bon Chrétien.

Name	Skin colour	Season of use	Notes
BETH	Pale yellow	Sept	Small fruit. High yield
CONCORDE	Pale green	Nov-Dec	Reliable. Good flavour
CONFERENCE	Green, russetted	Oct-Nov	Most reliable variety
DOYENNÉ DU COMICE	Yellow, flushed brown	Nov-Dec	Excellent flavour
WILLIAMS' BON CHRÉTIEN	Yellow, spotted red	Sept	Bartlett Pear. Very popular

PLUM

There are ordinary Plum varieties for eating fresh or for cooking, and sour Damsons for cooking and bottling. The yellow or green Gages are regarded as sweeter than ordinary Plums, but they are also more difficult to grow. Plums flower very early, so pollination is sometimes disappointing.

Many Plums are self-fertile, including the most popular dessert variety (Victoria) and the most widely grown cooker (Czar). Others need a pollination partner. Buy 2- or 3-year old partly-trained trees – choose a late-flowering variety if the site is unfavourable. A good plan is to grow the Plum as a fan against a south-facing wall.

Name	Dessert (D) or Cooking (C)	Skin colour	Season of use	Notes
CZAR	Plum C	Dark purple	Aug	Easiest to grow
MARJORIE'S SEEDLING	Plum C or D	Purple	Sept-Oct	Large fruit. High yield
MERRYWEATHER	Damson C	Purple	Sept	Best garden Damson
OULLIN'S GOLDEN GAGE	Gage D	Yellow, spotted red	Aug	Large fruit. High yield
VICTORIA	Plum C or D	Pink, spotted red	Aug	Most popular Plum

CHERRY

Before World War II Sweet Cherries were out of the question for a small garden – 10 m high trees and the need for a nearby pollinating partner made their cultivation impractical. Cherry growing is now a practical proposition with the introduction of self-fertile varieties and dwarfing rootstocks.

Sour Cherries are used for cooking, bottling etc, and the usual choice is the self-fertile Morello. Other varieties such as Nabella are available. The best site for a Sweet Cherry is a wall in full sun. Choose a self-fertile variety which has been trained as a fan – look for Stella or Sunburst. Birds will be a problem – see page 93.

See
THE FRUIT EXPERT
for a more complete list
together with full details
and photographs

CHOOSING SOFT FRUIT

The increased interest in grow-your-own has made soft fruit growing much more popular than ever before. Unlike vegetables you can crop the plants year after year once they are established, and unlike top fruit there is a place for at least one example in every garden. Plant Gooseberry bushes and Raspberry canes where space permits, or plant Strawberries in a tub or window box where the garden is tiny.

The need for care when buying is greater with soft fruit than with tree fruit. Virus-infected stock will never amount to anything, so do not plant gifts from friends – always go for certified stock where the scheme applies.

As you will read later, soft fruit needs attention – you cannot neglect the plants year after year and still expect high-yielding bushes and canes. In addition there are only a few general rules which apply to all types – the differences far outweigh the similarities.

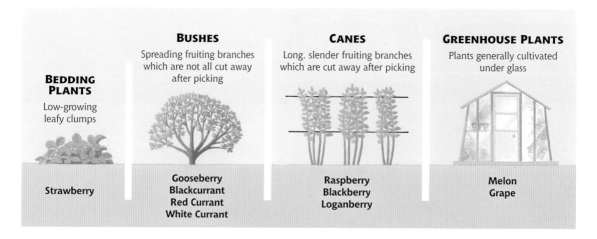

BEDDING PLANTS

Low-growing leafy clumps

Strawberry

BUSHES

Spreading fruiting branches which are not all cut away after picking

Gooseberry
Blackcurrant
Red Currant
White Currant

CANES

Long. slender fruiting branches which are cut away after picking

Raspberry
Blackberry
Loganberry

GREENHOUSE PLANTS

Plants generally cultivated under glass

Melon
Grape

STRAWBERRY

Strawberries are the most popular home-grown fruit. There are many reasons apart from their luscious taste. You don't need lots of room and you don't need lots of patience – plant in August and pick fruit next summer. The problem is that the picking period of popular varieties is fleeting – two or three weeks and it is all over.

You can extend the season by planting several different varieties – there are early, mid season and late types and also perpetual ones which bear several flushes between August and October. Buy young, healthy plants in late summer – make sure they are certified as virus free.

Name	Type	Season of use	Notes
BARON SOLEMACHER	Alpine	June-Oct	Tiny fruit. No runners
DOMANIL	Summer fruiting	Aug	Excellent flavour. High yield
ELSANTA	Summer fruiting	June-July	Large fruit. High yield
HONEYONE	Summer fruiting	June	Excellent flavour. High yield
RAPELLA	Perpetual	Aug-Oct	Not good for N. areas
ROYAL SOVEREIGN	Summer fruiting	June	No longer a good choice
TAMELLA	Summer fruiting	June-July	Good for N. areas

RASPBERRY FAMILY

The basic types are the Blackberry (used mainly for pies, jam-making and other culinary purposes) and the Raspberry (used mainly for dessert purposes – either immediately or frozen for later use). Then there are the hybrid berries – Loganberry, Tayberry, Boysenberry etc. Always buy stock which is certified virus free and follow the pruning instructions exactly.

Raspberries are by far the most popular cane fruit. Not all Raspberries are red and not all fruit in midsummer. The Summer-fruiting varieties (June-August) are the usual ones, but you can buy Autumn-fruiting varieties to extend the cropping season.

Name	Type	Season of use	Notes
AUTUMN BLISS	Autumn-fruiting Raspberry	Aug-Oct	Firm fruit. High yield
GLEN MOY	Summer-fruiting Raspberry	July	No spines. Large berries
HIMALAYA GIANT	Blackberry	Aug-Sept	Thorny variety. Very vigorous
MALLING JEWEL	Summer-fruiting Raspberry	July	Compact growth. Popular
TAYBERRY	Hybrid berry	July-Aug	Best of the hybrid berries

CURRANT FAMILY

Currants are usually obtained from the home plot or allotment rather than the supermarket. Red Currants are tart – use them for pies or jams. The White Currant is a sport of the red one and is eaten fresh – the flavour is grape-like. Blackcurrants are grown mainly for use in pies and puddings.

The choice of Red Currants and White Currants is limited. With Blackcurrants it is wise to choose one of the late-flowering varieties – older types flower in late April and are susceptible to frost damage.

Buy 2-year old plants – Red and White Currants should have at least 3 branches on the stem. Blackcurrants should have at least 4 shoots

Name	Type	Season of use	Notes
BEN LOMOND	Blackcurrant	July	Some mildew resistance. High yield
BEN SAREK	Blackcurrant	July	Some mildew resistance. High yield
JONKHEER VAN TETS	Red Currant	July	Best as a cordon
RED LAKE	Red Currant	July	Most popular variety
WHITE VERSAILLES	White Currant	July	Most popular variety

GOOSEBERRY

The Gooseberry is a long-suffering bush – a neglected plant will continue to give some fruit for many years. Annual pruning, however, will improve yields and make picking easier. There are cooking varieties (e.g Careless) and others more suitable for dessert purposes (e.g Leveller). The best cooking/dessert variety is Invicta.

A good plan is to buy a dessert variety from which you can pick unripe fruit in late May or June for cooking and then pick ripe fruit in July or August for eating fresh. Choose a 2- or 3-year old plant – it can be grown as a bush or cordon. Gooseberries are not generally troubled by virus.

*See
THE FRUIT EXPERT
for a more complete list
together with full details
and photographs*

The
FRUIT EXPERT
Dr. D. G. Hessayon

CHOOSING VEGETABLES

The boom in growing vegetables at home that began in the early years of the 21st century has been truly remarkable. The prime cause has been the desire to obtain produce which is known to be free from chemical residues. Listed on these two pages are the types you will find as seed or plants at your local garden centre or DIY superstore. Outdoor vegetables are nearly always grown in long rows as described on pages 74–75 – follow the spacing recommendations in *The Vegetable & Herb Expert* or on the seed packets. This is not the only way to grow them – there are two other ways (pages 76–78) which have their own distinct advantages.

Crop	Sow	Plant	Harvest	Time taken (weeks)	Easy to grow	Easy to store
ASPARAGUS	Apr	Apr	May-June	120 P → H	✗	✗
AUBERGINE	Feb ⌂	Apr ⌂	Aug-Sept	20 S → H	✗	✗
BEANS, BROAD	Feb-Apr	—	July-Aug	14 S → H	✔	✗
BEANS, FRENCH	May-June	—	July-Sept	10 S → H	✔	✗
BEANS, RUNNER	May-June	—	Aug-Oct	13 S → H	(✔)	✗
	Apr ⌂	May-June	Aug-Oct	14 S → H	(✔)	✗
BEET, LEAF	Apr	—	Aug-Nov	12 S → H	✔	✗
BEETROOT	Apr-June	—	June-Oct	11 S → H	✔	✔
BROCCOLI	Apr-May	June-July	Feb-May	44 S → H	(✔)	✗
BRUSSELS SPROUTS	Mar-Apr	May-June	Oct-Feb	30 S → H	(✔)	✗
CABBAGE, SPRING	July-Aug	Sept-Oct	Apr-May	35 S → H	(✔)	✗
CABBAGE, SUMMER	Apr	May-June	Aug-Sept	20 S → H	(✔)	✗
CABBAGE, WINTER	Apr-May	July	Nov-Feb	35 S → H	(✔)	✔
CABBAGE, CHINESE	July-Aug	—	Oct	10 S → H	✔	✗
CALABRESE	Apr-May	June-July	Aug-Oct	12 S → H	(✔)	✗
CAPSICUM	Feb ⌂	Apr ⌂	Aug-Sept	18 S → H	✗	✗
CARROT, EARLY	Mar-Apr	—	July	12 S → H	(✔)	✗
CARROT, MAINCROP	Apr-June	—	Sept-Oct	16 S → H	(✔)	✔
CAULIFLOWER, SUMMER	Apr	June	Aug-Sept	18 S → H	✗	✗
CAULIFLOWER, AUTUMN	Apr-May	June	Oct-Nov	24 S → H	✗	✗
CAULIFLOWER, WINTER	May	July	Mar-May	45 S → H	✗	✗

Runner Bean: Pickwick

Cabbage: Stonehead

Carrot: Amsterdam Forcing

Cauliflower: Purple Cape

Crop	Sow	Plant	Harvest	Time taken (weeks)	Easy to grow	Easy to store
CELERIAC	Mar 🏠	May-June	Oct-Nov	33 S → H	✘	✔
CELERY, TRENCH	Mar-Apr 🏠	June	Oct-Feb	40 S → H	✘	✘
CELERY, SELF-BLANCHING	Mar-Apr 🏠	June	Aug-Oct	25 S → H	✘	✘
CHICORY	May	—	Dec-Mar	25 S → H	✘	✘
COURGETTE	May-June	—	July-Sept	10 S → H	(✔)	✘
CUCUMBER, GREENHOUSE	Apr 🏠	May 🏠	July-Sept	12 S → H	✘	✘
CUCUMBER, OUTDOOR	May-June	—	Aug-Sept	12 S → H	✘	✘
ENDIVE	Apr-Aug	—	Sept-Feb	18 S → H	✘	✘
KALE	May	July	Dec-Mar	33 S → H	✔	✘
KOHL RABI	Apr-June	—	Aug-Oct	10 S → H	✔	✘
LEEK	Mar-Apr	June	Nov-Mar	45 S → H	(✔)	✘
LETTUCE	Mar-July	—	June-Oct	10 S → H	✔	✘
MARROW	May-June	—	Aug-Oct	14 S → H	(✔)	✔
MARROW	Apr 🏠	June	Aug-Oct	14 S → H	✘	✔
ONION, SETS	—	Mar-Apr	Aug	20 P → H	✔	✔
ONION, SEED	Mar-Apr	—	Aug-Sept	22 S → H	✔	✔
PARSNIP	Mar	—	Nov-Feb	34 S → H	✔	✔
PEA	Mar-July	—	May-Oct	12-32 S → H	✘	✘
POTATO, EARLY	—	Mar-Apr	June-Aug	13 P → H	✔	✔
POTATO, MAINCROP	—	Apr	Sept-Oct	22 P → H	✔	✔
RADISH	Mar-June	—	May-Sept	6 S → H	✔	✔
RHUBARB	—	Feb-Mar	Apr-July	65 P → H	✔	✘
SALSIFY	April	—	Nov-Jan	25 S → H	✔	✔
SHALLOT	—	Feb-Mar	Aug	20 P → H	✔	✔
SPINACH	Mar-May	—	June-Oct	10 S → H	(✔)	✘
SWEDE	May-June	—	Nov-Feb	22 S → H	✔	✔
SWEET CORN	May	—	Aug-Sept	14 S → H	✘	✘
TOMATO, GREENHOUSE	Feb 🏠	Apr 🏠	July-Oct	16 S → H	✘	✘
TOMATO, OUTDOOR	Mar-Apr 🏠	June	Aug-Sept	20 S → H	✘	✘
TURNIP, EARLY	Mar-June	—	May-Sept	8 S → H	✔	✘
TURNIP, MAINCROP	July-Aug	—	Oct-Dec	12 S → H	✔	✔

🏠 = under glass

S = sowing
P = planting
H = harvest

✔ = easy
(✔) = not really easy
✘ = difficult

✔ = can be stored for months
✘ = cannot be stored

The months listed above are based on a location in the Midlands. Southern areas will be about 2 weeks earlier – parts of Scotland may be more than 2 weeks later.

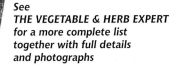

See
THE VEGETABLE & HERB EXPERT
for a more complete list
together with full details
and photographs

CHOOSING WILDFLOWERS

Garden Friendly

A recurring theme of this book is the growing awareness that the garden is part of the environment. It is therefore not surprising that there is an increasing number of people who want to grow some wildflowers in their garden.

The easiest approach is to grow individual plants or small clumps in the border or in a cottage garden. The idea of a Wildflower Meadow may sound attractive, but it is a difficult feature to create and maintain – see page 85.

Seeds and plugs of individual varieties can be bought through specialist suppliers, and wildflower mixtures are obtainable. There are mixes with and without grasses for acid, neutral or alkaline soils. Remember that these plants may grow happily in some parts of the country, but are not 'natural' in your garden … the natural ones are the weeds that grow in your beds, borders and wasteland.

Name	Type	Flowering period	Colour	Height
BIRD'S FOOT TREFOIL	HP	May-Sept	Yellow	10-30 cm
BLACK MEDICK	A	Apr-Aug	Yellow	5-30 cm
BLUEBELL	Bu	Apr-June	Blue	20-50 cm
BUGLE	HP	May-July	Blue	10-30 cm
COMMON KNAPWEED	HP	June-Sept	Purple	30-60 cm
COMMON SORREL	HP	May-June	Pink	50 cm-1 m
COMMON TOADFLAX	HP	July-Oct	Yellow	30-80 cm
COMMON VETCH	A	May-Sept	Purple	20 cm-1 m
CORN CHAMOMILE	A	June-Sept	White	15-60 cm
CORN MARIGOLD	A	May-Aug	Yellow	15-50 cm
CORNCOCKLE	HP	June-Aug	Red	30-80 cm
CORNFLOWER	HP	July-Aug	Blue	30-60 cm
COWSLIP	HP	Apr-May	Yellow	10-30 cm
FIELD POPPY	A	May-Oct	Red	25-50 cm
GOAT'S BEARD	A	June-July	Yellow	30-60 cm
GREAT BURNET	HP	June-Sept	Red	30-80 cm
LADY'S BEDSTRAW	HP	July-Aug	Yellow	15-80 cm
MEADOW BUTTERCUP	HP	Apr-May	Yellow	30-80 cm
MEADOW CRANESBILL	HP	June-Sept	Blue	30-80 cm
OX-EYE DAISY	HP	May-Aug	White	25-60 cm
PIGNUT	HP	May-June	White	25-50 cm
PRIMROSE	HP	Mar-May	Yellow	10-15 cm
RAGGED ROBIN	HP	May-June	Red	30-80 cm
RED CLOVER	HP	May-Sept	Red	10-70 cm
RIBWORT PLANTAIN	HP	Apr-Aug	Brown	15-25 cm
SAINFOIN	HP	June-Aug	Pink	15-80 cm
SELFHEAL	HP	June-Sept	Lilac	5-25 cm
SMALL SCABIOUS	HP	June-Aug	Mauve	15-60 cm
SOAPWORT	HP	July-Sept	Pale pink	30-80 cm
ST JOHN'S WORT	HP	June-Sept	Yellow	30-80 cm
TEASEL	Bi	July-Aug	Lilac	50 cm-1.5 m
WHITE CAMPION	HP	May-Sept	White	30-80 cm
WHITE MELILOT	HP	June-Aug	White	60 cm-1 m
WILD CARROT	Bi	June-Aug	White	30-80 cm
YARROW	HP	June-Nov	White	15-50 cm
YELLOW RATTLE	A	May-Aug	Yellow	10-50 cm

Ox-eye Daisy

Meadow Buttercup

Corncockle

A = Annual, **Bi** = Biennial, **Bu** = Bulb, **HP** = Hardy Perennial

CHOOSING GROUND COVER PLANTS

It is essential to blanket bare ground in order to prevent colonisation by weeds. You can put on a non-living blanket (a mulch) or grow a living blanket which is referred to as ground cover. This consists of reasonably or highly ornamental plants with a spread of leafy growth which is sufficiently dense to partly or completely inhibit weed development.

Most but not all are low-growing and most but not all are evergreen. Many have a fairly controlled growth habit, but some are rampant invaders which people are warned not to use. This warning is only partly correct – if the purpose of the ground cover is to clothe the soil between plants then these rampant ones should be avoided. But another use for ground cover is to clothe inaccessible areas such as banks where little else would grow, and here the vigorous invasive types may be a godsend. A word of warning. Do not try to fill all the bare spaces with ground cover rather than a mulch – if you do the garden will have an overcrowded look.

Lysimachia nummularia Aurea

Name	Type	Notes
AJUGA	HP : E	Decorative-leaved ground hugger. Height 10 cm, spacing 45 cm
ALCHEMILLA	HP : D	Lobed leaves and yellow flowers. Height 45 cm, spacing 45 cm
BALLOTA	HP : E	Grey woolly leaves. Height 30 cm, spacing 45 cm
BERGENIA	HP : E	Good under trees. Height 45 cm, spacing 45 cm
CALLUNA	S : E	Heather for acid soil. Height 15-45 cm, spacing 30 cm
COTONEASTER	S : E	Choose evergreen C. dammeri. Height 15-60 cm, spacing 60 cm
EUONYMUS	S : E	Choose a variegated one. Height 30-60 cm, spacing 60 cm
EUPHORBIA	HP : D	Masses of flower-heads. Height 60 cm, spacing 45 cm
GERANIUM	HP : D/E	Many types, choose carefully. Height 45 cm, spacing 45 cm
HEBE	S : E	Choose a dwarf variety. Height 30 cm, spacing 45 cm
HEDERA	S : E	Many leaf forms available. Height 15 cm, spacing 45 cm
HEUCHERA	HP : E	Lobed decorative leaves. Height 60 cm, spacing 45 cm
HOSTA	HP : D	Good under trees. Height 15-60 cm, spacing 60 cm
HYPERICUM	S : SE	Can be invasive. Height 60 cm-1.5 m, spacing 60 cm
IBERIS	S : E	I. sempervirens bears white flowers. Height 30 cm, spacing 30 cm
JUNIPERUS	C : E	Choose a dwarf spreading variety. Height 30 cm-1.2 m, spacing 75 cm
LAMIUM	HP : SE	White-marked leaves for shade. Height 10 cm, spacing 30 cm
LYSIMACHIA	HP : D	Creeping Jenny for damp soil. Height 5 cm, spacing 30 cm
NEPETA	HP : D	Aromatic grey-green leaves. Height 60 cm, spacing 45 cm
PACHYSANDRA	S : E	Good under trees. Height 10 cm, spacing 30 cm
POLYGONUM	HP : E	P. affine is invasive. Height 30 cm, spacing 60 cm
PULMONARIA	HP : D	White-spotted leaves. Height 30 cm, spacing 30 cm
ROSA	S : D	Choose a Carpet variety. Height 60 cm, spacing 45 cm
SEDUM	HP : E	Needs sandy soil in sun. Height 45 cm, spacing 45 cm
STACHYS	HP : E	Grey woolly leaves. Height 45 cm, spacing 45 cm
VINCA	S : E	Can be invasive. Height 15 cm, spacing 45 cm

HP = Hardy Perennial, **S** = Shrub, **C** = Conifer, **E** = Evergreen, **SE** = Semi-evergreen, **D** = Deciduous

CHOOSING COMPANION PLANTS

A companion plant is a variety or species which will help a vegetable which is growing nearby. Flowers, shrubs etc may also benefit – Victorian gardeners planted Chives next to Rose bushes and Apple trees. But companion planting is usually a feature of the allotment or home vegetable plot, and gardeners continue to debate its value.

It is claimed that these companion plants can work in various ways – vital nutrients may be supplied, root secretions may attack underground pests, and so on. In many cases, however, no explanation is offered for the benefits claimed for them.

There is little scientific evidence in support of companion planting, but it is part of age-old country wisdom and has become a feature of green gardening. For the believers, companion planting is a desirable technique as one or both plants benefit, but some combinations are claimed to be harmful. Examples are Cucumbers and Potatoes, or Brassicas and Beans.

Asparagus

Tomato

Companion plant	Vegetable
BEAN	**Crop :** Lettuce **Reason :** Unknown
CARROT	**Crop :** Lettuce, Tomato **Reason :** Unknown
CELERY	**Crop :** Pea **Reason :** Unknown
FRENCH MARIGOLD	**Crop :** Various **Reason :** Pests including eelworms, cabbage white butterflies and aphids are deterred. There is some scientific evidence for this effect
LETTUCE	**Crop :** Strawberry, Cucumber **Reason :** Unknown
MINT	**Crop :** Brassicas **Reason :** Cabbage white butterflies are repelled by the smell
NASTURTIUM	**Crop :** Various **Reason :** Beneficial hoverflies are attracted
ONION	**Crop :** Carrot **Reason :** Carrot root flies are repelled
PARSLEY	**Crop :** Carrot **Reason :** Carrot root flies are repelled
POTATO	**Crop :** Bean, Pea, Brassicas **Reason :** Unknown
RUE	**Crop :** Various **Reason :** Aphids are repelled by the smell
TOMATO	**Crop :** Asparagus **Reason:** Asparagus beetles are repelled
TURNIP	**Crop :** Pea, Bean **Reason :** Unknown

Chapter 4

CARING FOR THE PLANTS

In recent years there has been a growing awareness that the environment is affected by the way we live our lives. The way we travel, the way we manage our home … and the way we manage our garden.

As a result a more natural way of tending our plot has started to spread across the country. The age-old practice of planting annuals in parade-ground straight rows continues to give way to informal planting, the presence of a scattering of buttercups and daisies in the lawn is no longer regarded as a sign of neglect, and no longer do we seek to kill every insect we see on a leaf or flower bud. Once we struggled to keep the lawn green in times of drought with a sprinkler and a vast volume of water – now we accept that the grass can be left to recover quickly once the rain returns.

We are adopting a green approach, but at various levels of involvement. To some this means merely avoiding chemicals which call for a waiting period between spraying and picking in the vegetable garden. For others this is extended to all chemicals – the organic school avoids all products which are neither natural nor derived from living material.

Seeking to attract wildlife to our gardens is yet one more feature of this green trend, but despite all these changes in attitude the basic care principles remain. Plants must be given a suitable home as outlined in Chapter 2, and you must study the plants' needs and potential size *before* purchase. Proper planting is more than just digging a hole and dropping in the plant before returning the soil, and pruning is much more than just lopping off branches which have grown beyond their allotted space. Watering is vital for shallow-rooting or newly-planted flowers or shrubs, and serious pests and diseases must be kept at bay wherever practical. The basic rules remain, but we now use them alongside a number of new ideas to ensure that our garden is friendly to the environment.

CARING FOR BEDDING PLANTS

A bedding plant is a species or variety which is transplanted at the leafy stage to its place in the ground or in a container where it provides a display for a limited period. It is usually grown for its floral display rather than its foliage. Annuals and biennials are the dominant types, but you will also find rockery perennials (e.g Diascia), hardy perennials such as Polyanthus, and tender perennials (e.g Pelargonium and Canna).

Many gardeners find the promise of instant gardening irresistible, and sales continue to rise despite the scorn of horticultural purists. Bedding out in spring and autumn has traditionally been the main use for these plants, but these days containers have become the most popular home.

Choose a day when the ground is moist. Squeeze a handful of soil – it should be wet enough to form a ball and yet dry enough to shatter when dropped on a hard surface.

The Right Condition

Buy plants which are compact and sturdy, and are growing in compost which is moist. There should be no wilted leaves nor drooping stems. Pot plants are generally sold in flower. With strips and trays it is wise to buy plants in bud with just a few open blooms, but some (e.g Impatiens, Begonia and Marigolds) are nearly always sold in flower. Do not buy Geraniums or Petunias in flower unless they are in pots or packs.

The Right Time

Spring-flowering hardy annuals can be bought and planted out in April or early May when the weather and soil are suitable. Half-hardy annuals and perennials should be bought later as they must not be set out until the danger of frost has gone – this means waiting until mid to late May in southern counties and as late as early June in exposed northern areas. Spring-flowering plants such as Daisies and Wallflowers should be bought and planted in October.

TRAY

The tray is the traditional method of buying bedding plants. It is the cheapest way to buy for immediate planting, but roots are damaged when they are torn apart at planting time. Plastic trays have replaced wooden ones. Never buy a few plants wrapped in newspaper.

STRIP

The strip has become the most popular way to buy bedding plants. The plants are grown in a series of snap-off strips which are made of rigid white polystyrene or flimsy plastic. Each strip contains from 3 large plants (e.g Geraniums) to 10-12 small annuals (e.g Antirrhinums).

PACK

The pack is made of flimsy plastic and consists of 4-24 individual pots. Each pot contains a single plant and is usually detached at the time of sale. More expensive per plant than strips, but there is no root disturbance at planting time. Packs are becoming increasingly popular.

POT

The individual rigid pot is the most expensive way to buy bedding plants, but this is the container for top-quality stock. Pots are usually plastic but clay ones are still used. Peat pots can be planted directly into the soil. Pots are the way to buy a few choice plants.

PLUG

A plug is larger and more advanced than a seedling – it is a small but well-rooted plant raised in a cellular tray by the grower. Economical – they are bought in units of 35. Use for planting directly into a hanging basket or into a small pot of compost for growing on before planting out.

Spacing

As a general guide use the expected height for low-growing and average-sized plants as the spacing distance – see pages 24–25. For tall plants space at $2/3$ of the anticipated height.

Display

The creation of a formal bed calls for planting in geometric shapes. This entails marking out the pattern before you begin and after planting doing those tasks to ensure a uniform display. This means regular dead-heading and replacing poor specimens with plants kept in reserve. A lot of work for an out-of-fashion style.

It is better to use bedding plants as part rather than the whole of the bed or border planting scheme. Use them in informal clumps between other plants. Here differences between neighbouring plants are not a problem, nor is the loss of an occasional specimen. The other major use is in containers – see the feature on the right for details.

Using Containers

Garden Friendly

Pots, tubs, troughs, and baskets filled with bedding plants are a basic feature of the garden scene. An instant splash of colour is provided, and your container garden need never be empty. Summer bedding can be preceded by spring bedding and followed by winter bedding.

There are all sorts of advantages. Ground is not needed and plants can be grown on the patio or right next to the house. Small plants are easier to see and pendant ones look more attractive when raised from the ground. Eyesores can be hidden, plants which would not thrive in your soil can be grown and so on, but there is one big disadvantage. Regular watering is essential – this may have to be done every day in hot and dry weather.

There are a number of key points to remember when planting up containers. The tub or trough should be frost-proof, waterproof and strong enough to hold the compost and plants. There should be at least one hole (1.5 cm across or more) every 10-15 cm. The inside should be clean and the container should be raised from the ground or base if possible.

Cover the drainage holes with crocks with a mesh screen – add a layer of gravel to help drainage and stability. Add moist potting or general-purpose compost and plant firmly – see below. Leave a 3-8 cm watering space above the surface and water in plants immediately.

Planting

Prepare plants for the move. Always water plants prior to lifting – dry soil would fall away from the roots. Keep the soil ball intact.

1 Dig the hole to fit the roots. The hole should be much wider that it is deep – the roots at the base and at the side should never have to be bent to fit into the hole.

2 Use the right tool. A trowel is the right implement for small plants.

3 Plant at the right depth. Set all bedding plants so that the top of the soil ball is just below ground level.

4 Plant properly. For small plants, fill around the soil ball with loose soil and firm with the fingers or the trowel handle. With larger plants, fine soil should be added, each layer being gently compressed with the fists until the hole is full. Handle plants by the soil ball or the leaves – never by the stem. Water in after planting.

53

Sowing Seeds

INDOORS Tender plants are grown from seed in March or April and are set out in late May or early June. Sowing indoors is not restricted to half-hardy subjects – it is useful for hardy types which are to grow in a wet and/or cold area.

1 **CONTAINER & COMPOST** Use a seed tray, pan or pot. Drainage holes are necessary. Wash used containers before filling – soak clay pots overnight.

Fill with seed or general-purpose compost. Firm lightly with a piece of board. Sprinkle with water the day before seed sowing. It should be moist (not wet) when you scatter the seeds thinly over the surface. Cover with a thin layer of compost – do not cover small seeds. Firm lightly.

2 **'UNDER GLASS' METHOD** Place a sheet of glass on top and cover with brown paper. Keep at 16°-22° C – wipe and turn the glass every day. Remove the paper and prop up the glass when seedlings first appear. Remove the glass after a few days and move the container close to the light. Keep the compost moist, but not wet.

OR

'WINDOWSILL' METHOD Place a transparent plastic bag over the pot as shown. Secure with a rubber band and keep at 16°-22° C in a shady spot. Remove the bag when seedlings first appear and move the pot to a bright windowsill which is away from direct sunlight. Keep the compost moist, but not wet.

3 **PRICK OUT & HARDEN OFF** Fill a tray or pot with potting compost. Prick out seedlings into this as soon as the first set of true leaves have opened. Handle by the seed leaves, not the stems. Set them about 4 cm apart and keep in the shade for a few days.

The seedlings must be hardened off once they have recovered from pricking out. Move to a cool room and then move outdoors during daylight hours. Finally, leave outdoors for about 7 days before planting out.

OUTDOORS March-April is the usual time to sow hardy annuals – hold up operations if the weather is cold and wet, even though it may mean being a couple of weeks late. Half-hardy annuals should be sown once the danger of frost has passed.

1 **PREPARE SOIL** Choose a day when the soil is moist below but quite dry on top. Lightly tread over and then rake until the surface is even and crumbly.

2 **PREPARE SEED AREAS** **OR** **PREPARE SEED DRILLS**

| small seeds | medium seeds | large seeds |

Mark out zones for each variety with a pointed stick. You can scatter seed over each allotted area but this will make thinning and weeding difficult. It is better to sow the seeds in drills.

The depth of the drill depends upon the size of the seeds. The seeds should be covered with soil to about twice their size. Water gently before sowing if the soil is dry.

3 **SOW SEED & THIN OUT** Do not sow directly from the packet – place some seed in the palm of your hand and gently sprinkle with your thumb and forefinger. Carefully rake the soil back into the drill after sowing – firm with the back of the rake. Alternatively push the soil back with your finger. Do not water.

Thin out when the seedlings reach the stage shown above. Reduce the stand to one seedling every 2–5 cm. Repeat this thinning about 10 days later to the distance recommended on the seed packet.

Hardy perennials are the non-woody and non-bulbous plants which come up year after year. Most are herbaceous with leaves and stems which die in winter, but a few such as Bergenia and Stachys are evergreens which keep their foliage and so provide a little greenery during the dormant season. At the other end of the scale there are some hardy perennials which are killed by prolonged frosts – such plants should have their crowns covered with a mulch in winter.

The standard home for hardy perennials is in a border. A *border* is a plot which is designed to be seen from two or three sides, unlike a *bed* which is created to be viewed from all sides. In some books and catalogues you will find these plants listed as border perennials.

There are two types of border and these are described and illustrated in the next column. There are other ways of using these plants – in pots, in cottage gardens mixed with Roses, shrubs, herbs etc, and on their own as focal plants. Their smaller relatives are the rockery perennials or alpines which are usually grown in the rock garden, raised bed, containers etc, but are also used at the front of herbaceous and mixed borders.

The herbaceous and mixed border are stars of the green movement. They are not one of the danger areas for people in the garden, and are certainly friendly to wildlife – the wide range of flowers and the presence of seedheads make them attractive to birds, butterflies etc.

Choose the hardy perennials with care for your mixed border. There is a vast range of plants to choose from and with their partners such as shrubs and bulbs you can have colour all year round. There is one vital proviso – the subjects chosen must be suitable for the location in question, and not just the attraction of the picture in the catalogue or on the label.

To save work it is a good idea to avoid short-lived ones such as Anchusa, and those like Day Lilies which have to be lifted and divided every few years.

Display

HERBACEOUS BORDER

In the early years of the 20th century the herbaceous border was an essential feature of the larger garden. It was long and narrow with a backcloth of a wall or clipped hedge. Hardy perennials were used in tiers, with tall-growing varieties at the back and clumps of low-growing plants at the front. It is a lot of work and is lifeless in winter, and so its popularity has declined. These days the constant slope from back to front is often broken by including an occasional tall plant near the front.

MIXED BORDER

The mixed border has taken over from the herbaceous border as the most popular way of growing hardy perennials. Gone are most of the slavish rules about colour, height etc, and the flowering season has been extended by including other types of plants. Like all borders it is designed to be viewed from two or three sides and not from all angles. The shape is often irregular and no longer strictly rectangular. The usual pattern is a framework of flowering shrubs, Roses and decorative evergreens. Hardy perennials form large and colourful patches and close to the front pockets are left for bulbs, alpines and/or bedding plants.

Garden Friendly

Planting

Lifted Plants • Rooted Cuttings

Use the technique described on page 53 where the root ball is small and all or nearly all of the roots are covered with earth or compost. Use the method shown on page 62 where there are roots outside the soil ball.

Container Plants
•
Lifted Plants with Compact Soil Ball

Garden Friendly

Make up the planting mixture in a wheelbarrow on a day when the soil is reasonably dry and friable – 1 part topsoil, 1 part moist leafmould or compost and 3 handfuls of bone meal per barrow load. Keep this mixture in a shed or garage until you are ready to start planting. Planting can take place at any time of the year, but the soil must be neither frozen nor waterlogged.

1 The hole should be deep enough to ensure that the top of the soil ball will be about 3 cm below the soil surface after planting. The hole should be wide enough for the soil ball to be surrounded by a layer of planting mixture (see above). Put a 3 cm layer of the planting mixture at the bottom of the hole.

2 Water the pot or container thoroughly at least an hour before planting. Remove the plant very carefully – do not disturb the soil ball. With a pot-grown plant place your hand around the crown of the plant and turn the pot over. Gently remove – tap the sides with a trowel if necessary.

3 Examine the exposed surface – cut away circling or tangled roots but do not break up the soil ball. Fill the space between the soil ball and the sides of the hole with planting mixture. Firm down the planting mixture with your hands.

4 After planting there should be a shallow water-holding basin. Water in after planting.

Staking

Weak-stemmed plants, tall varieties on exposed sites and large-headed flowers all need some form of support. Put the stake or stakes in position when the plant is quite small so that the stems and leaves can cover the supports. For many plants brushwood is the best idea – twiggy branches pushed into the soil when the stems are about 15 cm high.

This will not do for tall plants such as Chrysanthemums which require staking at planting time. Stout canes are the usual answer, the stems being tied to the supports as growth proceeds. The single-pole method should not be used with bushy plants where it would produce an ugly 'drumstick' effect. A better plan is to insert three or four canes around the stems and enclose them with twine tied around the canes at 15-25 cm intervals.

Dead-heading

Standard gardening books extol the virtues of dead-heading – the removal of faded flowers. The bed or border keeps its well-maintained appearance and new flowering shoots may develop. The only exceptions quoted are flowers such as Honesty and Chinese Lantern which are grown for their decorative seed pods, and plants with flower heads which are impractical to remove.

The green gardener should treat dead-heading with more caution – many flowers produce fruits and/or seeds which serve as food for birds. So the general rule here is to cut back the dead flowers and stems in early spring before new growth begins. An exception to this rule involves a small group (e.g Lupin, Phlox and Delphinium) which will usually produce a second flower stalk if the first one is cut down after flowering.

Increasing Your Stock

Dividing Clumps

Division is a form of propagation which is often forced upon you – spreading hardy perennials will often deteriorate after a few years if not lifted and divided.

Choose a mild day in spring or autumn when the soil is moist. Dig up the clump with a fork, taking care not to damage the roots more than necessary. Shake off the excess soil and study where the basic divisions should be. You might be able to break the clump with your hands – if the clump is too tough for this technique then use two hand forks or garden forks. Push the forks back-to-back into the centre and prise gently apart. Treat the resulting divisions in a similar fashion or tear apart with the fingers.

Select the divisions which came from the outer region of the clump – discard the central dead region of an old plant. Replant the divisions as soon as possible and water in thoroughly.

Taking Stem-tip Cuttings

Stem-tip cuttings are 5-10 cm long pieces of non-flowering shoot tips – ideally they should be soft and green at the top and quite firm at the base. Spring and summer is the usual time for taking cuttings. Use a compost which is recommended for seeds and cuttings – some gardeners mix this compost with an equal amount of a fertilizer-free medium such as vermiculite or perlite. Plant the cuttings as soon as possible after severance from the parent plant. Some form of cover will be required to maintain a humid atmosphere – Pelargonium is the exception.

Cut off leaves from lower half of cutting

Leaf joint

Straight cut

Filling up the pot

1 Fill a 12.5 cm pot with a suitable compost.

2 Trim foliage of large-leaved plants by half.

3 Make a hole close to the edge with a pencil.

4 Insert cutting – firm around the base with a pencil. Label if necessary.

5 Water in very gently.

Polythene bag method

1 Place four canes in the pot and drape a polythene bag over them. Secure with a rubber band. Stand pot in a bright spot, away from direct sunlight.

2 Leave undisturbed until new growth appears. Harden off by giving more ventilation and then lift out each rooted cutting after watering – transfer into a compost-filled 7.5 cm pot.

Propagator method

1 Place pots in the propagator. Keep at 18°-24° C. Shade and ventilate on hot days.

2 Leave undisturbed until new growth appears. Harden off by giving more ventilation and then lift out each rooted cutting after watering – transfer into a compost-filled 7.5 cm pot.

Cold frame method

1 Place pots in a cold frame – shade glass and ventilate on hot days. Water gently when necessary. In frosty weather cover glass with sacking.

2 Leave undisturbed until new growth appears. Harden off by giving more ventilation and then lift out each rooted cutting after watering – transfer into a compost-filled 7.5 cm pot.

CARING FOR ROCKERY PERENNIALS

A rockery perennial is a hardy plant which does not produce woody stems – the leaves and shoots usually die down in winter and new stems appear in spring but a few are evergreen. They are sometimes called alpines, but this term is really meant to cover only those plants which come from mountainous regions such as the Alps and Himalayas.

The dividing line between rockery perennials and hardy perennials is an indistinct one. The non-woody plants which come up year after year are called hardy or border perennials if they grow to more than 30 cm – smaller ones are classed as rockery perennials, but there are exceptions.

Rockery plants are scattered around the garden – at the edges of beds and borders, in cracks in the path, in spaces in retaining walls and in containers. The two main sites are the rockery (rock garden) and the raised bed – details of these two features are described in the next column. Whichever home you choose for your plants you must remember their basic needs – really good drainage, soil or compost to which grit has been added, and a regular routine of weeding and trimming as necessary.

Choose the plants with care. There are easy but invasive ones such as Aubrieta, Arabis, Alyssum saxatile and Cerastium which can quickly overrun more delicate types. At the other end of the scale there are the difficult and non-invasive ones which cannot tolerate cold, soggy soil and need protection in winter.

Check details in *The Rock & Water Garden Expert* before buying – do not let their beauty on the garden centre bench be your only guide. The variety of rockery perennials is enormous, but do introduce a scattering of other types in your rockery or raised bed – a dwarf shrub or two, some bulbs etc.

For planting details see page 56. You can increase your stock by sowing seeds (page 54), dividing clumps (page 57) or taking cuttings (page 57).

Display

ROCKERY

A well-constructed rock garden is perhaps the ideal home, but it is laborious to make and will need regular attention. To qualify as a 'rock garden' rather than a bed with a few stones it needs to be at least 2.5 m x 1.5 m and the rocks should be partly buried to make the rockery look like a sloping outcrop. Use a planting mixture to fill the spaces between the stones – a standard mixture is 1 part topsoil, 1 part well-rotted leafmould or compost and 1 part grit or stone chippings.

RAISED BED

A height of 45-80 cm is recommended and the retaining walls can be made with bricks, stone, reconstituted stone blocks or railway sleepers. Lay a concrete foundation if the walls are to be more than 30-45 cm high. Provide weep-holes at the base if mortar-bonded bricks, blocks or stones are the building material. Fill with planting mixture (see Rockery above) – leave a 5 cm space at the top. Plant up after a few weeks.

CARING FOR BULBS

The bulbous plants include true bulbs (scales arising from a basal plate), corms, tubers and rhizomes. The popular spring-flowering ones are known to everyone, but if you pick wisely this group can provide colour all year round.

The soil should be fairly rich in organic matter. Bone meal is the best pre-planting fertilizer – never use fresh manure. In damp ground Daffodils do better than Tulips. Whenever possible try to naturalise hardy bulbs by planting them around trees or on banks where they can be left to grow undisturbed. Scatter them and plant them where they fall.

Buy the largest bulbs you can afford and choose ones that are plump and firm. When flowering is over the leaves must be left on the plant until they turn yellow. Do not tie Daffodil foliage in knots.

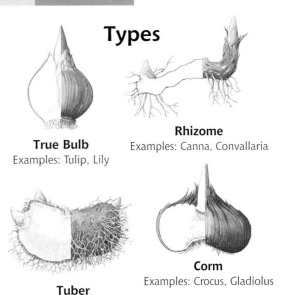

Types

True Bulb
Examples: Tulip, Lily

Rhizome
Examples: Canna, Convallaria

Tuber
Examples: Cyclamen, Anemone

Corm
Examples: Crocus, Gladiolus

Planting

As a general rule the bulbs should be planted as soon as possible after purchase, but the big four (Tulip, Narcissus, Hyacinth and Crocus) will come to no harm if stored in a cool, dry place before planting. However, they must go in the ground while they are still firm and without prominent sprouts. Bulbs with roots and without a protective tunic can be stored in moist sand for a little time but planting should not be long delayed.

2 The width of the hole should be about twice the diameter of the bulb. The depth will depend upon the variety you are planting – as a general rule, the common large bulbs such as Tulip, Narcissus and Hyacinth will need to be covered by twice their own height. Most small bulbs are covered to about their own height. The bottom should be reasonably flat and the sides reasonably vertical – avoid making 'ice cream cone' holes.

3 It is vital that there should not be an air space between the bottom of the bulb and the soil at the base of the hole. If the soil is heavy it is useful to put in a shallow layer of grit.

4 Push the bulb down to the base of the hole and twist gently. Make sure the bulb is the right way up.

5 Put the earth back and press it down gently. Use the dug-out soil for this job, but it is a good idea to mix it with coarse sand, well-rotted compost or leafmould if the ground is heavy. Rake over the surface if a large area has been planted and water in if the weather is dry.

1 Nearly all bulbs require free-draining soil. Dig about a week before the planting date if the soil is compacted – adding coarse sand or grit will help if the ground is heavy. Free drainage is equally or even more important when planting up containers – make sure that the drainage holes are large enough and not blocked.

6 Bulbs leave no above-ground indication of their presence after planting. It is therefore sometimes necessary to put in a label to remind you that there are bulbs below.

CARING FOR TREES AND SHRUBS

Woody plants have a special place in the garden – they provide the living framework. In summer they provide height, colour and fragrance – they give the garden its shape. In winter their role is equally important. When the flower garden has died down, the bare branches of deciduous trees and shrubs and the leaf-bedecked stems of the evergreens ensure that we are looking at living shapes and not bare plots of ground. For the green gardener there is an extra blessing – trees and shrubs are the home and a source of food for a vast collection of small and large creatures for all or part of the year. Most trees are too large for the average garden and the range and use of climbers are limited. Shrubs do not have these drawbacks – there is an abundance of varieties for gardens of every size.

The labour-saving aspect of trees and shrubs is well known – hardly any book on the subject fails to mention this virtue, but they are neither trouble-free nor child's play. There are three aspects which call for attention – choose sensibly, plant properly and prune correctly.

First of all, choice. Never buy a shrub or tree on impulse – the label may be detailed enough for this purpose, but it is usually better to consult a book such as *The Tree & Shrub Expert*. Make sure that the estimated mature height and needs of the plant are right for the situation you have in mind.

Next, planting. Page 62 provides a simple guide to the proper technique. You will see that there is a need to use a planting mixture to fill the hole – this soil/humus mix provides a bridge between the mineral soil and the organic soil ball.

Finally, pruning. Leaving sufficient space between the plants will save you from the task of having to cut back branches regularly to prevent over-crowding. Even with correct spacing there will be times when you have to prune – there will be dead branches to remove, and stems to cut back to regulate blossom and/or fruit production.

Tree

A tree is a perennial plant which bears only one woody stem at ground level. A mature tree may be as little as 60 cm high or as tall as 30 metres or more, depending on the variety.

Types

COLUMNAR (FASTIGIATE)   CONICAL   PYRAMIDAL

ROUND-HEADED   OPEN   WEEPING (PENDULOUS)

GLOBULAR (ROUND)   LOW-BRANCHED   PROSTRATE

Shrub

A shrub is a perennial plant which bears several woody stems at ground level. A mature shrub may be as small as a few centimetres or as tall as 6 metres, depending on the variety.

Hedge

A formal hedge is a continuous line of trees or shrubs in which the individuality of each plant is lost. Unlike a plant-covered screen or fence, it requires little or no support. An informal hedge is a continuous line of trees or shrubs in which some or all of the natural outline of the plants is maintained.

Buying

The purchase of trees and shrubs often represents a sizeable outlay and you don't want to waste your money, so choose with care. There are four basic types of planting material and each one has its own advantages and disadvantages. Conifers were once widely sold as balled plants but these are now rarely seen. Bare-rooted shrubs are less popular than they used to be, but are well worth considering – they are less expensive and some types root more readily when planted as bare-rooted stock. The pre-packaged plant is a bare-rooted specimen with its roots surrounded by moist material and the whole plant packed in a plastic bag. Colourful and inexpensive, but avoid packs with early growth signs such as opening leaf buds and small white roots.

Container-grown plants are the most popular type of planting material. Look for danger signs before you buy – these include wilted or diseased leaves, misshapen growth habit, dry soil or thick roots growing out of the base. Don't buy the biggest size you can afford – large and old specimens are often overtaken by younger and less expensive ones.

Container-grown plants can be left unplanted for several weeks if the compost is kept moist. Do not leave bare-rooted plants for more than 4 days before planting – soak roots for 2 hours if they look dry.

Container-grown

The most convenient way to buy both deciduous and evergreen shrubs. Suitable for planting all year round.

Bare-rooted

The traditional way to buy deciduous shrubs. Suitable for planting between October and March.

Balled

Once traditional way to buy evergreen shrubs. Suitable for planting in September, October or April.

Pre-packaged

The popular way to buy deciduous shrubs from shops and department stores. Suitable for planting between October and March.

61

Planting

Not all planting material sold by shops, garden centres, mail order companies etc is top quality and it is easy to blame the plant you have bought when a tree or shrub fails. Disappointment, however, is more likely to be due to mistakes at planting time. The instructions below may be a little more complex than you expected, but following the rules will save you time in the long run.

Soil conditions are as important as the calendar. The ground should be neither frozen nor waterlogged. Squeeze a handful of soil – it should be wet enough to form a ball and yet dry enough to shatter when dropped on to a hard surface.

Container Plants
•
Lifted Plants with Compact Soil Ball

Do not regard container-grown specimens as an easy way to plant trees and shrubs. If the environment surrounding the soil ball is not right then the roots will not grow into humus-starved soil. This means that it is not enough to dig a hole, take the plant out of the container, drop it into the hole and replace the earth.

See page 56 for basic instructions. With a large container make the hole about 20 cm wider than the soil ball and put a 10 cm layer of the planting mixture at the bottom of the hole.

Bare-rooted Plants
•
Lifted Plants with Large Roots beyond the Soil Ball

Planting time is the dormant season between autumn and spring – choose mid October-late November if you can, but delay planting until March if the soil is heavy and wet. Cut off leaves, dead flowers, weak stems and damaged roots. If the stem of a bare-rooted plant is shrivelled plunge the roots in a bucket of water for two hours before planting.

3 Work a couple of trowelfuls of the planting mixture around the roots. Shake the plant gently up and down – add a little more planting mixture. Firm this around the roots with the fists – do not press too hard. Half-fill the hole with more planting mixture and firm it down.

2 The old soil mark should be level with the soil surface – set a board across the top of the hole as a guide.

4 Add more planting mixture until the hole is full. Firm by pressing with the fists or gentle treading – on no account tread heavily. Loosen the surface once the hole has been filled – there should be a shallow water-holding basin after planting. Water in after planting.

1 The hole should be wide enough to allow the roots to be spread evenly. Put a layer of planting mixture (page 56) at the bottom of the hole – important if soil condition is poor.

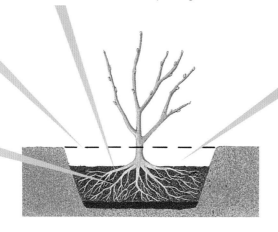

Staking

A tree or tall spindly shrub can be rocked by strong winds if its roots are not able to anchor it firmly in the ground. A newly-planted specimen does not have this anchorage, so it can be dislodged or blown over. Staking is the answer – it is a job to do at planting time and not after the damage has been done.

Bare-rooted Trees

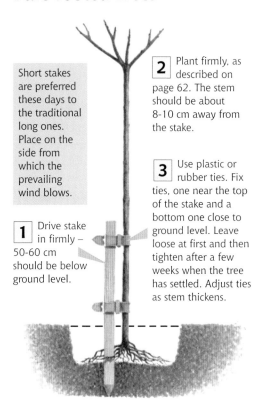

Short stakes are preferred these days to the traditional long ones. Place on the side from which the prevailing wind blows.

1 Drive stake in firmly – 50-60 cm should be below ground level.

2 Plant firmly, as described on page 62. The stem should be about 8-10 cm away from the stake.

3 Use plastic or rubber ties. Fix ties, one near the top of the stake and a bottom one close to ground level. Leave loose at first and then tighten after a few weeks when the tree has settled. Adjust ties as stem thickens.

Container-grown Trees

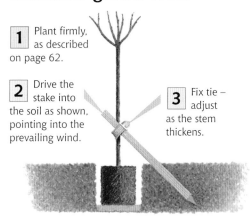

1 Plant firmly, as described on page 62.

2 Drive the stake into the soil as shown, pointing into the prevailing wind.

3 Fix tie – adjust as the stem thickens.

Spacing

It is easy to see why people plant too closely. The plants from the garden centre or nursery are usually small, and it is hard to imagine at this stage what they will look like when they are mature. But they will reach maturity, and if you have planted them too closely there are only two alternatives – you can either dig out some of the cramped shrubs (which is the more sensible but the less popular choice) or you can hack them back each year, which destroys so much of their beauty.

Of course, the better plan is to start correctly:

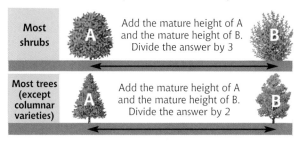

| Most shrubs | | Add the mature height of A and the mature height of B. Divide the answer by 3 | |
| Most trees (except columnar varieties) | | Add the mature height of A and the mature height of B. Divide the answer by 2 | |

Use the rule of thumb guide below if you do not know the expected mature height of the plants:

Trees – 5-8 m apart, depending on whether they are small, medium or large types.
Shrubs – 0.5 m-1.5 m apart, depending on whether they are small, medium or large types.

Do not plant trees close to water pipes, drains etc.

When you plant at these distances the border will look bare and unattractive. You can plant a little closer, but that is not really the answer. One solution is to plant a number of 'fill-in' shrubs between the choice shrubs and trees which you regard as permanent residents. These 'fill-in' shrubs, such as Forsythia, Ribes, Spiraea, Mahonia etc, can be bought cheaply as 'bargains' and will soon provide a colourful display. They are progressively removed as the choice shrubs develop and require more room. A second alternative is to fill the space between widely-spaced shrubs with bulbs, annuals, hardy perennials and ground cover plants.

After Planting

Proper after-care is just as important as good planting. Once the new tree or shrub is in place it should be watered in thoroughly. Cut back the branches of bare-rooted shrubs to about two-thirds of their length; container-grown and balled plants should not need trimming.

Evergreens pose a problem. Winter browning can take place when they are planted in autumn – protect choice specimens with a screen made out of polythene sheeting. When spring arrives, spray the leaves with water on warm days and apply a mulch around the stems.

Lastly, an extremely important point. Do not let grass grow closer than 30 cm from the trunk of trees until two years after planting.

Pruning

There is no need to prune if the tree or shrub has healthy branches and is not crowding into other plants.

Cutting back flowering trees and shrubs severely at the wrong time may lead to the loss of a whole season's floral display and sometimes to the death of the plant. The standard advice is to check the precise pruning requirement for each individual tree and shrub before reaching for the secateurs or shears. This is the correct path for the keen hobby gardener, but for most people the approach described below is much simpler and quite satisfactory.

A few general rules. Buy good quality tools and make sure they are sharp. Keep your free hand well away from the blade when using a knife, secateurs or saw.

Secateurs for stems up to 1.5 cm across
Long-handled loppers for stems up to 3 cm across
Pruning saw for stems over 3 cm across

Pruning for Growth

LIGHT PRUNING

Heading Back involves the removal of the ends of the branches. This pruning technique is called **Trimming** when all the tips are removed *en masse*. This stimulates the buds below the cuts to burst into growth.
The long-term effect is to produce a shrub which is smaller and denser than one left unpruned.

HARD PRUNING

Thinning involves the removal of entire branches back to the main stem. This diverts extra energy to the remaining branches.
The long-term effect is to produce a shrub which is larger and more open than one left unpruned.

When and how to prune

The following table is a general guide to pruning. There are a number of exceptions and the rule to follow is that if you are in doubt – don't prune.

Deciduous Shrubs which bloom before the end of May
Time: As soon as flowering is over – do not delay
Cut out all weak, dead and awkwardly-placed shoots and then remove overcrowded or invasive branches.
Flowers are produced on old wood. Some of the branches which have borne flowers should therefore be cut back – new, vigorous growth will develop and this will bear flowers next season.

Deciduous Shrubs which bloom after the end of May
Time: January-March – do not wait until growth starts
Cut out all weak, dead and awkwardly-placed shoots and then remove overcrowded or invasive branches.
Flowers are produced on new wood. If flowering has been poor cut back some of the old branches to stimulate fresh growth for next year's flowers.

Flowering Cherries & Conifers
Time: Late summer or autumn – never in winter
Cut out dead wood and overcrowded or invasive branches.

Evergreen Shrubs
Time: May
Cut out all weak, dead and awkwardly-placed shoots and then remove overcrowded or invasive stems. With some of these plants (Santolina, Rhododendron, Buxus etc) hard pruning can be used to regenerate bushes with leggy stems.

Hedges
Time: Trim an informal flowering hedge when blooms have faded
The established formal hedge should be kept at 1.2-1.8 m and the top should be narrower than the base. You can use shears but an electric hedgetrimmer will save time. Place plastic sheeting at the base of the hedge – this will make clipping removal much easier.

Increasing Your Stock

Dividing Clumps

Some small shrubs form clumps which can be lifted and then split up like hardy perennials into several rooted sections. Each section should be planted firmly and then watered in thoroughly.

Best time: Early winter
Examples: Cistus   Lavender
Hebe   Vinca

Many shrubs spread by means of suckers, which are shoots arising from an underground shoot or root. Remove and plant as described above.

Best time: Early winter for deciduous plants;
April or September for evergreens
Examples: Cotinus Mahonia
Kerria   Pernettya

Sowing Seeds

Seed sowing is the standard method of raising flowers and vegetables, but it is not widely used for propagating shrubs at home. Germination is not always straightforward – some seeds take many months to germinate and others need exposure to months of cold weather before they start to grow. It may be several years before the seedling is large enough to be decorative and many varieties will not breed true. Despite the drawbacks, there are several shrubs which can be readily raised from seed:

Best time: Spring. See page 54 for
step-by-step details
Examples: Cistus   Pieris
Genista Potentilla

Garden Friendly

Taking Softwood and Semi-ripe Cuttings

Softwood cuttings are green at the tip and base. Some small shrubs are propagated in this way. Basal cuttings are shoots formed at the base of the plant and pulled away for use as softwood cuttings.

Semi-ripe cuttings are green at the top and partly woody at the base. They are usually heel cuttings – side shoots pulled off with a heel attached. Most shrubs are propagated by this method.

See page 57 for step-by-step details for taking softwood and semi-ripe cuttings.

Best time: Summer
Examples: Buddleia Cistus Hydrangea Potentilla Spiraea

Taking Hardwood Cuttings

Hardwood cuttings can be used for many shrubs. Choose a well-ripened shoot of this year's growth.

Best time: November
Examples: Aucuba Cornus Forsythia Ribes Weigela

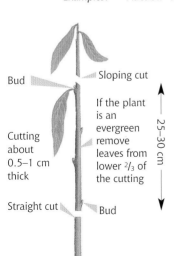

Bud

Sloping cut

If the plant is an evergreen remove leaves from lower 2/3 of the cutting

25–30 cm

Cutting about 0.5–1 cm thick

Straight cut

Bud

4 Leave the top 1/3 of the cutting above ground. Plant the cuttings about 10-15 cm apart. Label the cuttings.

3 Insert the cutting so that the base rests firmly on the bottom and against the vertical side of the trench.

2 Add a 3 cm layer of sharp sand.

1 Dig a 15-20 cm trench with one vertical wall in a well-drained part of the garden. Light shade is desirable.

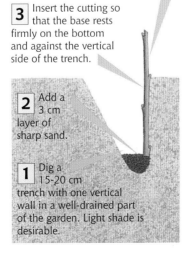

5 Replace the soil a little at a time. Tread down each layer. Fill to ground level – hoe to loosen surface. Water thoroughly.

Firm the soil after winter frosts. Water during dry weather. The cuttings should be ready for planting in about 12 months time.

65

Green gardeners should have no problem feeding their Roses, and keeping the major pests at bay by hand-picking or by using repeat applications of an organic spray. The snag is disease control – organic and natural fungicides are far less effective than the chemical systemic ones which penetrate the leaves and enter the sap stream. There is a disfiguring duo of fungal diseases – blackspot with its dark-spotted yellow patches on the leaves which fall prematurely, and mildew which distorts leaves, shoots and buds which it covers with white mould. Rust is much less common but is even deadlier – see pages 94–95 for details of these diseases.

The first rule for growing Roses the organic way is to choose wisely. You should check the disease resistance of a variety on the label or in the catalogue before buying – some types such as Ramblers and many old-fashioned Shrub Roses have little or no resistance to disease. The top twelve most disease-resistant Roses in the Royal National Rose Society poll were Silver Jubilee, Warm Wishes, Alexander, Elina, Pink Flower Carpet, Mountbatten, Thérèse Bugnet, Compassion, Freedom, Glorious, Amber Queen and Ispahan.

Next, you must pay extra attention to all the cultural rules so as to cut down the risk of disease infection. Pick a suitable site and then plant properly – see page 68. Feed in the traditional way by applying a dressing of fish, blood and bone in spring and put down a humus mulch (see page 16) in May or June. An added benefit provided by mulching is the prevention of disease spores being splashed up from the soil by raindrops.

Make sure the bushes do not go short of water – dryness at the roots stimulates mildew. Keep watch for aphids – use insecticidal soap if they are clustered on young growth. Pick off caterpillars and rolled leaves – dead-head faded blooms. Pick off leaves which are badly affected by blackspot. Remove fallen leaves in winter.

Flowering Period

Just one flush e.g Canary Bird **Several flushes e.g Fellowship**

Repeat-flowering Roses produce two or more flushes of blooms during the flowering season. Modern Roses generally produce blooms at intervals throughout the summer months and into the autumn – one of the main reasons for the unrivalled popularity of Hybrid Teas and Floribundas. Repeat-flowering varieties, also known as recurrent and remontant varieties, may produce some flowers between the main flushes. When this feature is strongly marked the descriptions perpetual and continuous flowering are sometimes used, but they are not strictly correct.

Once-flowering Roses produce a single flush of blooms which usually lasts for several weeks. Occasionally a few flowers may appear in autumn, but this flowering is far too sporadic to be considered a second flush. The once-flowering varieties most frequently bloom in June/July, but there are varieties of Shrubs and Ramblers which bloom in late spring, early summer or late summer.

Easy-care Roses

Multi-petalled, shapely flowers borne singly or in clusters above large leaves are a splendid sight in summer, but they are a sorry spectacle if they are disfigured or defoliated by disease, or turned into soggy balls by heavy rain.

To avoid these problems there are two outstanding groups which are repeat flowering and disease resistant. The Ground Cover Roses have small leaves which are semi-evergreen. Look for the Flower Carpet and County series – at the end of the year simply trim the bushes to shape with garden shears. For larger bushes choose one of the Rugosa group – leaves stay green all season and the flowers are followed by attractive hips.

Types

Garden Friendly

Hybrid Tea

The classic Rose – a pointed bud opening into a many-petalled flower with a high central cone. But it is not the ideal Rose – many Hybrid Tea bushes are upright and rigid, and the blooms of many varieties are ruined by heavy rain. In general they flower less frequently and provide less colour than Floribundas. New varieties appear every year – check the catalogues and pick ones with good disease resistance.

Floribunda

The typical Floribunda produces blooms which lack the size, beauty and fragrance of their more elegant rival – the Hybrid Tea Rose. But there are advantages – these bushes provide a larger splash of colour and have a longer flowering season. The average Floribunda is also hardier, easier to care for and more reliable in wet weather than its Hybrid Tea counterpart. Follow the modern way to prune on page 69.

Patio

These dwarf Floribunda Roses have become increasingly popular for planting at the front of the border and in containers. When grown in pots you must make sure that they are watered regularly in dry weather, and in early spring the bushes should be pruned in the same way as their larger relatives – see page 69. Make sure you choose a variety which claims good disease resistance in the catalogue or on the label.

Miniature

These tiny-leaved plants are smaller than Patio Roses, and are generally grown in pots to provide a colourful season-long display. Maintenance is not quite as easy as some people think. Pruning is straightforward (see page 69), but pests and diseases can be a problem. Regular watering in dry weather is essential, and the fairy-like form may disappear in time. Plant pot-grown specimens in spring.

Shrub

This class is a wide-ranging rag-bag of varieties as noted on page 40. There are tiny ones and giants, types which bloom for a few short weeks and others which are in flower all season long. Some, such as the Rugosas, are extremely easy to grow as they are remarkably resistant to disease – there are others which have little or no resistance. The rule is to check the label and/or catalogue description carefully before buying.

Climber

The two distinct types are described on page 41. Ramblers have long pliable stems with large flower trusses. There is generally only one flush, and they are not a good choice for the green gardener. They have little resistance to mildew and the need for regular pruning is a chore. Climbers are a better choice. Larger flowers are borne on stiffer stems which provide a permanent framework – maintenance and pruning are easier.

Ground Cover

Shrub Roses with a distinctly spreading or trailing growth habit have been moved to a class of their own – the Ground Cover Roses. The leafy mounds are useful for covering banks or manhole covers, but nearly all varieties can grow to 60 cm or more when mature. There are a few which reach only 45 cm or less.

The four basic growth types are ground cover, bush, standard and climbing (see chart below). A bush may be a Hybrid Tea, Patio, Miniature, Floribunda or Shrub Rose.

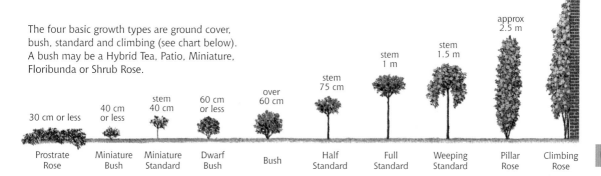

Prostrate Rose	Miniature Bush	Miniature Standard	Dwarf Bush	Bush	Half Standard	Full Standard	Weeping Standard	Pillar Rose	Climbing Rose
30 cm or less	40 cm or less	stem 40 cm	60 cm or less	over 60 cm	stem 75 cm	stem 1 m	stem 1.5 m	approx 2.5 m	

Planting

GETTING THE PLANT READY

There is little to do if you have chosen a container-grown plant. Water thoroughly before removing from the pot – keep the soil ball intact when planting.

A bare-rooted plant should be carefully unpacked and very long roots trimmed to about 30 cm. Remove any leaves, buds or hips which may be present.Plunge roots in a bucket of water if roots appear dry or if stems are shrivelled. If planting is to be delayed you can keep the unopened package in an unheated shed or garage. For a longer delay it is necessary to heel in the plants in a shallow V-shaped trench in the garden.

THE RIGHT SPOT

SUITABLE SOIL is necessary, and fortunately this can be achieved in nearly all gardens. Ideally it should be a medium loam, slightly acid and reasonably rich in plant foods and humus. A high clay content is not necessary, and is actually harmful if not improved by adding humus. A high lime content is harmful. Soil in which Roses have grown for more than 10 years is not suitable for all Roses – see below.
Roses cannot thrive if the soil is poor.

REASONABLY FREE DRAINAGE is essential, so break up the subsoil if necessary.
Roses cannot stand being waterlogged.

SHELTER FROM COLD WINDS is helpful. A nearby hedge or fence is useful, but it should not be close enough to shade the bush. Avoid planting in the lowest part of the garden if it is a 'frost pocket'.
Roses do not thrive in exposed, low-lying sites.

PLENTY OF SUN is required to produce top-quality Roses, but slight shade during early afternoon is beneficial.
Roses cannot stand deep and continuous shade.

PLENTY OF AIR is required to produce healthy plants. Bush and standard Roses do not like being shut in by walls and overhanging plants.
Roses cannot stand being planted under trees.

Replanting

Grafted Roses often do badly when planted in soil which has grown Roses for 10 years or more. Varieties grown on their own roots are not affected by this soil sickness – Miniature Roses and Rugosa varieties will grow quite happily.

THE RIGHT WAY TO PLANT

Container-grown bushes

These Roses can be planted at any time of the year, but some times are better than others. The soil must be in the right condition and autumn or spring allows some root development before the summer drought. See page 56 for planting details.

Bare-rooted bushes

Plant between late October and late March. November is the best time in most gardens – plant in March if the soil is very heavy. The ground must be neither frozen nor waterlogged. Squeeze a handful – it should form a ball and yet be dry enough to shatter when dropped. See page 62 for planting details. Dig a fan-shaped hole when roots run along in one direction – see below.

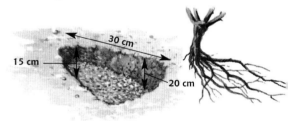

Bare-rooted climbers

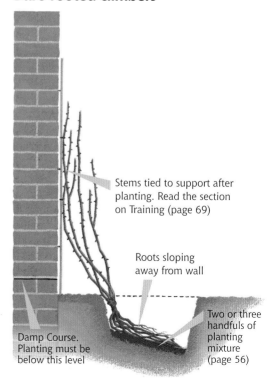

Stems tied to support after planting. Read the section on Training (page 69)

Roots sloping away from wall

Two or three handfuls of planting mixture (page 56)

Damp Course. Planting must be below this level

Garden Friendly

Pruning

Miniature & Shrub Roses

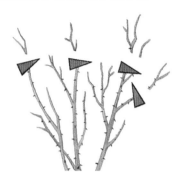

Don't cut back these Roses like Hybrid Teas and Floribundas – very little pruning is required. Cut out dead and sickly growth and then merely trim to shape as necessary to avoid overcrowding.

Secateurs are the usual tool used for pruning, but Ground Cover Roses are trimmed with garden shears.

THE RIGHT TIME

Early spring pruning is recommended for autumn- and winter-planted Roses and for established plants. If the bushes or standards are to be planted in the spring, prune just before planting. The best time to prune is when growth is just beginning. The uppermost buds will have begun to swell but no leaves will have appeared.

Hybrid Teas • Floribundas • Patio Roses

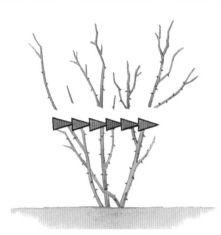

It came as a surprise to many Rose experts that the Easy-care Method of pruning has proved to be so successful. Extensive trials carried out by the Royal National Rose Society and other organisations in the 1990s have shown that this technique is at least equal to the laborious Traditional Method which is recommended in the standard textbooks. The blooms are sometimes larger and more numerous and the bushes are no less healthy than with the standard method.

Nothing could be simpler – the bush is cut to half its height with secateurs or a hedge trimmer. Leave all the weak and twiggy growth – cut out dead wood at the base if it is unsightly.

Training

Some shrubs with lax spreading stems may require support after a few years. Use three or more unobtrusive stakes with a secure band joining the top of each stake.

Climbing Roses must be trained from the outset. This does not mean that the main stems should be allowed to grow vertically – when this happens the usual result is a mature plant which bears its leaves and flowers at the top. To prevent this happening, train the main shoots as horizontally as possible. This interruption of the free upward movement of the sap causes lateral branches to appear. It is these laterals which grow upwards, and they bear the flowers. The wire ties used to attach the main stems to the supports should not be tied too tightly – these stems thicken with age and a tight tie can strangle growth. Wind stems in an ascending spiral to cover tripods or pillars.

Spacing

Rose Type	Distance Apart
Miniature Roses	30 cm
Patio Roses	45 cm
HT & Floribunda Bushes Compact varieties	45 cm
HT & Floribunda Bushes Average varieties	60 cm
HT & Floribunda Bushes Tall varieties	75 cm
Standards	1.2 m
Ground Cover Roses	expected spread
Shrubs	$1/2$ expected height
Weeping Standards	2 m
Climbers	2 m

APPLE

The choice is between a dessert or cooking variety, although a few are dual-purpose. The ones you choose can be bought in a number of growth forms (see page 42) and the rootstock will largely determine its eventual height. A mature dwarf bush will grow about 2 m high and provide about 20 kg of fruit – a mature standard will reach 10-12 m and yield up to 150 kg of fruit.

Plant half standards 6 m apart – fans, espaliers and bushes 5 m apart, 3 m for dwarf bushes and 2 m for dwarf pyramids.

The Catalogue Words

Biennial bearer. A variety which produces a good crop every other year with little or nothing in between.

Tip-bearing variety. A variety which bears most of its fruit at the ends of 1-year old shoots.

Spur-bearing variety. A variety which bears all or most of its fruit on very short branches.

Early variety. Fruit is picked in July-early September.

Mid-season variety. Fruit is picked in September-October.

Late variety. Fruit is picked in October-November.

Planting

Follow the basic rules set out on pages 56 and 62. Before putting in the tree the soil should have been limed if it is very acid and some form of windbreak created if the site is exposed. Plant to the old mark – the union with the rootstock should be about 10 cm above ground level. Keep the soil moist after planting. Do not grass over the soil above the planting hole for at least 2-3 years.

Pruning

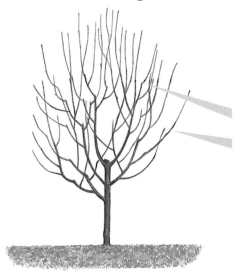

It is necessary to prune bushes and standards between November and February – see below for the easiest way to prune established trees. Espaliers, fans and cordons are pruned in mid July (southern districts) or early August (other areas). See *The Fruit Expert* for details.

Spur-bearing variety

Remove dead and badly diseased wood. Cut back crossing branches and vigorous laterals crowding into the centre. Then:

Inside the head – leave leaders alone. Cut back each lateral which is growing into and beyond the branch leader.

Outside the head – leave both leaders and laterals alone.

Overcropping and undersized fruit may become a problem. If this has happened, thin some of the fruiting spurs and cut out some laterals.

Tip-bearing variety

Remove dead, diseased and overcrowded wood. Then:

Cut back some leaders – leave alone all laterals with fruit buds at their tips.

Picking

Lift the fruit gently in the palm of your hand and give it a slight twist. It is ripe if the fruit comes away easily with the stalk attached. Harvest the fruit at daily intervals rather than trying to gather them all at once. Pick the brightest coloured ones first and handle gently. Never tug the fruits away from the shoot.

Feeding

The organic way to feed fruit trees and bushes has been used for generations. Sprinkle a couple of handfuls of fish, blood and bone per square metre around the plants – this dressing should extend to the whole area under the branches. In May put a mulch of compost or rotted manure around the base.

PEAR

Pears are obviously closely related to Apples, and the planting, pruning and spacing instructions are the same – see page 70. There are, however, a number of important differences. First of all, the soil. Pears are better able to cope in heavy soil but are less successful than Apples in sandy and chalky soil. Next, the site. Pears need more sun and more wind protection and there is an increased risk of frost damage – blossom appears 2-4 weeks before Apple blooms open. On the credit side Pears are less likely to suffer from pests and diseases, although bud damage by bullfinches can be a problem.

Picking

Follow the Apple instructions for mid-season varieties. For early-ripening ones you should cut the stalks when they are full-sized and leave to ripen indoors – do not store. Late varieties can be stored.

Storage

Mid-season and late varieties can be stored, but their shelf-life is limited. Fruit which is neither bruised nor damaged should be kept on slatted shelves – do not wrap. Softness near the stalk indicates ripeness.

PLUM

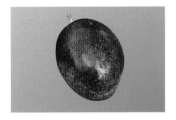

Plums are the most popular stone fruit and they are also the easiest to grow. However, they are not for everyone. The first problem is size. A bush or pyramid on standard rootstock can reach 6 m or more – dwarfing-rootstock plants are available, but the best plan is to grow a fan against a south-facing wall. The second problem is the danger of frost – Plums flower very early in the season.

A moisture-retentive but free-draining soil is required. November is the best time for planting.

Pruning

Prune in June-late July, not in winter. Keep pruning to a minimum to cut down the risk of the dreaded silver leaf disease. Remove dead, broken and diseased branches – cut back overcrowded ones.

Picking

Ripe fruit is easily removed from the tree. With Plums the stalk usually remains on the tree – with Gages and Damsons the stalk comes away with the fruit. Pick dessert varieties when thoroughly ripe.

CHERRY

Buy a dwarf bush or a fan if your choice is a Sweet Cherry – netting will be essential to keep the birds away. The best plan is to grow a fan against a wall in full sun. Acid Cherries such as Morellos are less demanding – they will grow in some shade and birds are less of a nuisance.

Cherries need soil which is moisture-retentive but free-draining. Keep grass away from the trunk.

Pruning

With bushes follow the Plum routine described above – leave as much healthy old wood as you can. Pruning fans is a complex affair – see *The Fruit Expert*. A simplified routine for Sweet Cherries it to pinch back the tips of new shoots in July and shorten to 3 or 4 buds in September.

Picking

Leave Sweet Cherries on the tree or fan until they are ripe – pick immediately if they have started to crack. Eat as soon as possible after picking – they can be frozen but not stored. Use scissors or secateurs when harvesting Acid Cherries – cut off with the stalk attached.

STRAWBERRY

There is a wide choice of growing methods and an even larger choice of varieties – growing them in a barrel makes picking easier and keeps slugs at bay. In the garden choose a bed or border which is sunny and sheltered – dig in compost a month before planting and scatter fish, blood and bone over the surface just before planting. Plant in July-September, leaving 60 cm between plants and rows. Keep weeds down and water regularly – mulch in May. Netting may be necessary. Cut back leaves to about 10 cm above the ground when the last fruits have been picked.

Picking

Once maximum size has been reached the fruit ripens very quickly. Inspect the bed daily – pick fruit which have reddened all over. Nip the stalk between thumbnail and forefinger – do not tug the fruit away. Pick when dry – eat as soon as possible.

Propagating

New plants can be raised from runners if the mother plant has healthy leaves. Bury a pot of compost under the runner – peg down beyond the plantlet and nip off the runner end. Sever the rooted plantlet after 4-6 weeks – remove and plant about 1 week later.

RASPBERRY

The Raspberry family is a large one, consisting of the True Raspberries and the Briar Fruits (Blackberries, Loganberries etc) – see page 45. They are easy to grow, but a post-and-wire system is needed for support and plants start to deteriorate after about 8 years. Plant bare-rooted canes in November or December. Apply fish, blood and bone in March and mulch in May. Canes must be tied to the wires as they grow and all the canes which have fruited are cut down after picking – the best, young unfruited canes are tied to the wires. There are several training methods – see *The Fruit Expert*.

CURRANT

The Currants are split into two groups – Red Currants and White Currants which have a single central stem and the Blackcurrants which have a group of stems at soil level.

Blackcurrants are planted as bare-rooted bushes in November, leaving 1.5 m between plants and rows. The old soil mark is set about 5 cm below the surface and a mulch is placed around the bushes after planting. Drape nets over the bushes when fruit starts to colour – old wood on mature plants is removed in winter.

Red Currants and White Currants are usually grown as bushes and are planted, pruned and cared for like Gooseberries – see below.

GOOSEBERRY

Gooseberries are planted as bare-rooted plants in October-November, leaving 1.5 m between plants and rows. The old soil mark is set at soil level and a mulch is placed around the bushes after planting. Use netting to protect the buds in winter and the ripening fruit in summer. Pick small green fruit in late May for cooking. The remaining fruit on dessert varieties should be left to ripen – they are ready when rather soft to the touch when gently squeezed. In winter branches crowding the centre are removed and side-shoots are reduced.

CARING FOR VEGETABLES

The vegetable plot is at the centre of the organic gardening movement. For millions of people the ornamental garden is somewhere to be treated with standard fertilizers and modern sprays – lawns and paths receive their weedkiller and Roses are sprayed with fungicide to prevent mildew and black spot. For an increasing number of these people the vegetable plot is rather different – here the plants or their produce are eaten. For this reason a natural growing system is sought. Their worries may not all be based on scientific fact, but they are all understandable.

Plan your sowings and plantings before the start of the season. You should not grow a vegetable in the same spot year after year. If you do then soil pest and nutrient imbalance problems may increase. The answer is to follow a crop rotation plan – see below.

Traditional Rotation

Year 1	Year 2	Year 3	Year 4

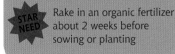
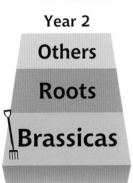
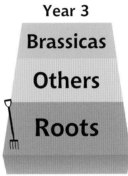
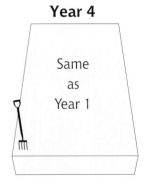

Year 1: Roots / Brassicas / Others

Year 2: Others / Roots / Brassicas

Year 3: Brassicas / Others / Roots

Year 4: Same as Year 1

Roots
Beetroot • Carrot • Chicory Jerusalem Artichoke • Parsnip Potato • Salsify • Scorzonera

- Do not add manure if soil has been enriched previously

- Do not lime

STAR NEED Rake in an organic fertilizer about 2 weeks before sowing or planting

Brassicas
Broccoli • Brussels Sprout Cabbage • Cauliflower • Kohl Rabi Kale • Radish • Swede • Turnip

- Add some well-rotted manure or compost at digging time if soil is known to be short of humus

STAR NEED Lime the soil unless you are sure it is already alkaline

STAR NEED Rake in an organic fertilizer about 2 weeks before sowing or planting

Others
Aubergine • Bean • Capsicum Celeriac • Celery • Cucumber Endive • Leaf Beet • Leek Lettuce • Marrow • Onion • Pea Spinach • Sweet Corn • Tomato

STAR NEED Add a liberal amount of well-rotted manure or compost at digging time

- Lime only if the soil is known to be acid

- Rake in an organic fertilizer about 2 weeks before sowing or planting

Simple Rotation

Grow a root crop this year where an above-ground vegetable was grown last year, and then back to an above-ground vegetable next year.

There are two extra points. Do not grow Potatoes on land which was limed last year, and if a vegetable has done badly this year then never follow it next year with one from the same group shown in the table above.

THE TRADITIONAL PLOT

You will get the longest Beans and the heaviest Potatoes by following this system, but the work involved is laborious and it can be a muddy chore in wet weather. The only choice for the allotment, but there are alternative growing systems for the home plot.

For nearly all gardeners this is the only system they have ever used for growing vegetables. The whole plot or allotment is cultivated and the plants are either sown or set out in long rows. Strips of bare earth are left between each row or group of rows so that the gardener is able to walk along for watering, cultivating, harvesting etc.

There is a lot of work involved but for many that is part of the pleasure of growing vegetables at home. The traditional gardener digs over the plot every autumn or early winter, and the organic-minded ones will always incorporate compost or well-rotted manure – see below. Another autumn or winter job is to draw up your plan using the information on pages 46–47.

Three vital routines are necessary to prevent the plot developing a run-down look as the season progresses. Hoe regularly to keep down weeds, take action against pests and diseases as soon as they appear, and pick or cut the vegetables when they are ready whether or not you can use them.

Digging

Digging is an annual routine in the traditional plot, especially if the soil is heavy, weed growth is abundant and/or the surface has been compacted by foot traffic. However, you should consider the no-digging route outlined on page 9 if conditions are more favourable. The time for digging is during a dry spell in late winter or early spring if you plan to sow or plant in spring. Follow the routine illustrated on page 9 – read the feature on manuring on this page before you begin.

Choose a spade which is suited to your height and strength. Keep the blade clean. Never bring subsoil to the surface – raw clay, chalk or sand will ruin the fertility. Leave heavy soil in lumps – frost will break down the clods.

Manuring & Liming

Manuring is the start of the year for the vegetable grower. A layer of humus maker such as compost or well-rotted manure is spread over the surface at the rate of a bucketful per square metre. This organic matter is forked into the surface, and the area is then turned over with a spade if digging is necessary. Manuring is essential for 'other crops' (see page 73) and also for brassicas if the soil is low in organic matter. Do not manure land to be used for root crops if it was enriched last year. By following this routine the organic content of the whole area is maintained over the years.

Do not lime as a matter of routine – see the Traditional Rotation plan on page 73.

Preparing the Seed Bed

The pattern for most vegetables is to sow seeds outdoors and then either leave them to grow where sown or to sow them elsewhere and then transplant them as seedlings. Either way, a seed bed is required.

Early spring is the usual time to start – the ideal time is when there is a thin dry layer on the surface and moist soil below. Break down the clods using a fork or cultivator – do not let the prongs go deeper than 15 cm. Spread a general fertilizer such as fish, blood and bone over the surface and rake into the top few centimetres.

Now you are ready to prepare the seed bed. Don't tramp heavily over the surface to make it smooth and level – walk over it and use a rake to break down mounds and fill in the hollows.

Sowing & Thinning

Not too early, not too deeply and not too thickly are the golden rules. Proper timing is extremely important. Seeds will only germinate when the soil temperature is high enough to allow growth to begin – sowing in wet and near-freezing conditions is bound to lead to disaster.

Use a length of taut string to mark out the row and sow the seeds, following the instructions on page 54. Remember to feel the soil at the bottom of the drill before sowing – if it is dry, water gently through the rose of a watering can. Never water in after sowing – cover the surface with newspaper if the weather is dry.

Emerged seedlings are usually too close together. Begin thinning as soon as the seedlings are large enough to handle – carry out this job in stages until the recommended spacing is reached.

Large seeds such as Sweet Corn are sown in shallow holes made with a trowel or dibber where they are to grow. Plant two or three at each station – remove the weaker seedlings after germination.

Feeding & Watering

A base feed will have been added during the preparation of the seed bed – see above. There should be no need to apply any extra fertilizer to vegetables which are harvested relatively quickly after sowing or planting, but crops which take some time to reach maturity may need a top dressing during this season. This can be a powder such as fish, blood and bone or liquid manure. Keep solid fertilizers off the leaves and rake into the surface if rain seems unlikely.

By increasing the organic matter content of the soil you will have done all you can to ensure a good moisture reservoir in your soil – the rest is up to the weather. If there is a prolonged drought then watering will be necessary, especially for Tomatoes, Cucumbers, Marrows, Beans, Peas, Celery and Onions. The rule is to water the soil gently every 7 days during the critical period – between flowering and full pod development for Peas and Beans, and from seedling to maturity for leaf crops. Apply 10 litres/sq m – water slowly close to the base of the plant.

Weeding

Weeds are a threat and must be kept at bay. Apart from giving the plot an untidy appearance they compete for space, nutrients and water etc. In addition they can harbour pests and diseases.

There is no single miracle cure – a number of tasks will have to be carried out. The first one begins before the crop is sown, at which time the roots of perennial weeds have to be dug out. If the plot has been neglected and is a sea of grass and other weeds then you have a problem on your hands. For the green gardener the only answer is digging and hand pulling – for the not-so-green gardener there is glyphosate which rapidly breaks down in the soil and leaves no residues.

New weeds will appear among the growing plants. Hoeing is the basic technique to keep them under control – carry it out at regular intervals in order to keep annual weeds in constant check and to starve out the underground parts of perennial ones.

THE BED SYSTEM

A series of rectangular beds are separated by permanent paths. Care is much simpler than with the traditional plot method. Dwarf or early-maturing varieties are chosen, and are grown closely together so that leaves of adjacent plants touch when mature.

The bed system has several distinct advantages compared with the standard allotment pattern. The close spacing results in most weeds being smothered and the gravel- or bark-covered paths mean that there are no muddy walkways. Perhaps the most important advantage is that annual digging is not necessary.

The yearly round begins in autumn or early winter when a layer of organic matter such as rotted manure or garden compost is worked into the surface with a fork. In spring fish, blood and bone is raked into the top few centimetres. Walk over the surface about 2 weeks later and rake to form a seed bed. Sowing and planting take place in the usual way, but the row spacing and plant spacing are equal to each other. Sow short rows every 1-3 weeks to avoid gluts. Yields per sq metre are higher than you would obtain by the traditional plot method, but the size of each individual vegetable is usually smaller. Do not grow the same vegetable in the bed year after year.

Making the Bed

The diagram on the right is a general guide to the dimensions to aim for – note that the beds are narrow enough to allow all the plants to be reached from the paths. If possible construct the beds so that they run north to south.

The flat bed as illustrated in the photograph above is the easier type to construct but you do need free-draining soil. Use the dimensions given for raised beds in the drawing. Turn the soil over and work in a 3 cm layer of organic matter. Let it settle for at least a couple of weeks before sowing or planting.

The raised bed is the type to make if drainage is poor. You will have to build retaining walls – railway sleepers, bricks or reconstituted stone blocks can be used, but stout planks with square wooden posts at the corners are the usual choice. The raised bed should be at least 10 cm high – fork over the bottom and then fill with a mixture of 2 parts topsoil and 1 part organic matter.

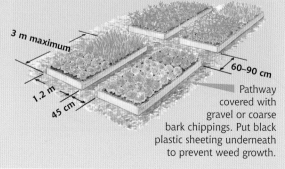

3 m maximum

60–90 cm

1.2 m

45 cm

Pathway covered with gravel or coarse bark chippings. Put black plastic sheeting underneath to prevent weed growth.

Easy-care Vegetables for the Bed System

Name	Sow	Depth	Plant	Distance* between Plants	Harvest	Time** Taken (weeks)	Notes
BEAN, BROAD	February – April	5 cm	–	15 cm	July – August	16 S → H	Favourite varieties include Aquadulce and Bunyard's Exhibition – the favourite dwarf is The Sutton. Begin picking when pods are 8 cm long – cook whole
BEAN, FRENCH	May – June	5 cm	–	15 cm	July – September	10 S → H	The popular Flat-podded or English varieties tend to become stringy as they mature. The Pencil–podded or Continental varieties (e.g Sprite) are stringless
BEETROOT	April – June	2.5 cm	–	8 cm	June – October	11 S → H	Grow a globe variety – harvest when no larger than a tennis ball. Reliable varieties include Boltardy, Monopoly and Monodet
CARROT	March – July	1 cm	–	10 cm	July – October	14 S → H	Pick a quick-maturing short-rooted variety such as the round Early French Frame or the finger-long Amsterdam Forcing
COURGETTE	May – June	2.5 cm	–	45 cm	July – September	10 S → H	Courgettes are marrows cut at the immature stage when 8-10 cm long. Varieties include Gold Rush (yellow) and Defender (green)
KALE	May	1 cm	July	40 cm	December	30 S → H	Pentland Brig is the variety to grow. Pick young leaves in winter, young shoots in early spring and spears (cook like Broccoli) a little later
LETTUCE	March – July	1 cm		25 cm	June – October	12 S → H	Grow a Miniature e.g Tom Thumb or Little Gem or a loose-leaf variety (e.g Salad Bowl) – a few leaves can be removed each time over many weeks
ONION	–	Tip showing	March– April	8 cm	August	20 P → H	Grow sets rather than seed – harvest 2 weeks after stems topple over. Popular varieties include Stuttgarter Giant and Sturon
POTATO	–	12 cm	March– April	30 cm	June– July	13 P → H	Grow an early variety for new Potatoes in early summer – examples include Arran Pilot, Foremost, Pentland Javelin and Sharpe's Express
RADISH	March– July	1 cm	–	5 cm	May– Sept	6 S → H	Nothing is easier to grow. There are many varieties – e.g Cherry Belle (round/red), Sparkler (round/white-red) and Large White Icicle (long/white)
SPINACH BEET	April	2.5 cm	–	20 cm	August– Nov	15 S → H	This type of Leaf Beet is similar to Spinach but it is not prone to bolting and the leaves are large and fleshier
TOMATO	–	–	June	45 cm	August– Sept	12 P → H	An easy crop, but only if you choose a bush variety such as The Amateur and grow it in a warm, sunny and sheltered spot
TURNIP	March– June	1 cm	–	15 cm	May– Sept	10 S → H	Early or bunching varieties (e.g Snowball) are sown early in the year and picked at golf-ball size for salads or stews

* Distance between plants
These spacings are the recommended distance between the rows and also between the mature plants in the rows

** Time taken (weeks)
S = Sowing
P = Planting
H = Harvest

THE POTAGER

This is a section of the garden containing a geometric pattern of beds divided by paths. The beds are often enclosed by dwarf hedging. The main component of the beds is an assortment of vegetables, but one or more other types of plants are included – Roses, herbs, fruit, flowers or bulbs.

'Potager' is the French word for kitchen garden, but in this country it has acquired a special meaning. It describes a plot in which vegetables are grown and are usually accompanied by herbs and fruit. What makes it different from an ordinary vegetable bed (see pages 76–77) is the fact that the ornamental aspect is as important as the productive one. To heighten the ornamental effect a variety of flowers, bushes, bulbs etc are included.

In the potager there is a series of beds which are compact enough to allow easy access from the pathways. They are made of paving slabs or gravel, and in the de-luxe version there are archways draped with Grapes, Roses etc.

There is no specific ratio of food crops to ornamentals – it is a matter of personal taste. As a general rule the vegetables should dominate, but it is usual for some of them to be colourful varieties, and fruit is often grown as pyramids or cordons. A word of warning. The annual and perennial ornamentals will require regular attention if the potager is not to acquire a run-down look.

Colourful Potager Vegetables

Aubergine
Bambino
Black Enorma

Brussels sprout
Rubine

Cabbage
Red Drumhead

Capsicum
Gypsy

Cauliflower
Purple Cape

Celery
Giant Red

French bean
Kinghorn Wax
Purple Podded

Globe Artichoke

Leaf beet
Ruby Chard
Swiss Chard

Lettuce
Lollo Rossa

Rhubarb

Runner bean
Hestia
Painted Lady

Cauliflower – *Purple Cape*

CARING FOR LAWNS

For generations the lawn has been the centrepiece of most gardens. To maintain a lawn in first-rate condition is something we all strive for, but it involves a lot of hard work.

The 'bowling green' type of lawn will have been mown, trimmed, fed, watered, aerated, scarified and top dressed, but not all of these treatments are used on the average home lawn. For the strictly organic gardener there are added problems. The quick-acting nitrogen fertilizers which are used to green up the grass cannot be used, nor can the chemical weedkillers which kill the roots of perennial weeds.

As a result of these difficulties it is not easy to write about caring for the lawn in a green garden. Some organic gardening guides leave out lawns altogether and some others deal with them very sketchily. This won't do – lawn care in the organic garden calls for special emphasis on techniques which are often ignored in the chemical-friendly garden.

Details appear on the following pages – briefly set out here are the main points. Avoid cutting the lawn too closely – the velvet look is not for you. Use a grass box only when the clippings are long – always leave it off for routine mowing. Apply an organic fertilizer in spring if the grass is patchy and pale. Deal with weeds in the way described later, but do not aim for the spotless look which was the goal we used to aim for. A sprinkling of buttercups and daisies is part of the green garden scene.

Both scarifying and top dressing are important for the lawn in the green garden, and aerating the turf is beneficial if the soil is heavy. Liming is only necessary if the soil is very acid with a pH of less than 5.5.

People were maintaining beautiful lawns before quick-acting fertilizers and systemic weedkillers appeared and you can do the same, but it will be necessary to pay more attention to good cultural practice than your spray-happy neighbour.

The New Lawn

The obvious but not the only site for creating a new lawn is on the bare earth left around a newly-built house. Do not choose a luxury-grade turf or seed mixture – the promised velvet look may sound an attractive idea, but it will not stand heavy traffic and needs constant attention. Choose instead utility-grade turf which has been grown from seed and not cut from a meadow. Alternatively use a utility-grade seed mix.

There should be a gap of at least three months between the start of soil preparation and the laying of turf or the sowing of seed – there are a number of jobs to do and the soil must be given time to settle before the final smooth surface is created. Weeds must be removed and perennial roots killed or removed before you begin. This calls for hoeing, forking and/or digging by organic gardeners or an overall application of glyphosate by their not-so-green counterparts. See *The Lawn Expert* for a step-by-step guide.

The worn-out lawn with its cover of moss, coarse grass, weeds and bare earth is another site for a new lawn. Here it is even more important to get rid of surface vegetation and underground perennial roots before preparing the ground for turf or seed.

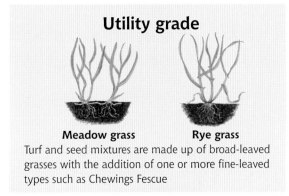

Utility grade

Meadow grass   **Rye grass**

Turf and seed mixtures are made up of broad-leaved grasses with the addition of one or more fine-leaved types such as Chewings Fescue

Luxury grade

Bent   **Fescue**

Turf and seed mixtures are made up of fine-leaved grasses. The broad-leaved grasses are not used, but may appear in mature lawns

Feeding

The feeding programme for the non-organic and not-so-green gardener is to apply a nitrogen-rich fertilizer in spring to produce a rapid green. The really keen lawn owner then follows up with a summer feed and in autumn a dressing with phosphate, potash and some slow-acting nitrogen is used.

The orthodox organic gardener follows a much simpler programme. Clippings are left on the lawn to nourish it and the surface is lightly raked several times during summer to encourage their decomposition and to avoid the build-up of thatch. Extra treatment is needed if the grass is pale and lacking vigour – apply fish, blood and bone at 100 g/sq m in April.

Top Dressing

Top dressing is the application of bulky material to the surface of the soil. This annual treatment has long been a matter of routine for the groundsman, and is now being adopted by an increasing number of green gardeners. Its purpose is to fill in the minor hollows and to build up an ideal soil layer over the years.

There are several recipes – examples are 1 part sieved compost/4 parts soil/2 parts sharp sand (1.5kg/sq m) or 1 part sieved compost/1 part sharp sand (1 kg/sq m). The best time to apply the top dressing is early autumn – using a spade to put down small heaps over the surface. Use the back of an ordinary garden rake to spread it over the grass.

Watering

During a period of drought there is a loss of springiness in the turf and a general dullness over the surface. Later on the grass turns straw-coloured and unsightly. During a prolonged dry spell you will have to choose between two courses of action.

Firstly, you can decide to do nothing and just wait for rain. In recent years this has become the preferred action – lawn grasses are very rarely killed by drought and they soon recover once the rains return. Furthermore, watering is often banned for garden use in times of prolonged drought. The main problem with leaving it to nature is that drought-resistant weeds such as yarrow and clover are spread rapidly.

There are two situations where watering during prolonged dry weather is desirable. Newly-sown grass or newly-laid turf can be seriously damaged if kept short of water, and lawns where the grass is thin and sparse may need to be kept growing to prevent serious weed invasion.

If you have to water then you must do it thoroughly – at least 20 litres/sq m once a week until rain returns. Do not try to save water by sprinkling every few days to dampen the surface – it will do more harm than good.

ROTARY SPRINKLER

Rotating arms produce a circle of fine droplets. Very popular and many brands are available. Some are adjustable for area covered

OSCILLATING SPRINKLER

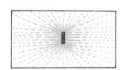

A horizontal tube bearing a series of fine holes slowly turns from side to side. A rectangular spray pattern is obtained – all are adjustable for area covered

Scarifying

Lightly rake over your lawn several times during summer to discourage weeds and coarse grasses. Scarifying is a different technique, involving the use of a garden rake or rake-like tool with considerable downward pressure. Never scarify in spring – the time for this treatment is early autumn, before aerating and top dressing. This treatment is used when thick thatch has built up on the surface – disturbing it stimulates the production of the side-shoots and runners which grass develops at this time of the year. Apply grass seed to any bare patches which have appeared.

Aerating

Aerating creates holes or slits so that air and water can penetrate. The purpose of these air channels is to break through the compaction layer which occurs at 5-8 cm beneath the surface. Spiking is the technique to use, and it is used on areas of the lawn showing symptoms of compaction, such as waterlogging, moss, worn-out patches and poor grass vigour. For small areas use a garden fork – drive prongs to a depth of about 10 cm and rock back and forth. For larger areas there are hollow-tine forks. September is the best month.

Mowing

The purpose of mowing a utility-grade lawn is to keep the grass long enough to ensure vigorous root activity but short enough for it to be attractive. But mowing does much more than keeping the lawn looking neat and tidy. Cutting the grass regularly but not too closely prevents the development of excess leaf growth. The result is that the loss of nutrients and the menace of weeds are reduced. The lawn develops a dwarf growth habit and the production of tillers is stimulated – it is the growth of these side-shoots which thickens the turf in summer.

Busy gardeners sometimes try to save time by cutting at the lowest setting so they can wait at least a couple of weeks before the next scalping is necessary. This technique is almost guaranteed to ruin the lawn – the grass is shocked and vigour is reduced. The result is thin and open turf infested with moss and weeds.

Don't use a grass box. Leaving short clippings on the surface returns some of the nutrients to the soil so that feeding is much less necessary, and the baking effect of the sun is reduced during dry spells in summer. An added benefit is that you do not have to stop at regular intervals to empty the container. The drawback is that you lose an important source of material for the compost heap. One answer is to collect cuttings from the first few mowings in spring and then leave off the grass box.

A striped effect is sometimes regarded as a sign of a healthy and cared-for lawn. It is nothing of the sort – it merely shows that the lawn has been cut in parallel strips with a mower fitted with a roller.

START

Begin in **March** or **early April**, depending on the locality and the weather. It is time for the first cut when the soil is reasonably dry and the grass is starting to grow actively. With this first cut set the blades high so that the grass is merely tipped, not shorn.

MARCH

MOW REGULARLY

As a general rule the cutting height should be 2.5 cm and mowing should take place at weekly intervals. However, there are several exceptions to this standard procedure:

- Set the blades at 3-4 cm for the first couple of cuts in spring and for the last few cuts in autumn.

- Set the blades at 4 cm during periods of prolonged drought if the lawn is not being regularly watered. The longer grass will help to cut down water loss.

- Cut at fortnightly rather than weekly intervals if the grass is growing very slowly – for example under trees or during prolonged drought.

- If you have had to be away for a couple of weeks or more in summer then merely tip it at the first cut following your return. Reduce the height at the next cut and then continue with 2.5 cm high cuts.

APRIL

MAY

JUNE

JULY

AUGUST

SEPTEMBER

FINISH

Stop in **October** when the growth of the grass has slowed right down and the soil has become very moist. Put the mower away, but rake off fallen leaves on the surface of the lawn. Keen gardeners lightly 'top' the grass occasionally in winter when the weather is mild, but it is not essential. Avoid walking on the lawn when it is frozen or covered in snow.

OCTOBER

Weed Control

It is inevitable that some weeds will appear in your lawn. Millions of gardeners get to work with repeat treatments using a systemic weedkiller which attacks the roots. The green gardener does not have this armoury of bottles, powders etc, and so the approach must be to encourage weed prevention by cultural means rather than relying on modern chemicals to remove them after they appear. Towards this end you must mow properly, leaving clippings on the surface, rake during the season, and then when required aerate, scarify, top dress and feed as described on the previous pages.

When weeds do appear follow this three-part programme to keep them under control:

- Learn to live with scattered clumps of daisies, buttercups, clover etc. Their leaves are reasonably small and are not unsightly in an environment-friendly lawn.

- A few weeds make large rosettes which do stand out – examples include plantains, thistles and dandelions. Grub these out with an old knife, apple corer, daisy grubber or narrow trowel.

- Patches of small-leaved weeds can be dealt with by sprinkling lawn sand sparingly on the leaves.

Lawn Sand

Lawn sand is sold under various proprietary names and is a blend of ammonium sulphate, iron sulphate and sharp sand. It is an age-old treatment for moss and for burning off the top of lawn weeds as well as serving as a green-up feed for the grass. Chemical-friendly gardeners have largely switched over to the modern systemic weedkillers which go inside the plant, but some traditional lawn owners stick with the old remedy.

Opinion is divided over its use in the green garden. Copper sulphate is acceptable in Bordeaux mixture used on Potatoes, and iron sulphate is no more 'chemical' than a copper salt. A pinch in the heart of a lawn weed should be inoffensive to anyone, but its use as an overall treatment is not acceptable to the strict organic gardener.

Take care if you decide to use lawn sand. Fine grasses will be scorched if carelessly handled.

Buttercup	*Cat's ear*	*Chickweed*	*Clover*	*Daisy*	*Dandelion*
Pearlwort	*Plantain*	*Self heal*	*Speedwell*	*Thistle*	*Yarrow*

Moss Control

Small patches of moss are not a problem, but large mossy areas are unsightly. Unfortunately there is no easy solution. The not-so-green gardener can burn it off with lawn sand, but this offers only short-term relief. If you don't remove the basic cause or causes then the moss will return. Poor drainage is an important culprit, so making holes with a fork in a mossy patch on compacted soil will help. Other causes are shade, lack of nutrients in sandy soil and over-acidity (lime will help, but do test first). The best advice is to apply a fertilizer in spring, spike the affected areas in autumn, remove the cause of shade if possible, top dress, and always cut at the recommended height – closely shaving the lawn is a common cause of moss infestation.

Lawn Problems

Toadstools

The usual cause is buried organic debris, and removing this will often eliminate a small clump of toadstools. Fairy rings are more serious – two dark green circles in the grass with a bare space in between. The ring grows wider every year and the usual cause is Marasmius – a brown-capped 5-10 cm high toadstool. Many cures have been proposed, but replacing the soil and re-turfing is the only satisfactory answer. A lot of work – the usual approach is to live with the problem.

Earthworms

The worms which inhabit the lawn are not efficient soil aerators like their relatives which live in the beds and borders. Their casts on the surface are a problem – they are unsightly when flattened by the mower and the worms attract moles. Brush away dry casts before mowing.

Weeds & Moss

See page 82.

Moles

See page 93.

Broken Edges

Cut out a square of turf carrying the broken edge. Use a spade to prise up the cut square and move it forward so that the damaged part projects beyond the border. Now trim to line up with the rest of the lawn. Use the piece you have removed to fill the gap at the back of the square of turf. Put soil in the hollow area, firm down and sow with grass seed.

Bumps & Hollows

Do not try to roll out bumps – the area will become more unsightly than ever. Remove the bump by cutting the grass and rolling back the turf above the affected area. Remove soil to level the surface – roll back the turf and fill cracks with sifted soil. Small hollows can be gradually filled in by working sifted soil (no more than 1 cm thickness at a time) into the turf at regular intervals. Deep hollows call for surgery as described above, adding rather than removing soil.

Disease

Diseases cause brown patches. They are much less widespread than the major pests (worms, moles and leatherjackets) but they can be more dangerous. Some like red thread are merely unsightly but ophiobolus patch can be a killer. If you feel that disease is the cause of your brown patches, send off a sample to an advisory service run by your gardening magazine or the Royal Horticultural Society.

Leatherjackets

The worst of all insect pests, especially in heavy soil after a wet autumn. The 3 cm grey or brown grubs devour roots and stem bases in the spring – the grass turns yellow and brown. Tackle the problem by watering in the evening and spreading a plastic sheet over the surface. Remove next morning and brush away the grubs.

Bitch Urine

The brown patches are roughly circular in outline, with a ring of dark lush grass surrounding each patch. The effect is worst in dry weather. The problem is a difficult one – there are no effective repellents which can be used over the whole lawn, and the only thing you can do is to water the patches copiously. If one or more of the patches is an eyesore then re-seeding or re-turfing the area is the answer.

Thatch

Thatch is a fibrous layer on top of the soil surface. When it is more than 3 cm thick it forms a semi-waterproof cover – downward passage of rain is restricted and aeration is impeded. Disease is encouraged and the turf begins to thin out. Scarify the surface with a lawn rake in autumn. You can hire a powered scarifier if the area is large.

Pale Grass

A pale green look usually indicates a lack of nitrogen. Mowing is a serious drain on the soil's reserve, and unless it is replaced the turf may become thin and sparse. There are three things to do. Do not use a grass box when mowing, apply an organic fertilizer in spring, and spread a top dressing in autumn.

Moles

Earthworms

Weeds

Toadstools

CARING FOR WILDFLOWERS

The Wildflower Meadow should provide a mass of colour in late spring – a reminder of the flower-filled fields of times gone by. Unfortunately coarse weed grasses can soon become a problem, and the area will look dull when the flowers are absent.

The Wildflower Patch is the better choice for most gardens. Various native flowers growing closely together among rocks and/or native shrubby plants provide a natural look. In addition you are spared the hard work involved in making and maintaining a Wildflower Meadow.

In this environment-conscious age it is not surprising that the idea of having an area of fine-leaved and low-growing grasses liberally sprinkled with a wide variety of wildflowers has caught the public imagination for several reasons. Cornflowers, Ox-eye Daisies, Poppies etc are less common than they used to be, and the Wildflower Meadow in the garden seems to be a way of redressing the trend in a small way. Another attractive feature is the fact that mowing is an occasional rather than a regular task, but the often-quoted benefit that native plants are more attractive to wildlife than our garden ones does not seem to be correct. You do not need a Wildflower Meadow in order to create a haven for birds, butterflies and bees in your garden.

Having an area of native flowers around your house is indeed a desirable feature in the green garden, but you should think carefully before creating a Wildflower Meadow. Unless you are really into the Green Movement it is unwise to turn your whole garden into grassland and native plants – for much of the year it will have a drab and uncared-for appearance. For most people this feature should be created at the back of the traditional garden areas – it will be a plot which has an irregular outline with wattle fencing, rustic seating etc and sprinkled with flowers of the field among fine-leaved grasses.

The starting point is soil which is too infertile to grow good garden plants and is free from perennial weeds. Now that is a problem for most people – how to achieve it is outlined on the next page. It is best to start from scratch, but as noted later you can transform an area of existing grassland provided the soil is not rich and the grass varieties are fine-leaved and relatively slow-growing.

For the average-sized garden the Wildflower Meadow is not really a practical idea. A better plan is to aim for one or more Wildflower Patches – groups of native flowers growing in beds, borders or rockery.

The Wildflower Meadow

Preparing the Ground

The basic principle is that you don't want the grass to grow too quickly and that means the soil should have low fertility for good results – sandy free-draining soil is best. The next principle is that getting rid of weeds at the preparatory stage is vital. The not-so-green gardener might use glyphosate to kill the roots of perennial weeds, but for the organic gardener this means digging out the roots when cultivating before preparing the seed bed. The best time to sow is September or October – prepare the land well in advance (see *The Lawn Expert*). There are a few variations to the standard method of preparing for a new lawn. For a Wildflower Meadow you must not add fertilizer and the chore of producing a truly level surface is not necessary. On the other hand the top few centimetres of soil will have to be stripped off before seed bed preparation if the land is fertile and if the area is not too large.

Mowing & Maintenance

You will need to adjust the frequency of cutting to the vigour of the grass, the wildflower and bulb species present and the growing conditions. There are no hard and fast rules for the established Wildflower Meadow, but the plan for the newly-established one is more clear-cut.

In the first year the goal is to prevent the grass from swamping the wildflowers and to make sure that the perennials put their strength into leaf and not flower production. The grass should therefore be cut in March, May, July and September at a height of 6-10 cm – do not expect flowers in this first season although some annuals may bloom. Always use a grass box to remove the clippings and get rid of docks, thistles and nettles by grubbing out.

A popular maintenance plan for the established Wildflower Meadow is to make the first cut when the spring flowers have all faded and set seed. This is generally in late June or early July, and a second and final cut of the season is made in September or October. There are, however, several variations of this basic plan. If growth is vigorous in summer an August cut may be necessary and if you have autumn-flowering plants then the final cut should be delayed until late October or November. When cutting you should aim at a height of 6-10 cm and this can pose problems. If your mower cannot be set to this height you will have to either scythe or use a strimmer. Never apply a fertilizer and always remove the clippings – leave them on the surface for a few days before removal so that the seeds will have been shed.

Sowing the Seed

The first step is to buy a good-quality mixture of fine grasses and meadow wildflowers. You can buy a 'natural' mixture obtained from agricultural meadows, but this may contain weed-type wildflowers which are undesirable. It is better to use a mixture which is made by mixing individual types of seed. Here you have a choice – ready-made mixes under various names (Flower Lawn, Flower Meadow Mixture etc) are available or you can blend your own from packets bought from a specialist supplier. With either route the grass element should consist mainly or entirely of Bents and Fescues, and the wildflower element should contain numerous varieties which will grow in your situation. Some annuals as well as the more usual perennials may be present and the wildflower seed content of branded mixtures is in the 5-10 per cent range.

Sow in autumn. Follow the instructions on the package or use 5 g/sq m with a home-made mix. Add 5 parts of fine sand to 1 part of the mixture to help to ensure even distribution and be careful not to bury the seed when raking it into the surface.

Converting a Meadow

In most cases the gardener does not start from scratch – it is more usual to convert an area of rough grassland in the garden into a Wildflower Meadow. Naturalise some bulbs and plant some suitable wildflowers – cut the grass to about 5 cm before you start in order to make the job easier. Unfortunately sprinkling a wildflower seed mixture over the area is not the way to do it – you will have to start with robust seedlings, or divisions obtained from large plants.

The Wildflower Patch

You will find packets of mixed wildflower seeds at your local garden centre. Choose a site in a bed or rockery where the soil is poor and relatively weed- and grass-free – dig out the roots of any perennial weeds. Prepare a seed bed, following the guidelines on page 54 – autumn is the best time but you can sow in March or April if necessary. Mix the seed with 10 parts of dry sand and sow, again following the instructions on page 54. Do not clean up the site at the end of the flowering season before all the seeds have been shed.

Chapter 5

TACKLING THE PROBLEMS

A variety of troubles are going to occur in your garden. The nature of the plant is important here – some hardy shrubs may remain trouble-free for all their lives, an old-fashioned Rose may be a host to an assortment of pests and diseases every year. The weather is another important factor – there will be slugs when it's wet, greenfly when it's dry, frost damage when it's cold and red spider mite when it's hot. Both green and non-green gardeners can expect problems. The big difference is that expert organic gardeners will have built up their soil to ensure strong plant growth and they will know what problems to watch for. Steps will have been taken to reduce the likelihood of pest and disease attacks, and troubles will be tackled as soon as they are spotted.

Garden troubles are tackled in two ways – culturally and chemically. Green gardeners rely almost exclusively on cultural methods of control, but there are times when a spray may be necessary.

What to use? There is no problem for chemical-friendly gardeners – they choose one of the pesticides on the shelves of the garden centre and hopefully follow the instructions and precautions to the letter.

There is also no difficulty in making a choice for the orthodox green gardener. No synthetic chemical insecticide, fungicide or weedkiller can be used – only mineral or organic products are acceptable.

It is the not-so-green gardeners who are in a difficult situation. Like the organic group they ignore non-serious pests and would not dream of using a modern synthetic pesticide on a food crop. But there are serious problems where they may be tempted to turn to a modern chemical product approved by the Government, provided that it does not leave a long-lasting residue and is known to have no risk to humans. Examples here are glyphosate on perennials weeds, and iron sulphate for moss control. Where to draw the line between organic and acceptable chemicals poses a problem.

KEEPING PLANTS HEALTHY
Prevent Trouble Before it Starts

Prepare the ground thoroughly

Pull out the roots of perennial weeds when cultivating soil prior to planting. It is essential to incorporate some organic matter every year, especially if the soil is in poor condition. This will help to open up heavy soil, where waterlogging in winter is a major cause of root-rotting diseases. It will also help sandy soil by building up the water- and food-holding capacity. Nutrients essential for healthy growth will be provided by the incorporated humus maker – extra nutrients can be supplied by adding fish, blood and bone.

Choose the right plants

There are several points to think about here. Firstly, make sure the plant is suited to the site. Avoid sun-lovers if shade is a problem, do not pick tender types if the garden is exposed and prone to frosts, and forget about acid-loving plants if the ground is chalky. Secondly, buy good quality stock – reject soft bulbs, lanky bedding plants and sickly perennials. Thirdly, try to choose varieties which are noted for their pest or disease resistance, and make sure that your Raspberry, Strawberry, Blackcurrant or Potato purchase is certified stock.

Plant properly

Trouble lies ahead if you don't follow the rules for good planting in Chapter 4. These rules ensure that there will be no air pockets and that the roots will spread into the garden soil in the minimum possible time.

Care for the plants properly

Most troubles arise from poor growing conditions rather than a specific pest or disease. Incorrect watering is the most important cause of poor growth and death. Failure to water in dry weather can lead to death as everyone knows, but daily sprinklings can be almost as damaging. The rule is to water thoroughly, let the soil partly dry out and then water again. At the other end of the scale there is damage caused by overwatering – plants in pots may die if kept waterlogged in winter.

Remove rubbish and weeds

Rotting plants can be a source of infection – some actually attract pests to the garden. Boxes, old flower pots etc are a breeding ground for slugs and woodlice. Rake away fallen Rose and Apple leaves in winter. Remove Brussels Sprout and Broccoli stems after harvest. Weeds growing close to plants will compete for light, water, nutrients and space if not removed.

Follow hygiene rules under glass

The humid atmosphere of a greenhouse is a paradise for pests and diseases. Control is often difficult, so prevention is far better than cure. Use compost or sterilised soil. Ensure the house is adequately ventilated – dry air encourages pests and poor growth, but constantly saturated air encourages diseases. Try to avoid sudden fluctuations in temperature. Water regularly – try to do this job in the morning, although watering in the early evening is acceptable if the weather is warm. Remove dead leaves and plants immediately.

Use a pest barrier where possible

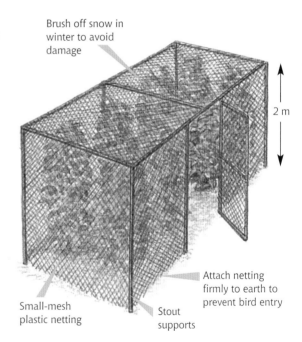

Brush off snow in winter to avoid damage

2 m

Attach netting firmly to earth to prevent bird entry

Small-mesh plastic netting

Stout supports

A number of animals and pests can be kept away from plants by using barriers or traps. Use netting to protect seedlings, vegetables and soft fruit from birds. Erect a fruit cage as illustrated above, or drape netting over Strawberries etc – use sticks etc to keep the net off the plants. A cylinder of wire netting is the best way to keep squirrels, rabbits, cats and deer away from the base of trees. Sticky bands around the trunks of Apple trees will save fruit from the winter moth caterpillar, and felt collars around the stems of brassica plants will keep cabbage root fly away. A ring of sharp grit or pine needles around plants will give slug protection. In addition slugs can be caught in saucers filled with beer and greenhouse slugs can be killed by using nematodes (see page 92).

Tackle Trouble Without Delay

Garden Friendly

Pull up and destroy if the trouble is incurable

Some disease and pest problems (e.g virus, chrysanthemum eelworm, damping off of seedlings, root aphid) are incurable. Remove the affected plants and destroy them. Look in the *Expert* books to find the cause and to see if replanting is permissible.

Examine dead plants

Don't just throw them away after lifting – look at the soil ball and the ground which held the plant. If roots have not developed from the original soil ball, then re-read the planting instructions in Chapter 4. If there is an infestation of grubs in the soil, remove as many as you can by digging and then hand picking. There is no soil insecticide for you to use, but there are biological methods for controlling chafer grubs, leatherjackets and slugs – see page 89.

Cut out dead wood

When pruning in autumn or spring cut out all dead and badly diseased wood and burn it. If a large canker is present on a branch of a tree cut back to clean wood.

Don't try to kill everything

Not all insects are pests – many are positive allies in the war against plant troubles. Obviously these should not be harmed and neither should the vast majority of the insect population – the ones which are neither friends nor foes. There will be times when a plant pest or disease poses a serious problem, such as an infestation of slugs in the vegetable garden or a crippling attack by aphids on the Roses. But even here small infestations of minor pests can be ignored (e.g cuckoo spit) or picked off by hand (e.g caterpillars, rolled leaves and leafminer-damaged foliage).

Use cultural methods when you can

Unlike your chemical-friendly neighbour you won't be able to reach for a bottle or sprayer when there is a serious attack by harmful insects or pathogenic fungi. There is a limited range of organic and mineral sprays you can turn to, so green gardeners must place much greater reliance on cultural methods of pest control. This has the added benefit of avoiding any harm to friendly organisms. Examples include putting down guards around plants to protect against slugs once damage is seen (see page 92) and pinching out the tops of Broad Beans once five trusses of pods have formed in order to guard against blackfly. Use yellow sticky cards when whitefly appear in the greenhouse.

Use a spray or dust only if you have to

There are three reasons why the green gardener should not be as reliant on insecticides and fungicides as the chemical-friendly gardener. First of all, the presence of insects and minor blemishes are less distasteful when gardening this way. Next, we have to face up to the fact that organic and mineral pesticides are much less effective than their modern chemical equivalents and kill only those insects which are hit by the spray or dust. There is no systemic action to enable them to enter the sap stream, and they are not long-lasting. Finally, some organic sprays can harm friendly insects which are caught by the spray, so don't use an insecticide unless the attack is serious enough to warrant such action.

Still, there are times when it may be necessary to turn to insecticidal soap, pyrethrins, copper, sulphur etc, and there are rules to follow. Read the label carefully – make sure that the product is recommended for the plant you wish to spray. Follow the instructions – do not make the mixture stronger than recommended. An easy approach to spraying is to buy a ready-to-use solution packed in a trigger-operated container.

Choose a sunless day when the leaves are dry. During the flowering season treat in the evening, when bees will have stopped working. Use a fine forceful spray. Keep sprays off your skin – wash off any splashes. Spray thoroughly until the leaves are covered with liquid which is just beginning to run off. Dust to provide a fine but complete cover. Wash out equipment after use, and wash hands and face. Do not keep any spray solution you have made up until next time and store packs in a safe place.

PESTS

Animals, varying in size from microscopic eelworms to majestic deer, may attack your plants. The general term 'insect' covers small pests – mites, slugs and true insects such as aphids. See pages 83 and 90–93.

There are three types of chemical insecticide – the short-lived contact ones, the long-lasting stomach-acting ones, and the systemic insecticides which enter the sap stream. The green gardener is restricted to the organic contact insecticides described below – sadly the EC ceased to approve the use of Derris in 2008, despite 100 years of no-problem use. But there are also the biological ones. These are predatory mites, beetles, nematodes and wasps used for killing leatherjackets, slugs, thrips, caterpillars, greenfly etc – order cards are available at large garden centres.

	Insecticidal Soap	Pyrethrins
Uses	Controls whitefly, greenfly, blackfly, red spider mite, mealy bug	Controls greenfly, whitefly, small caterpillars, thrips, raspberry beetle
Notes	Safe to ladybirds. Described as 'fatty acids' on the label	Now hard to find. Mixtures based on an extract from Pyrethrum flower-heads

DISEASES

Plant troubles caused by living organisms which are transmitted from one plant to another. Fungal diseases are the most common but there are other diseases caused by bacteria and viruses. See pages 83 and 94–95.

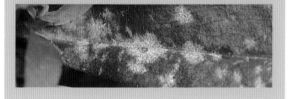

Disease control is difficult when you restrict yourself to green products. There are powerful synthetic chemical fungicides which can be used to control a wide range of diseases, and some of them have a systemic action whereby they enter the sap stream and work from within. For the green gardener there is a very limited range – there are just two basic types on the organic shelf. Neither is organic, but both are simple types which have been used for generations. It is important to remember that they are protectants and not cures – they must be applied before the disease takes hold, and repeat applications are essential.

	Copper	Sulphur
Uses	Controls downy mildews, blights, some rusts	Controls powdery mildews, storage rots
Notes	Bordeaux mixture is the standard spray. Cheshunt compound is a copper fungicide used to control damping off of seedlings	Usually sold as ready-to-use puffer. Apply to Roses, ornamentals and fruit before disease takes hold. Safe to bees but keep away from fish

DISORDERS

Plant troubles which may have disease-like symptoms but are not due to a living organism – they are caused, not caught. Common causes are too much shade, too little food, frost, waterlogging and drought. See page 96.

WEEDS

Plants growing where you do not want them to be – no plant is inherently a 'weed'. Self-sown annual flowers in a Rose bed are weeds – dandelions in a wild garden are not. All broad-leaved plants are weeds in a lawn. See pages 82 and 97–98.

PESTS Above ground

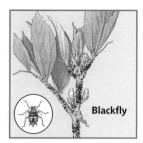

Blackfly

Pest	Background	Control
Apple Sawfly	A ribbon-like scar appears on the skin. A creamy grub is inside – sticky 'frass' surrounds the surface hole. Fruit usually drops in July	Pick up and destroy fallen fruit. Spray with pyrethrins a few days after petal fall if you are really keen
Blackfly	A serious pest of Broad Beans in spring and French Beans in July. Large colonies stunt growth, damage flowers and distort pods	Pinch out tops of Broad Beans once 5 flower trusses have formed. Use insecticidal soap if serious
Caterpillars	Many types attack plants – usual sign is the presence of large irregular holes in the leaves. Cabbage white butterfly can be serious	If practical pick off by hand. Where damage is widespread use insecticidal soap
Codling Moth	Pale pink grubs inside fruits of Apples, Pears and Plums in July and August. Sawdust-like 'frass' surrounds eaten-out area	Live with it. The only practical alternative is to tie a grease band around the trunk
Cuckoo Spit	Frothy white masses on the stems of many plants. Within are pinkish froghoppers which suck the sap	Wash off with a forceful jet of water if you wish, but not worth bothering about
Earwig	A pest which can attack vegetables and fruit – Chrysanthemums and Dahlias are the major targets. Leaves and petals are torn	Shake plants – destroy earwigs which fall. Trap in upturned flower pots filled with straw
Eelworm	Microscopic worms which affect leaves, stems and/or roots of numerous plants including Chrysanthemums and Potatoes	No cure – do not replant for 3–6 years if you are sure eelworms are present
Flea Beetle	Tiny yellow and black beetles which jump when disturbed. Small round holes appear in young leaves of the Cabbage family	Live with it, or use an insect spray if the attack is serious
Greenfly	An all-too-familiar pest – green, brown, yellow or pink. Rapid build-up in warm, settled weather. Young growth is weakened – viruses are transmitted	Water plants in dry weather. Spray greenfly clusters with pyrethrins or insecticidal soap
Leafhopper	Small green insects produce pale mottled patches on leaves of ornamentals, e.g Pelargonium. Direct damage is slight but viruses are transmitted	Spraying is not worthwhile
Leaf Miner	Winding tunnels, blisters or blotches occur on the leaves of many plants, including Chrysanthemums and Carnations	Pick off and destroy mined leaves
Mealy Bug	An indoor pest, infesting house plants and greenhouse ornamentals. Clusters of cottony fluff occur on stems and the underside of leaves	Deal with the trouble promptly. Wipe off with a damp cloth or a moistened cotton bud
Pea & Bean Weevil	Young Peas and Beans can be severely retarded by the beetles which bite notches in the leaves	Hoe around plants in April and May. Use insecticidal soap if the attack is severe

Codling moth

Chrysanthemum eelworm

Flea beetle

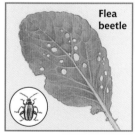

Leaf miner

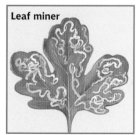

Pea & bean weevil

Pest	Background	Control
Pea Moth	The cause of maggoty Peas. Eggs are laid on the leaves in summer – the greenish grubs bore through the pods and into the seeds	Early- and late-sown crops usually escape damage. Hoe the soil to expose after crop has been lifted
Raspberry Beetle	The cause of maggoty Raspberries, Loganberries and Blackberries. The grubs can soon ruin the crop	If attacks occurred last year, use pyrethrins when flowers open and again at petal fall
Red Spider Mite	A general pest of greenhouse and house plants. Leaves turn an unhealthy bronze – fine silky webbing is a tell-tale sign	Encouraged by hot and dry conditions. Damp down under glass. See page 89
Root Aphid	Greyish 'greenfly' and white powdery patches occur on the roots. Many plants can be affected but Lettuce is the favourite host	There is no cure. Lift and destroy affected plants. Grow an aphid-resistant Lettuce variety (e.g Avoncrisp)
Rose Slugworm	Areas of the leaf are skeletonised. Affected areas turn brown. Greenish grubs on surface	Pick off affected leaves. If serious use insecticidal soap
Scale	Non-moving insects which attack a wide range of plants. The small discs are found on stems and the underside of leaves	Wipe off with a damp cloth or a moistened cotton bud
Thrips	Silvery flecking and streaking occur on flowers, leaves and pods. Minute black or yellow flies are just visible	Not usually treated
Wasps	A nuisance in the garden as ripening tree and soft fruits are damaged. Only blemished fruit is attacked	Live with the problem. If close to the house it may be necessary to destroy the nest
Whitefly	A serious greenhouse pest – clouds of small moth-like flies in the air and greenish larvae under the leaves	Chemical control is difficult – hang up yellow sticky cards
Winter Moth	Green 'looper' caterpillars devour the young leaves of fruit trees. Petals, flower stalks and fruitlets may also be attacked. Leaves are often spun together	Encircle each trunk in autumn with grease bands if you are really keen
Woolly Aphid	A pest of ornamental and fruit trees and shrubs – the white waxy wool on the stems is produced by the aphids within	Rub or scrape off – brush large areas with an old toothbrush and methylated spirits

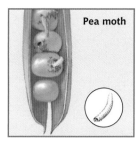

Pea moth

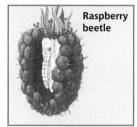

Raspberry beetle

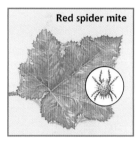

Red spider mite

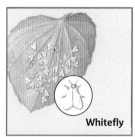

Whitefly

Woolly aphid

PESTS On surface or below-ground

Pest	Background	Control
Cabbage Root Fly	Young Cabbages, Sprouts, Radishes, Turnips etc die – older ones are stunted. Leaves are blue-tinged. Look for small white maggots on the roots	Place a collar around the base of each seedling when planting out if you are really bothered. Lift and destroy affected plants
Carrot Fly	A serious pest of Carrots and Parsnips. Seedlings are killed – mature roots are riddled and liable to rot. Look for reddish leaves and for small creamy maggots in the roots	Try to avoid thinning – the smell of crushed leaves attracts the flies. Next year sow in March or June
Cutworm	Large grey or brown caterpillars just below the surface. Young plants are attacked at night – stems are severed at ground level	July–August is the danger period. Hoe around affected plants – destroy caterpillars brought to the surface.
Leatherjacket	Dark grey grubs – 2.5 cm long and slow moving. Can be a problem on the lawn – look for brown patches and intense bird activity. May also be serious in new, badly-drained plots	Tackle the problem when digging and hoeing. Pick up and destroy the easily-recognisable grubs. See page 89
Onion Fly	Small white maggots burrow into the bulb bases – young plants are killed, old ones fail to develop. Look for yellow, drooping leaves	Try to avoid thinning – grow sets or transplants. Destroy damaged leaves. Firm the soil around the plants
Slugs & Snails	Serious garden pests, especially when the weather is wet and cool. They hide under debris during the day and come out at night, devouring seedlings and roots, stems, leaves and even flowers. Slime trails are a tell-tale clue	Remove rubbish and hand-pick at night. There are barriers (sharp grit, copper wire etc), traps (beer-filled saucers etc) and biological control – see page 89. Try oat bran around the plants – it is lethal once it has been eaten
Vine Weevil	An important pest of container plants – look for white grubs in the compost	Pick out and destroy if seen – use a nematode-type insecticide (page 89)
Wireworm	A pest in grassland dug for the first time – 1 cm long shiny, yellow grubs attack the roots of many plants	Avoid growing Potatoes and root vegetables for about 3 years in infested land. Destroy grubs when digging

Carrot fly

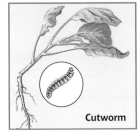

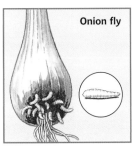

Cutworm

Onion fly

Slugs & snails

PESTS Animals

A number of animals other than flies and creepy-crawlies can damage your garden, but the approach to them must be different to the way we tackle insect pests. The object here must be to protect the plants and/or discourage the invaders without causing them actual harm. There are exceptions – rats must be killed and the mole too, if all else fails.

Pest	Background	Control
Birds	The flower garden is least affected – but Polyanthus, Primula wanda and Crocus may be stripped of buds and flowers. Vegetables can suffer badly, especially Peas and the Cabbage family. Seeds and seedlings are eaten, sparrows tear flowers and pigeons strip away the soft portion of leaves. Bullfinches and sparrows devour buds of Cherries, Gooseberries etc – the fruit is also attacked	Small areas can be protected with soft plastic netting – make sure all the plants are covered and the base of the net is properly secured. For a large number of plants a fruit cage is undoubtedly the best answer. Spray-on repellents are of limited value and are removed by rain – mechanical scarers soon lose their ability to frighten away birds
Cats	Cats can be a pest of the flower and vegetable garden. Seed beds and young transplants are disturbed by their scratching	Protection is not easy if cats have chosen your flower bed as a toilet. Remove surface soil and insert stout twigs over the area
Deer	Deer can be a serious pest in rural areas close to woodland. Young trees are grazed – the bark may be stripped in winter. Rose buds are a favourite meal	Tall fencing is the real answer but may not be practical. Ring the trunks of trees with a wire netting cage
Dogs	Dogs, like cats, will scratch in soft ground. Remove dog droppings at once – they are a health risk. The most serious effect, however, is the brown patches caused on lawns by bitch urine	Train your dog not to foul the beds. Hedges and prickly shrubs will deter stray dogs. Copiously water affected areas on the lawn
Foxes	A new but not serious pest in urban areas – plants are not attacked but dustbins are disturbed	Do not leave plastic bags containing waste food standing out overnight
Mice, Rats & Voles	Mice, rats and voles attack stored fruits and vegetables – in the garden whole rows of larger seeds such as Peas may be removed	Harmless traps are available for mice and voles. Rats *must* be destroyed. If you see one, get in touch with the Council
Moles	An invasion by moles can cause havoc. Severe root damage occurs and the hills thrown up by their tunnelling are unsightly. Small plants may be uprooted. The lawn is most at risk – the surface is disfigured and uneven	Begin with simple remedies. Moles dislike soil disturbance – try a mechanical scarer. If all else fails you may have to call in a professional exterminator
Rabbits	Rabbits are very fond of young greens, but in winter they will gnaw the bark at the base of trees. A serious problem in rural areas – they can easily burrow underneath ordinary fencing	Individual tree guards can be used, but an anti-rabbit fence is the only complete answer. The wire netting should be 90 cm above ground, and 15 cm below
Squirrels	Nice to watch, but they can be a nuisance. Bulbs, soft fruit, nuts etc are removed and bark is stripped in winter	There is little you can do. Fruit netting helps and wire-netting guards will protect individual trees

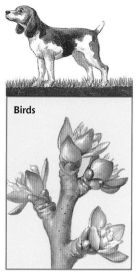

Birds

Cats

Moles

Rabbits

93

DISEASES

Disease	Background	Control
Apple Scab	Appears first as dark green or brown spots on leaves. Fruits are cracked and disfigured with corky patches	Rake up and remove fallen leaves. Prune scabby twigs
Bacterial Canker	A serious disease of Cherries, Plums and other stone fruit. Gum oozes from the bark – affected branches soon die	Cut out diseased branches. Spray with copper in autumn
Black Spot	A major Rose problem – black spots with yellow fringes on the leaves. Premature leaf fall often takes place	Rake and dispose of all fallen leaves in winter – apply a mulch in spring. Choose varieties with good disease resistance – space plants well apart
Brown Rot	Apples are susceptible. Fruit turns brown and concentric rings of yellowish mould appear on the surface	Destroy all affected fruit promptly. Store only sound fruit and inspect at regular intervals
Bulb, Corm & Tuber Rots	Browning and decay of underground storage organs	Dry thoroughly before storing. Discard any soft or rotten bulbs
Canker	A serious disease of Apples and Pears which can be fatal. Bark shrinks and cracks in concentric rings	Cut off damaged twigs. Cut out canker from stems and branches
Club Root	Swollen and distorted roots are the tell-tale sign of this disease of Stocks, Wallflowers and all the Cabbage family. Leaves wilt in sunny weather	Make sure land is adequately limed and well-drained. Destroy diseased plants – do not grow Cabbage family plants for several years
Damping Off	The most serious seedling complaint. The base of an affected plant becomes withered and blackened – the stem topples over	Use sterilised compost, sow thinly and never overwater. Remove affected seedlings
Die-Back	A common problem with woody plants such as Roses, fruit trees, ornamental shrubs etc. Die-back spreads slowly downwards from the tip	Cut out all dead wood. Try to improve drainage
Downy Mildews	Less likely to be troublesome than powdery mildew in the ornamental garden, but it can be serious on the vegetable plot. Upper leaf surface turns yellow – greyish mould occurs below	Make sure the soil is well-drained – practice crop rotation of vegetables. Pick off diseased leaves
Grey Mould (Botrytis)	Grey and fluffy mould appears on stems, leaves, flowers and soft fruit. Worst out-doors in a wet season and in unventilated damp conditions under glass	Avoid the basic causes – poor drainage, overwatering and inadequate ventilation. Remove affected leaves and fruit

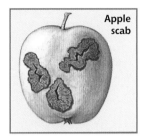

Apple scab

Tuber rot

Club root

Damping off

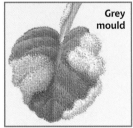

Grey mould

Disease	Background	Control
Leaf Spot	Blotches, spots or rings appear on leaves – especially Celery and Blackcurrant. Leaves may fall early	Feed with a fertilizer containing potash. Pick off diseased leaves and avoid overcrowding
Peach Leaf Curl	Large reddish blisters develop on the foliage of Peaches, Cherries, Apricots etc. Unsightly, and the tree is weakened	There is not much you can do, so expect attacks every year. Pick off and destroy affected leaves promptly
Potato Blight	Spreading brown patches appear on the leaves and infected tubers rot in store. Attacks occur in warm, wet weather	You can spray with Bordeaux mixture but it is not usually worth it. Remove infected stems a fortnight before lifting
Potato Scab	Ragged scurf patches occur on the tuber surface. The disease is only skin-deep – eating quality unaffected. Worst on light land	Use compost but not lime before planting. Grow a resistant variety
Powdery Mildew	A general menace all round the garden. White powdery deposit occurs on the leaves, stems, buds and fruit. Worst in hot, dry weather. Serious on Roses	Mulch in spring and water during dry periods in summer. Sulphur is the standard spray
Root & Foot Rots	Many plants, especially vegetables, can succumb. Leaves wilt and turn yellow – roots and sometimes the stem bases blacken and rot	Avoid cold and overwet conditions. Use a sterile compost. Rotate vegetable crops. Lift and destroy infected plants
Rust	Raised pustules (orange, brown or black) appear on the leaves. Numerous plants may be attacked, but rose rust is the one to fear – attacks may be fatal	Use a fertilizer containing potash. Remove affected leaves. Copper fungicides have some preventative action against rust on soft fruit
Sooty Mould	A black fungus which spots or covers the the upper surface of the foliage. Grows on the honeydew deposited by sap-sucking pests	Wash off if unsightly. Control by spraying or dusting to get rid of greenfly etc
Stem Rot	A brown patch develops at or near the stem base – roots are not affected. This disease can be serious on Tomatoes	Disinfect the greenhouse between Tomato crops. Cut out diseased areas if attack is slight. Remove and destroy plant if badly affected
Storage Rots	Soft grey or brown sunken areas appear on Apples and Pears in store	Discard unsound fruit at storage time. Remove and destroy diseased fruit promptly
Tulip Fire	Scorched areas occur on the leaves – flowers are spotted. Young shoots are covered with a grey mould and the bulbs rot	Diseased shoots should be cut off just below ground level. There is no cure
Virus	All sorts of distortions, discolorations and growth problems are produced, depending on the plant	No cure. Destroy infected plants if you are sure of identification. Keep sap-sucking insects under control
White Rot	The leaves of Onions and Leeks turn yellow and wilt. Fluffy white mould appears on the base of the bulbs. Worst in hot, dry weather	Rotate crops. Destroy diseased plants – do not replant with Onions or Leeks for at least 8 years
Wilt	Leaves wilt even in moist soil and tissue inside stems is often stained brown	No cure – do not grow susceptible plants in the same soil

Peach leaf curl

Powdery mildew

Rust

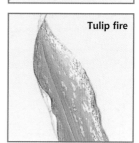

Tulip fire

White rot

Wilt

DISORDERS

Not all troubles are caused by pests and diseases – split Tomatoes and bolted Beetroots do not appear in the pest charts but they are still the effects of important disorders. These disorders are due to faults in cultivation or an adverse environment. It is important to try to find the cause because many can be prevented once you know what went wrong. Important disorders and their causes are listed below, but there are others. Blindness of Tulips and Daffodils is usually due to planting undersized bulbs, and the forking of Carrots is due to poorly prepared ground or the use of fresh manure.

Frost damage

Disorder	Background
Bolting	A number of vegetables have the annoying habit of occasionally bolting or running to seed. The cause is a set-back to steady growth, so try to avoid checks. Prepare the soil properly, plant out firmly and at the right time and make sure the plants are watered in dry weather. Lettuce, Onion, Celery and Beetroot are prone to bolting – grow a bolt-resistant variety if you can
Drought	See pages 75 and 80
Dry Air Damage	In the home or greenhouse the effect is a browning of leaf tips. Both outdoors and indoors the most obvious result is a poor set of those vegetables which form fruit or pods – Tomatoes, Beans etc
Frost Damage	With non-hardy plants frost threatens life itself – transplant or sow when the danger of frost has passed. A hard frost can damage the tender new growth of hardy plants such as Potatoes, Asparagus, Apple etc. Affected leaves may be bleached, blistered, cracked or scorched along the margins. The worst effects of frost are seen in the fruit garden – blossom turns brown and drops off
Incorrect Planting	Incorrect planting can lead to slow development or even death of transplants. Inadequate soil consolidation and loose planting lead to several distinct disorders in the vegetable garden – blown Brussels Sprouts, heartless Cabbages, button-headed Cauliflowers etc
Irregular Watering Damage	The outer skin of many vegetables hardens under drought conditions, and when heavy rain or watering takes place the sudden increase in growth stretches and then splits the skin. This results in the splitting of Tomatoes, Potatoes, Carrots etc. Avoid by watering before the soil dries out. A common disorder due to the irregular watering of growing bags is blossom end rot – a sunken, dark-coloured patch appears at the bottom of Tomatoes
Major Nutrient Shortage	See page 18
Sun & Heat Damage	Bright sunshine can damage plants grown under glass. Leaves and fruit may be scorched – the pale papery patches are referred to as sun scald. The answer is to apply shading material such as Coolglass in summer
Trace Element Shortage	Leaf discoloration is a common symptom. Iron and manganese deficiency lead to yellowing between the veins – the effect is most marked in non-acid soils. See page 18
Waterlogging	The plant is affected in 2 ways. Root development is crippled by the shortage of air in the soil. The root system becomes shallow, and also ineffective as the root hairs die. Leaves turn pale and growth is stunted. The second serious effect is the stimulation of root-rotting diseases
Weedkiller Drift	Traces of hormone lawn weedkiller from a nearby garden can cause severe distortion of Tomatoes and members of the Cabbage family. Tomato leaves become fern-like and twisted. Fruit is plum-shaped and hollow. There is no cure – ask neighbours not to spray on a windy day
Wind Damage	Wind is often ignored as a danger to plant growth, yet a cold east wind in spring can kill in the same way as frost. More frequently the effect is the browning of leaf margins. Another damaging effect is wind rock, which can lead to rotting of the roots

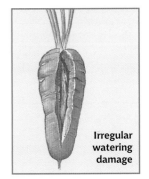

Irregular watering damage

Manganese shortage

Sun & heat damage

WEEDS

Weeds have no place in a well-ordered garden, even if its owner is organically minded. Have a wildflower area and patches of unmown grass by all means, but that is not the same thing as having rampant weeds swamping your garden plants and competing with them for water, nutrients and light. Worst of all, they give the garden a neglected look. So the menace of weeds must be tackled, and tackled quickly before they take hold. Many efficient weedkillers are now on the shelves of the garden centres, but they are modern chemicals which orthodox green gardeners will not use. The basic approach here is to use a combination of some of the non-chemical methods of control described overleaf.

ANNUAL WEEDS

These plants complete at least one life cycle during the season. They spread by seeding, and all fertile soils contain a large reservoir of annual weed seeds. The golden rule is that emerged annuals must be killed by hand pulling or hoeing *before* seeding. Burning off with a contact weedkiller such as diquat is only for not-so-green gardeners.

A

PERENNIAL WEEDS

These plants survive by means of underground stems or roots which act as storage organs over winter. The golden rule is that their leaves must be regularly removed to starve out the underground storage organs. See the next page for control measures – killing the roots with a systemic weedkiller such as glyphosate is only for not-so-green gardeners.

P

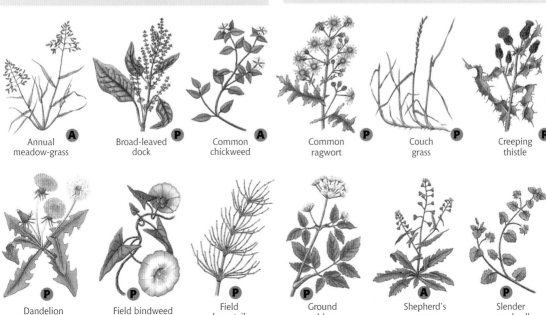

Annual meadow-grass **A**	Broad-leaved dock **P**	Common chickweed **A**	Common ragwort **P**	Couch grass **P**	Creeping thistle **P**
Dandelion **P**	Field bindweed **P**	Field horsetail **P**	Ground elder **P**	Shepherd's purse **A**	Slender speedwell **P**

Weed Control

Herbicides

During the past 30 years many garden weedkillers have appeared, both contact ones which burn off the above-ground parts and translocated ones which get down to the roots. The not-so-green gardener will not use any of these weedkillers around vegetables or fruit, but may turn to glyphosate when preparing land for planting or a long-lasting herbicide for keeping down weeds in paths. None of these chemicals are used by orthodox green gardeners, although some do use simple (but not very efficient) aids such as salt, vinegar and boiling water.

Digging

Weed control on neglected land which is to be brought into cultivation begins at the digging stage. The roots of perennial weeds should be removed and burnt. The surface layer of annual weeds should be buried by inverting the spadeful of soil. This will not end your weed problems – seeds which have been buried for years are brought to the surface by digging.

Ground cover

One way to reduce the invasion of annual weeds is to reduce the area of bare earth around flowers and shrubs by planting living plant material. This can be done by setting bedding plants more closely together and by using the bed method for growing vegetables – see pages 76–77. Ground cover is achieved in the shrub border by planting perennials between the woody specimens – see page 49.

Hoeing

Hoeing is the traditional method of weed control – it will effectively kill annuals when done properly, but it has no long-term effect on perennial ones. Choose a day when the soil is dry – aim to sever the weed stems rather than merely dragging them out. Hoe with care – roots of some plants lie close to the surface and damage can be done by hoeing too deeply. Don't hoe if weeds are absent as disturbing the soil brings up a fresh crop of weed seeds. Keep the blade clean and sharp.

Flame gunning

This technique involves the use of an oversized blow torch for burning off the top growth of weeds and destroying weed seeds on the surface. Flame gunning was once fairly popular but is not often used these days. The organic gardening experts are divided on the wisdom of this technique. Opponents point out the risk in careless hands and the destruction of both insects and organic matter in the soil just below the surface. The experts who recommend the technique feel that the ecological dangers are not serious if the flame gun is used to scorch and not burn away the weed leaves.

Hand pulling and grubbing out

Pulling out weeds by hand is a technique we use all the time – removing well-grown but easily uprooted annual weeds in beds and borders, getting rid of weeds growing among the alpines in the rockery, etc. A few rules – choose a day when the soil is moist, hold the stem as close to soil level as possible and pull upwards slowly and steadily. Grubbing out is a way of removing deeply-rooted perennial weeds – an implement such as a hand fork, trowel, old knife or daisy grubber is used. This is the technique used for removing isolated weeds from lawns and between paving slabs. Loosen soil around the weed before pulling it out firmly but without tugging.

Perennial weeds growing within a flowering plant clump pose a problem. You may be able to gently pull out the weeds but this is often not possible. Lift the clump in autumn and divide it into segments for replanting, removing all the weed roots before you do so.

Mulching

Organic mulches will help to suppress annual weeds – read the mulching section on pages 14–16. There is an introduction to the weed-control mulch on page 16 – a weed-infested patch can be covered with black plastic sheeting and then covered with bark chippings or gravel. The weed-control mulch really comes into its own when creating a new shrub or Rose border – done properly it will mean that weeding becomes a thing of the past. Lay woven polypropylene sheeting over the soil – this material allows water to seep through the myriad holes between the threads. Make cross cuts where the planting holes will be, fold back the flaps and plant in the usual way – after planting replace the flaps, remove any soil on the surface and cover the sheeting with bark chippings or gravel.

Chapter 6

CARING FOR YOU & THE FAMILY

Few pastimes can match the health-giving properties of gardening and the feeling of satisfaction it gives when the day is over. For millions it is a time to escape from mental stress and to indulge in physical exercise which the working day may deny.

Against this background it is hard to talk about the dangers of gardening, but facts must be faced. Each year about 400,000 people have an accident, and of these a large number need hospital treatment. A shocking figure, but the consoling thought is that in nearly every case the cause is either ignorance or carelessness. In about three quarters of the incidents involving adult gardeners the cause is known at once and the patient knows what he or she has done wrong. Unlike flying, driving, playing rugby etc your safety and that of your family is in your own hands, and by following a number of rules you can avoid becoming an accident statistic.

First of all, get rid of hazards. Level uneven paths, fix loose stones, hang up tools, remove dangerous branches etc. Next, wear suitable clothing. Footwear must always be right for the job – gloves and goggles may be required. Then learn how to use equipment before you start – read the instructions carefully. Finally, think what you are doing. The Royal Society for the Prevention of Accidents wrote some years ago 'when attention is concentrated on the job, sensible precautions are often forgotten'.

Accidents cannot be prevented by going green – the table below shows it is not a green v. non-green issue. It all began right at the beginning, when Eve ate a poisonous fruit in the garden and Cain was felled by the improper use of a spade.

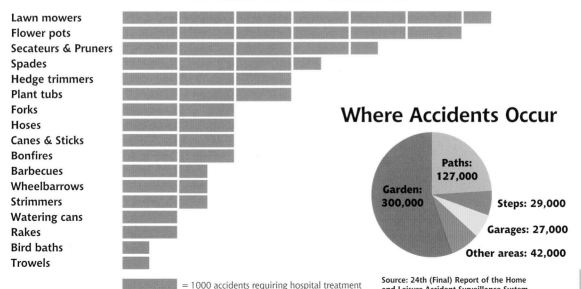

The Causes of Accidents

Lawn mowers
Flower pots
Secateurs & Pruners
Spades
Hedge trimmers
Plant tubs
Forks
Hoses
Canes & Sticks
Bonfires
Barbecues
Wheelbarrows
Strimmers
Watering cans
Rakes
Bird baths
Trowels

Where Accidents Occur

Paths: 127,000

Garden: 300,000

Steps: 29,000

Garages: 27,000

Other areas: 42,000

= 1000 accidents requiring hospital treatment

Source: 24th (Final) Report of the Home and Leisure Accident Surveillance System

Caring for YOU

Falls account for more than one in every three garden accidents requiring hospital treatment. Tripping over equipment and tools, falling off ladders, slipping on slimy or icy paths … you must do everything you can to reduce the risk. Most falls result in a bump or strain which does not require a visit to the hospital, but many are serious and some are fatal. So take care, especially if you are over sixty.

About 90,000 accidents around the garden happen to people who are actively gardening. The biggest threats here are cuts, followed by falls and then being hit by things. Do read these two pages. By wearing the right clothing and working in the right way you can avoid being in next year's casualty list.

CLOTHING

Correct clothing is important. It should keep you warm and protected in winter – cool and protected in summer. The key word is 'protected'. Avoid loose bits like ties and scarves when working with fast-moving machinery.

Head protection is not usually necessary, but you will need an industrial hard hat if you are planning to lop off tree branches which are more than head-high. It is also a good idea to wear a brimmed hat to keep branches off your face when working amongst trees – e.g pruning, spraying and harvesting.

Ear protectors are recommended if you are using a noisy power tool for a prolonged period. Remember the neighbours do not have ear protectors – try to agree with them the best time to do a really noisy job.

Goggles are sometimes necessary – see the Eyes section.

Gloves are necessary to protect your hands when undertaking many garden tasks, and you may need more than one type. Leather gloves protect against prickles, sharp objects and caustic materials such as lime. The problem is that they are heavy, rather inflexible and uncomfortable in hot weather. Cotton gloves are much more comfortable but are no protection against Rose thorns. Most people compromise by using all-purpose gloves – fabric ones with leather palms or fabric gloves impregnated with green plastic. You will need gauntlets if you propose to use a chainsaw, and rubber gloves if you plan to handle corrosive or toxic liquids.

Stout **footwear** is essential when digging, forking, mowing and carrying heavy loads. Wellington boots are a popular choice – choosing ones with reinforced toes and shin guards has prevented many accidents.

EYES

Serious eye injuries are perhaps the most distressing mishaps of all. Do take simple precautions. Place a small cream or yoghurt pot on top of each cane in areas where you will be working amongst the plants – people really do bend down and drive bamboo canes into their eyes. Remove stones from the grass before using a power mower and be careful of twigs and branches when pruning trees.

More than one in 10 people who garden or carry out DIY jobs at home injure their eyes at some time. To avoid problems you should wear goggles when doing any job which has a history of accidents – drilling holes in masonry, cutting tiles or concrete slabs, using an axe, hedge clipping, using a chainsaw, lopping trees etc.

HANDS

Bruises are commonplace and generally look after themselves. Cuts definitely do not – they require immediate attention. The simple drill is to wash out any dirt immediately with soap and warm water after which the wound should be covered with a porous elastic dressing or absorbent gauze and a bandage. Do not use an airtight plaster. Remove splinters or embedded thorns with a needle which has been sterilized by immersion in boiling water.

Prevention, of course, is always better than cure. Wear gloves when handling soil as buried bits of glass or broken pot can result in a nasty gash. Make sure that the branches of thorny bushes do not overhang pathways. Handle glass with great care. If you are a regular gardener and just cannot seem to avoid picking up cuts and scratches, a routine anti-tetanus injection really is a good idea. The bacterium which causes the disease lives in the soil and its effects are serious – several people die each year from tetanus.

Most cuts require neither a doctor nor hospital treatment, but if blood loss is excessive you should seek medical help immediately. This also applies if a home-treated cut starts to hurt after a day or two or the area around becomes swollen or discoloured.

BACK

Falls are the major cause of gardening accidents requiring hospital treatment, but it is back strain which is by far the most common reason for discomfort and days off work. Most gardening problems arise from carelessness, but back strain is different. The problem here has three causes. Lack of knowledge concerning the right way to prepare for bending and lifting, incorrect posture when carrying out the tasks, or doing the wrong thing when the job is over. Do read the instructions on the next page even if you are an experienced gardener – few people know all the rules.

FEET

Pushing a garden fork through one's foot is an all-too-common occurrence – each year 2000 accidents requiring hospital treatment are caused by the improper use of a fork. There are two rules to follow. You must protect your feet properly – sandals, track shoes etc are definitely out when using a digging tool or a lawn mower. Stout boots or shoes are essential – see Clothing section above. You must also keep your mind on what you are doing when digging, forking or cutting the lawn – carelessness is nearly always involved in foot injury.

BEFORE YOU BEGIN

Spring is the worst time, as any physiotherapist will tell you. Muscles which may have been inactive for months are suddenly called into play, and the weather is usually cold. It is therefore a good idea to carry out a simple exercise programme before going out to dig or plant – consider it essential if you are over forty, have a sedentary job and it is early in the year. This calls for bending over and then stretching back several times while standing with your legs apart. Then bend from side to side and tense your buttocks for a few seconds. Repeat several times and you are ready to go.

WHEN WORKING

Make sure your clothing is right. You should be warm and comfortable with no part of your back exposed to cold winds. Try to remain as upright as possible with the back arched. This calls for digging and cultivating tools with handles which are longer than you might be used to, and cutting the grass with the mower handles held close to the body. With a hover mower move the machine backwards and forwards. Kneeling instead of stooping is the golden rule, and never jerk suddenly to pull up a weed or lift up a load. Don't do any strenuous task for more than half an hour at one time.

AFTER FINISHING

Clean the tools, put them away safely and *don't* flop in a chair. Muscles must be stretched after work if backache the next morning is to be avoided. Sit upright in a straight chair for a little while if the jobs have not been particularly strenuous – put a rolled-up towel between the chair and the small of your back. If you've had a physically exhausting day you should do some stretching exercises instead. Lie on your back. Lift your right leg in the air and lower it to the floor on your left-hand side. Put your legs together and now do the exercise with your left leg. Repeat the procedure 10 times.

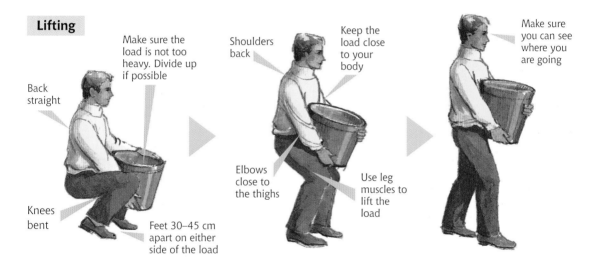

Lifting

Make sure the load is not too heavy. Divide up if possible

Back straight

Knees bent

Feet 30–45 cm apart on either side of the load

Shoulders back

Elbows close to the thighs

Keep the load close to your body

Use leg muscles to lift the load

Make sure you can see where you are going

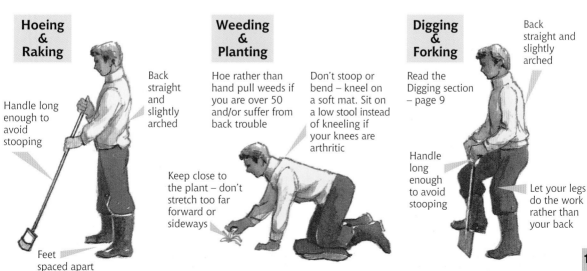

Hoeing & Raking

Handle long enough to avoid stooping

Back straight and slightly arched

Feet spaced apart

Weeding & Planting

Hoe rather than hand pull weeds if you are over 50 and/or suffer from back trouble

Don't stoop or bend – kneel on a soft mat. Sit on a low stool instead of kneeling if your knees are arthritic

Keep close to the plant – don't stretch too far forward or sideways

Digging & Forking

Read the Digging section – page 9

Handle long enough to avoid stooping

Back straight and slightly arched

Let your legs do the work rather than your back

Handling TOOLS & FURNITURE

A wide range of tools and equipment is listed in the accident chart on page 99. Cutting, digging and cultivating tools have always posed a risk to the young and the careless, but the wide scale introduction of power tools during the second half of the 20th century has greatly increased the number of mishaps. Some of the safety rules which appeared on previous pages are worth repeating here. Keep shears, knives and secateurs closed when not in use. Keep children well away when using power tools. Stand hoes and rakes upright – do not leave them laying about. When not in use, store all tools safely in a shed or garage – hanging them on the wall is the best way to avoid problems.

Buy good quality equipment and replace when the useful life of a tool is over. Many accidents occur every year resulting from metal splinters on rusty wheelbarrows, mowers etc.

People Friendly

LAWN MOWER

A lawn mower is absolutely essential if you have an area of grass, but it is also gardener enemy No. 1 in the list of tools and equipment. The 7000 accidents noted on page 99 are nearly all avoidable – just follow the rules below.

Before you begin

Choose a safe model if you are buying a new one. Make sure that it has been approved by an official body such as the British Standards Institute. Make sure that plastic and not metal blades have been fitted if you are buying a hover mower – these blades won't cut through a cable or the toe of your shoe. Read the instructions carefully. If you already have a hover mower, replace metal blades with plastic ones.

Put on the right clothes – wear slacks and boots, Wellingtons or stout flat-heeled shoes. Take care when moving the mower on to the lawn – many sprained backs and slipped discs occur annually due to heavy mowers being lifted up stairs or allowed to topple off paths.

Check the mower. Are the plugs firmly in place and is the cable sound? Are the blades properly set? A circuit breaker should be fitted if the mower is an electric one – see page 104 for details.

Walk over the lawn. Remove stones and other debris. You are now ready to begin … but not if it is raining and you have an electric mower.

Mowing

Drape the cable of an electric mower over your shoulder. Move in a forward direction away from you – never swing from side to side. Cut across slopes – not up and down. Keep children and pets well away. A power mower may suddenly stop, and that spells trouble if you are not careful. The simple drill is to remove the plug of an electric mower or disconnect the sparkplug lead of a petrol one *before* touching the motor or blades. Now you can free clogged grass etc, but do keep your fingers away from the cutting edges. Finally, remember never to leave a power mower unattended when it is on the lawn – a quarter of all lawn mower accidents occur with machines which are not in use.

After you have finished

Clear away all mud, cut grass etc while it is still easy to remove. When putting the mower away in a garage turn the machine away from the line of traffic.

ROTARY CULTIVATORS

Cultivators are not a major source of accidents, but most of them are powerful machines which should be treated with respect. As with all power tools, buy a reputable brand and study the instructions carefully before you start. Put on a stout pair of boots or Wellingtons with reinforced toe-caps and you are ready to start, once you have made sure that no bricks or pieces of rubble are laying on the ground which is to be cultivated.

Don't try to dig too deeply in heavy earth and do let the machine and not your muscle power do the work.

WHEELBARROWS

A surprising inclusion in this section on items of equipment which cause problems, but the humble wheelbarrow is an all-too-frequent cause of back strain. This is nearly always associated with carrying too heavy a load – always consider making two trips instead of one. Unfortunately it is not always possible or practical to divide up the load, and here you have to pay special attention to two points. Firstly you should raise the wheelbarrow legs off the ground as if you were lifting a heavy object – see page 101. Back straight, bend your knees and then straighten your legs. Next, keep the load level and keep away from the edge of the path. Tripping over is a common cause of torn ligaments and strained muscles.

HEDGE TRIMMERS

An electric hedge trimmer is a boon for a person with a large garden – gone are the hours of snipping away with shears. The fast-moving blades make short work of clipping an extensive hedge, but these fast-moving blades can't distinguish between twigs and fingers. The result is that the number of accidents with this tool is frighteningly high.

Before you begin make sure that the plug is in place and that the foliage is not wet – never work in the rain. Put on goggles, gloves and loop the cable over your shoulder. You are now ready to start. The golden rule is that both hands must be firmly on the machine and both feet firmly on a sound base when the hedge trimmer is on. Keep children and pets well away, and stop the machine each time you step forward.

KNIVES & SICKLES

It is a pleasure to watch a skilled gardener using a knife – pruning, grafting, dead-heading and so on. You should not try to copy the technique – in the hands of the inexperienced a knife is a dangerous weapon. Carry a folding pocket knife for cutting twine etc, but use a pair of secateurs for cutting stems. Never leave an open knife laying about – an all-too-common cause of accidents. Scythes, sickles and grass hooks still cause about 1000 mishaps requiring hospital attention every year, even though their use is no longer necessary. An electrically-driven nylon-cord strimmer will trim long grass much more quickly, safely and easily.

CHAINSAWS

The recommendation here is simple – do not use one unless you have been trained. Your local supplier or horticultural college should have details of courses. They will tell you to wear goggles, to hold the saw with both hands at all times, to keep both feet firmly on the ground and so on. But even a properly maintained machine can be unpredictable and dangerous, and many hired machines are not up to standard. Hit a nail or knot with a chainsaw and the blade can hurtle towards you. In untrained hands a chainsaw can be a lethal instrument.

CHAIRS

It is surprising at first glance that furniture should rank so high in the accident list, but then we remember the time we trapped a finger when putting up or closing a deckchair. The old fashioned wooden type has long been something of a menace until the art of opening and folding is mastered. Modern metal chairs, sunbeds, tables etc are usually (but not always) easier to put up, but the same safety rules apply. Keep your fingers well away from the edges and joints when opening or closing. Make sure that both the frame and covering are in sound condition and check that the stays are properly in place before use. Now sit down and relax.

HIRING TOOLS

There are times when we need to use a piece of equipment for a short time but where the high cost rules out purchase. Examples including concrete mixers, hedge trimmers, cultivators and large lawn spreaders. To answer this problem the tool hire industry has grown rapidly in the past few years, and in the main provides a useful service.

Powerful cutting tools are a special case. Unlike a new or carefully maintained machine the hire model will have been used by all sorts of people, and surveys reveal problems. In many instances hire machines such as chainsaws and hedge trimmers have been found to be defective, either electrically or mechanically. When hiring, check the following points. The supplier should be a reputable one and the tool should be clean and sound. Check that the wiring is secure. Try to arrange a demonstration – a complete set of printed instructions is essential. Buy or hire the necessary protective clothing.

Avoiding DANGER SPOTS

ELECTRICITY

Electricity has a vital part to play in the garden these days and you have got to learn to live with it. Outdoor electricity has special rules and you won't learn these from your experience with fitting plugs on table lamps. Do read through the following list – the incidence of fatal electrocutions in the home and garden has increased rapidly in the past few years.

- Look for the BEAB label or BSI kitemark when buying equipment.

- Always check the lead and plug before use. Make sure that there are no loose connections, frayed wires, missing insulation etc. Make sure you know how to wire a three-pin plug correctly – badly-wired plugs cause many accidents every year.

- Leads and connectors should be outdoor quality and not designed solely for indoor use. Take care with extension leads – special weatherproof connectors must be used and these should be joined before plugging into the mains. Never join wires together with insulation tape.

- Wear rubber- or plastic-soled shoes. Do not use an electrical appliance in the rain.

- Make sure the cable is out of the way before you start. With an electric lawn mower, hedge trimmer etc place the cable over your shoulder and work away from it.

- Always switch off and unplug if you have to do any cleaning, adjusting, inspecting or stopping for a tea break. Playing with the switch of a power tool has a fascination (sometimes a fatal fascination) for children.

- Never pick up the wires before unplugging if you are unfortunate enough to cut through the cable. Obvious, of course, but a cause of numerous deaths every year.

- You should always consult an electrician if there is a fault involving the home electrical system or an item of electrical equipment.

- The purpose of a circuit breaker (also called a power breaker) is to cut off the current if the circuit is broken. The type of circuit breaker you want when working with garden electricity is a Residual Current Device (RCD) as this cuts off in three hundredths of a second.

PATHS

The main site of accidents is on paths and driveways – you must therefore pay attention to this area of the garden. Keep all paved areas in good repair – level uneven stones and secure loose slabs. When laying a new path choose a paving material which has a rough surface. Make sure that steps are firm and level.

The next job is to keep the surface clear. Remove toys, boxes etc which can pose a hazard for the elderly visitor, absent-minded adult or running child. Sweep away leaves in autumn and de-ice in winter. A vital job is to remove slippery algae from the surface – use a cleaner recommended for this purpose.

BARBECUES

Start early. Choose a level site well away from overhanging branches, fences and buildings. Use firelighters or charcoal soaked in a recommended barbecue fuel – never use paraffin, petrol, methylated spirits etc. Never pour fuel on the charcoal once it has been lit. Avoid wearing loose clothing (ties, scarves etc) and keep children well away. Finally, use long-handled utensils and remember that sausages and chicken must be cooked all the way through before serving.

CHEMICALS

You are almost certain to have chemicals in your shed or garage. Even if you only use mineral or organic remedies, there are still going to be containers of paints, preservatives, solvents, adhesives etc. Keep them all properly closed. Do not keep packages if the labels are no longer readable and never decant liquid chemicals into unlabelled bottles.

BONFIRES

Standing next to a bonfire on a cold day has long been one of the rituals of autumn. Feeding it with cuttings and prunings, breathing in the smoke and damping it down with leaves and greenstuff all make for a pleasant scene, but bonfires are a waste of valuable recyclable material and a hazard for both you and your neighbours – see page 127.

LADDERS

Using a ladder calls for safety measures – do keep children well away. Place the feet so that the distance from the wall is about a quarter of the height of the top from the ground. Make sure it is firm and straight before you start to climb – place the feet on a large board if the ground is soft. Get someone to hold the sides or place a heavy sack or other large weight against the feet of the ladder. The top must be secure – if in doubt lash it to the tree, window, wall etc. Finally, don't stretch out sideways – move the ladder instead.

PRUNING

Pruning of reasonably-sized trees and shrubs is a straight-forward job for the average gardener, but think carefully before undertaking major tree surgery. Removing large branches which are more than head high is a skilled job – injury to person or property can easily occur.

Harmful Plants

Plants not for eating

Scores of garden plants can cause stomach upsets and other undesirable effects when the berries, seeds or other parts are swallowed. Nearly 2000 children go to hospital each year for observation and occasionally for treatment, and so the danger must be taken seriously. But don't panic – fatalities are very rare. Seek medical advice promptly if any part of a plant listed below has been eaten.

Box (leaves)
Bryony (any part)
Cherry laurel (berries)
Cotoneaster (berries)
Daphne (any part)
Datura (seeds)
Deadly nightshade (any part)

Dieffenbachia (stems)
Foxglove (berries & leaves)
Hellebore (any part)
Holly (berries)
Ivy (berries)
Juniper (berries)
Laburnum (pods)

Lords & ladies (berries)
Mistletoe (berries)
Privet (berries & leaves)
Spindle (berries & leaves)
Sweet pea (berries)
Winter cherry (berries)
Yew (berries)

Taxus baccata
(Yew)

Laburnum anagyroides
(Laburnum)

Daphne mezereum
(Daphne)

Euonymus europaeus
(Spindle)

Ligustrum vulgare
(Privet)

Plants not for touching

Much less has been written about plant allergies than plant poisoning, but they are much more common and are less easy to avoid. About one in every five gardeners is affected at some time. It is wise to wear gloves when handling any of the plants below if you have suffered from a rash, itching or swollen patches on the skin after gardening. Do be careful with the plants which are marked * below – the sap in the leaves can induce sunburn without prolonged exposure to sunlight.

Bamboo (stems & leaves)
Borage (leaves)
Bugloss (leaves)
Bulbs (sap)
*Carrot (leaves)
*Celery (leaves)
Chrysanthemum (stems & leaves)

Cucumber (stems & leaves)
Daphne (leaves)
Geranium (leaves)
Hellebore (sap)
Marrow (stems & leaves)
Nettle (stems & leaves)
*Parsnip (leaves)

Poinsettia (sap)
Primula (leaves)
Radish (leaves)
Rhus (leaves)
*Rue (leaves & sap)
Strawberry (leaves)
Tomato (leaves)

Primula obconica
(Poison Primrose)

Chrysanthemum hybrid
(Chrysanthemum)

Rhus typhina
(Sumach)

Pelargonium hortorum
(Geranium)

Raphanus sativus
(Radish)

Caring for CHILDREN

Getting children out from under your feet and into the garden is often a great relief for you and them. A chance to play in the open air, but sombre accident statistics tell us that about 100,000 children are treated in hospital each year as a result of mishaps in the garden. Some are fatal, yet nearly all are avoidable if you follow a few commonsense rules.

The danger time is the toddler stage. Between the ages of two and five children are active with little sense of danger. It is therefore necessary to keep dangerous objects out of their reach and out of their path. You should supervise them at play if danger areas are present.

PLAY AREA

Play should be a danger-free activity, but 5000 toddlers go to hospital each year as a result of an accident on outdoor play equipment such as a swing or slide.

Siting of a play area is important – place it in sight of the kitchen window if possible. The surface is even more important – use a base of sand, rubber pads, grass or a 10 cm layer of shredded bark. Never put a swing, climbing frame or slide on stone or concrete.

Buy equipment made to a British Standard specification. Secure firmly and maintain regularly. Swings are the major cause of accidents – make sure children don't stand too close when waiting for their turn.

WATER

A toddler can drown in 8 cm of water – never allow a child under three to go near an unguarded pond or into a paddling pool without supervision. This doesn't only apply to your own children – half of the accidents involving water happen to children in other people's gardens.

Some basic rules. Protect a pond with a fence or wire mesh cover if children play nearby. Turn it into a sand pit only as a last resort – garden ponds are now vital for frogs, common toads, etc. Empty paddling pools when not in use and cover water butts.

KEEP OUT OF HARM'S WAY

Tools & machinery should be kept away from children, especially when in use. Mowing, pruning, hedge trimming and spraying are strictly grown-up jobs where little helping hands should be discouraged. Hang up cultivating tools in the garden shed or garage and keep cutting tools out of reach.

Paths are for walking – the lawn is for running. Cycling, roller-skating and skate-boarding are too dangerous in a small garden and should be discouraged. Keep paths free from moss, algae and lichens, and make sure that toys and equipment are moved before someone trips over them.

Seeds & plants may be poisonous. Teach young children not to eat *any* berries, leaves etc – later on you can show them the dangerous ones (see page 105). Remember not to set a bad example by picking and eating fruit and vegetables when in the garden with small children.

Chemicals, DIY products & flammable liquids should be kept well out of the way.

GLASS

Glass and children definitely don't mix – both can harm each other. Balls can break glass – glass can cause horrific injuries to a colliding child. Try to keep the greenhouse and cold frame as far away as possible from the area where children play, and don't leave objects on which children (and you) can trip close to patio windows, greenhouses etc.

Use a shatterproof glass substitute for both greenhouse and cold frame. If this is not feasible you should cover the lower part of a greenhouse with PVC or wood.

CAT & DOG DROPPINGS

Parasites occur in about a quarter of cat and dog droppings. These rarely affect human beings, but if they do the effect can be extremely serious. As a result children are admitted to hospital every year, and you should therefore dispose of droppings promptly without handling them. It is especially important to cover a sand pit when not in use.

GATES & FENCES

You must make sure that small children can't wander into the road. In most gardens this calls for secure fencing and a gate which can be locked beyond the reach or ability of little fingers. Fencing is not possible in an open-plan garden – constant supervision is the only answer here.

Chapter 7

CARING FOR WILDLIFE

No matter how small your garden may be, you will still have to share it with animals. In a tiny urban plot you may be denied the pleasure of watching squirrels scampering over the lawn or hedgehogs ambling along the path, but in summer you will still have birds in the morning and butterflies in the afternoon.

Once gardeners just accepted that the land had to be shared with these 'outsiders'. Some put down scraps for the birds and a saucer of milk for the hedgehogs, but for most householders the wildlife outside the window was to be watched and admired if attractive, or deterred or killed if it attacked the plants. Little was done by the majority of gardeners to attract or care for wildlife.

Things have changed. Nowadays 80 per cent of garden owners are either doing something to encourage wildlife or would do so if they knew how to go about it. Six in every ten adults feed garden birds, and the bird care market has seen a six-fold increase in 5 years.

There are three reasons for this surge in interest. First of all, we have become much more interested in the wildlife around us – about three-quarters of all gardeners claim to be interested in the butterflies, birds etc around their home. Secondly, there is a growing realisation that we should do something to stop the decline of many of our birds, insects, pond animals etc – practical measures are outlined in this chapter.

There is one more reason for encouraging garden-friendly creatures. Much has been written about the way wildlife in the green garden can earn its keep by keeping plant-attacking insects at bay. A hedgehog can consume 500 slugs in a single night and a family of young tits devours 500 caterpillars in a day. A ladybird may have a daily diet of 500 aphids.

However, do not expect too much. You cannot expect the garden-friendly creatures to keep your plants totally free from pests. Just sit back and enjoy the sight of the frogs and the song of the birds for their own sake.

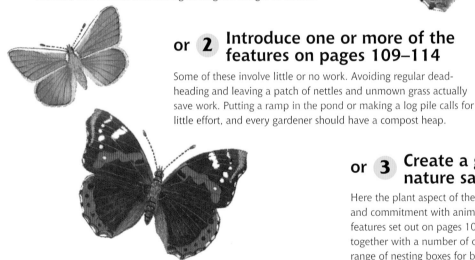

ATTRACTING WILDLIFE TO YOUR GARDEN

Animal Friendly

Thousands of different wildlife species live in or visit your garden – nearly all are lowly creatures such as insects but there will also be a number of larger animals. Deer are the largest. Birds, butterflies, hedgehogs and squirrels are the ones considered most appealing – moles and rats share the doubtful honour of being the least desirable. Some, but not all, of the friendly creatures can be encouraged to visit your plot and a relatively small number can be induced to breed there. This latter group includes tits, nuthatches, house martins, frogs, toads, newts, hedgehogs and bats. With regard to the wildlife in your garden you have three options:

1 Do nothing

You may be totally committed to the idea that your garden is a place for plants – friendly wildlife is welcome but should be left to its own devices. This is regrettable, but it is your garden and you are free to choose the way to look after it. Despite this you should not do anything to harm your friendly visitors. Do not fill in a pond. Do not use any pesticide in a way which could be lethal to birds or animals, and think twice before grubbing out hedges or shrubs.

or 2 Introduce one or more of the features on pages 109–114

Some of these involve little or no work. Avoiding regular dead-heading and leaving a patch of nettles and unmown grass actually save work. Putting a ramp in the pond or making a log pile calls for little effort, and every gardener should have a compost heap.

or 3 Create a garden/ nature sanctuary

Here the plant aspect of the garden must share space and commitment with animal welfare. All of the features set out on pages 109–114 will be introduced, together with a number of others. There may be a range of nesting boxes for birds, boxes for bats, etc.

PETS

There are pets as well as wildlife to consider and here the position is rather different. Virtually nobody wants to attract pets from outside on to the lawn or the flower beds, but we must ensure that the garden is safe both for our own pets and those which unfortunately stray in from outside.

- Keep the garden free from litter which can be dangerous. Included here are open tin cans, broken glass and patches of spilt oil.

- Ponds are not usually a problem, but kittens and even adult cats sometimes drown. Make a gentle sloping area so that an escape route is provided.

- Glass can be a problem. Put some form of marking on the lower panes of a newly-erected greenhouse.

- Tethering a puppy to prevent it from straying or causing damage is certainly not a good idea. Frustration is certain – strangulation is a possibility.

- The danger to cats and dogs from eating sprayed plants is minimal, but you must always follow pesticide instructions and you must never use a professional product which has no garden recommendations. A general rule is to keep pets off the lawn or paths which have been sprayed until the area is dry.

Install a BIRD TABLE

These days the advice is to feed all year round, not just in winter. Continue when you start – the birds will come to rely on you. Many food types are available – obtain a copy of a bird care catalogue from your garden centre. A mixed diet is best – each bird type has its own preferences.

NEST BOX

Nest boxes come in all sorts of shapes and sizes, so think before you buy. Choose wood rather than plastic and buy ones suited to the bird variety. There are two basic types of box. The small hole box is the usual type – with a 25 mm hole for tits and a 28–32 mm hole for sparrows and nuthatches. Starlings and the great spotted woodpecker need a larger hole. Other birds prefer the open-fronted nest box with only half of the front of the box enclosed. Residents include wrens, robins, blackbirds and song thrushes.

A few general rules. The top should be protected from direct sunlight and the hole should be pointed away from the prevailing wind. Clean out the box in winter for the spring nesting season.

Roof to keep out rain and fallen leaves

Table should be about 1.5 m high and at least 2 m from the nearest branch or wall

Spread out food so that a number of birds can feed at the same time

Provide bacon, fat, suet, proprietary wild bird food, cereals, nuts, bird cake, live or dried worms, dried fruit, cheese and wholemeal bread crumbs

Avoid salted peanuts, desiccated coconut, pieces of white bread, uncooked meat and spicy food

Low wall to prevent spillage

Gap for drainage

Plastic mesh bag or wire tube filled with peanuts, cheese, fat etc

Upturned biscuit tin to deter mice

BIRD BATH

Birds require water for drinking and bathing, especially in a dry summer and a cold winter. Do not fill too deeply – change frequently.

COMMON BIRD TABLE VISITORS

Blackbird	Finches	Sparrow
Collared Dove	Nuthatch	Starling
Dunnock	Robin	Tits

Thrushes, robins and dunnocks prefer to feed at ground level. Spread out food on the lawn so that many birds can feed at the same time. Always remove food before nightfall

Plastic drainpipe to deter cats and squirrels

Create a WILD AREA

Having a wildflower meadow (pages 84–85) in your garden may sound a good idea if you have the space. A sprinkling of native flowers growing among fine grasses – a natural look maybe, but not a wild area. The wildflower meadow cannot be left to look after itself – it usually requires quite careful management.

A wild area is a patch of the garden which is left undisturbed – no dead-heading, no cultivation, no routine pruning. You can have a green garden without a wild area, especially if your plot is small and you like things to be neat and tidy. There is indeed a vast acreage of neglected grassland and woodland outside the garden fence, but this acreage is shrinking. New houses, roads etc continue to appear and old hedges continue to be removed. This means that the garden wild area has an important part to play in wildlife conservation by providing small mammals, insects etc with a place to hide, feed and nest.

Rough Grassland

A patch of unmown grass and the weeds which accompany it will provide a place where a wide range of small creatures can live as permanent residents, and not just visit for food. Nettles may not be as attractive to egg-laying butterflies as once we thought, but the grassy/weedy wild area is regarded by environmentalists as an important site for wildlife conservation.

The usual place for the rough grassland area is out of sight at the bottom of the garden. If your lawn area contains attractive wildflowers you could consider a meadow strip, as illustrated below.

A strip is left in the mown lawn to provide a decorative meadow feature. Leave it undisturbed, although any tall weeds can be trimmed back in early spring.

Wildlife Thicket

A wildlife thicket is a woody area which is planted primarily with native species and is arranged in several layers. First of all there are the trees if you have room, below which are the shrubs and then the wildflowers. At the base is the litter – a layer of dead leaves, twigs etc. Most gardeners do not have room for full grown trees and shrubs, so it is quite usual to trim the larger specimens. In this way a mixed hedge is produced.

The wildlife thicket is a haven for animals. Hedgehogs, shrews, voles and mice nest in the surface litter. Birds, bees and butterflies gather around the flowers, seeds and berries. Blackbirds, dunnocks and greenfinches make their nests in the woody branches. Leaves serve as food and nesting material for animal types which shun the 'foreign' foliage offered by garden plants.

Try not to disturb the wildlife thicket – cleaning it up will frighten away some of the animals. However, some work is necessary for the first couple of years. Water in dry weather during the first year after planting and prune back the shoots during the first winter so that bushy growth will be encouraged. Mulch with bark and old leaves for 2 or 3 years.

Trees & Shrubs	Climbers & Wildflowers
Alder	Bluebell
Aldex Buckthorn	Crane's-bill
Birch	Foxglove
Blackthorn	Hart's-tongue Fern
Buckthorn	Honeysuckle
Dog Rose	Ivy
Dogwood	Lily of the Valley
Elder	Old Man's Beard
Field Maple	Primrose
Guelder Rose	Snowdrop
Hawthorn	Solomon's Seal
Hazel	Violet
Holly	White Campion
Rowan	

Make a POND

The purpose of an ornamental pond is to delight the eye with its blend of clear water, attractive fish and range of aquatic plants. The wildlife which arrive (frogs, dragonflies etc) are a bonus. The purpose of a wildlife pond is quite different.

The Wildlife Pond

A wildlife pond provides a haven and in some cases a breeding ground for insects, amphibians, birds and small mammals – to do this it should be as natural as possible. Fish should be omitted or must be chosen with care – the native stickleback is acceptable but goldfish and other exotics are not. The aquatic plants should be native species. For the deep water part of the pond you can choose the Wild Water Lily if the area is large or Nymphoides and Aponogeton if the pond is small. For planting close to the margin there are Menyanthes, Typha, Eriophorum, Scirpus and Iris.

The plants mentioned so far are grown in baskets rather than in the soil layer so as to limit their spread, but Oxygenators such as Myriophyllum or Ceratophyllum are usually planted in the mud. Finally there are the native Bog plants – Lychnis, Cardamine and Geum are examples.

Make an informal pond with a flexible liner – incorporate the special needs shown below. The benefits to be derived from a wildlife pond are the knowledge that you are providing a small habitat for our native fauna and flora, and the enjoyment of watching the pond's population in a 'natural' home. It will not be as visually attractive as an ornamental pond – exotic Water Lilies are not grown and there is a semi-wild look. Some algal growth is inevitable, but do scoop away excess blanketweed and duckweed to stop the pond from becoming choked.

Paved area for birds and people

Shallow pebble beach to allow small animals access to the water without drowning

Add a bucketful of water from an established pond to introduce aquatic life

Deep-water aquatics grown in baskets

Deepest part of the pond should be at least 60 cm to protect pond life in winter

Bog plants – choose native species

Butyl liner

5 cm layer of sand above and below the liner

5–8 cm layer of heavy soil on top of the sand layer

Oxygenators planted into the soil layer

Marginal plants grown in baskets and placed on a shelf

Bog garden – see *The Rock & Water Garden Expert*

Old logs and tall grass to encourage insects and animals

Grow Wildlife–Attracting Plants

For nearly everyone the primary role of the garden is to give pleasure from the plants we grow, rather than to serve as a sanctuary for wildlife. So we choose garden varieties of vegetables, flowers, shrubs and trees from the garden centre, seed catalogue etc rather than growing wildflowers and native woodland plants.

A growing number of gardeners do find a place for some native species, and there is some satisfaction in bringing a little of the countryside to the garden. But do not be too worried if you don't grow wildflowers for the birds and butterflies – recent research has shown that the long-held view that our native flowers are generally more attractive to these visitors than garden plants is not correct. By choosing carefully from the plants at the garden centre and by following the Golden Rules, your garden can act as a magnet for birds and butterflies. Plants in your garden play a role in some or every stage of the life cycle of the wildlife species which are temporary or permanent residents.

● Trees and shrubs provide both nesting sites and insects for birds. Native species are important here – look for Hawthorn, Rowan, Spindle, Guelder Rose, Ivy, Bird Cherry, Buckthorn and Birch. Important garden varieties include Honeysuckle, Virginia Creeper, Climbing Rose.

● Nectar plants are vital for bees and butterflies. Buddleia is the favourite butterfly flower and Foxglove is sought after by bees, but there are many others in the list on the next page. Wherever practical it is a good idea to grow nectar plants in clumps rather than as isolated individuals.

● Unfortunately these flowering plants do not provide food for butterfly caterpillars – eggs are laid on weeds and other countryside plants and not in the garden. Stinging nettles are chosen by several butterflies, including red admiral, but small patches of the weed are generally avoided by the egg-laying insects.

● Remember to grow seed-bearers (e.g Alder, Cornflower, Sunflower, Teasel) and fruiting plants (e.g Hawthorn, Holly, Cotoneaster, Elder) for the birds.

THE GOLDEN RULES

Aim for a wide range of shrubs and some trees, plus flowers to provide blooms from early spring to late autumn. Choose from the list on page 113, making sure that you have seed-bearing and fruiting types as well as ornamental floral ones. Avoid dead-heading some or all of the spent blooms

Alder 🐦

Alyssum 🦋

Aubretia 🦋

Aucuba 🐦

Berberis 🐝 🐦

Bluebell 🐝

Bramble 🦋

Broom 🐝

Buddleia 🐦 🦋

Bugle 🦋

Callicarpa 🐦

Candytuft 🦋

Carnation 🦋

Ceanothus 🐝

Cherry Laurel 🐦

Chrysanthemum 🦋

Cistus 🐝

Clematis 🐦

Cornflower 🐝 🐦 🦋

Cotinus 🦋 🐦

Cotoneaster 🐦

Dahlia 🦋

Daisy Bush 🐝

Daphne 🦋 🐦

Elder 🐝 🐦

Escallonia 🐝

Firethorn 🐝 🐦

Flowering Currant 🦋 🐦

Foxglove 🐝

Fuchsia 🦋

Geranium 🐝

Globe Thistle 🐝 🐦 🦋

Gorse 🐝

Grape Hyacinth 🐝 🐦 🦋

Hawthorn 🐦

Hebe 🦋

Helichrysum 🐝 🦋

Heliotrope 🦋

Holly 🐦

Honesty 🐦 🦋

Honeysuckle 🐝 🐦

Ice Plant 🦋

Ivy 🐦

Japonica 🐝 🐦

Jasmine 🐝

Lavender 🦋

Lilac 🐝 🐦 🦋

Mahonia 🐝 🐦

Marjoram 🐝 🦋

Michaelmas Daisy 🐦 🦋

Monkshood 🐝

Pernettya 🐦

Phlox 🦋

Polyanthus 🦋

Poppy 🦋 🐦

Pot Marigold 🐦

Potentilla 🦋

Privet 🦋

Rhododendron 🐝

Rose 🐦

Rowan 🐦

St. John's Wort 🐦

Scabious 🐝 🦋

Sea Buckthorn 🐦

Skimmia 🐝 🐦

Snapdragon 🦋

Snowberry 🐝 🐦

Spindle 🐦

Spiraea 🦋

Sunflower 🐦

Sweet William 🦋

Teasel 🐝 🐦

Viburnum 🐝 🐦

Virginia Creeper 🐦

Weigela 🦋

Yarrow 🐦

Yew 🐦

🐝 Bees   🐦 Birds   🦋 Butterflies

Build a LOG PILE

You cannot create an area of woodland in the average-sized garden, but by making a log pile you can attract and care for numerous small and not-so-small creatures which inhabit such areas. Though not particularly unsightly it is best constructed in an out-of-sight spot in semi-shade. Pick a spot away from trees as the pile may become a home for honey fungus.

Experts agree on the best material to use – logs from native deciduous trees such as Ash, Oak or Sycamore. There is no agreement, however, on the best method of construction. Some green gardeners choose the pyramid – a square base of logs with a decreasing number of them placed in layers above this base. Others choose a random pile of logs – at the other end of the scale there is the log garden, as illustrated.

This is a raised bed with logs used to make the retaining walls – at one or more sides place a pile of logs of various sizes and ages. The bed and some (not all) of the log crevices should be filled with humus-rich soil – plant woodland types such as Ferns, Primroses, Bluebells, Violets etc.

A few rules. Partly bury the bottom layer of logs and try to have one or more standing upright. Water during periods of dry weather.

Log Pile Inhabitants

Beetles are the usual pioneers. Numerous types will appear – the fearsome-looking stag beetles appear once the logs have started to rot. All sorts of insects will make the pile their home – solitary bees, wasps, spiders, woodlice, centipedes, millipedes etc. Higher up the animal chain you can expect mice, voles, shrews, frogs, toads, newts, slow-worms, hedgehogs and so on. Wrens, thrushes and blackbirds will use it as an insect larder. Lichens, mosses and toadstools soon remove the newly-made look of your log pile.

Make a COMPOST HEAP

There are two basic reasons for creating a compost heap. It provides a method of disposing of waste plant material such as grass clippings, fallen leaves and prunings without having to resort to burning or filling plastic bags. Secondly, it provides valuable humus-making material which is the cornerstone of green gardening.

To ensure that the resulting compost is friable, pleasant smelling and full of goodness you should follow the technique on page 13. This calls for a container with thick walls to stop the heat vital for good compost making from escaping.

Good compost, but not so good for wildlife. Grass snakes need a place to escape from the summer sun – amphibians and small mammals require a warm site where they can hibernate. Birds need a pile of decomposing vegetable matter where they can search for insects. A wildlife compost heap is the answer – no sides and no cover. Leaves and grass clippings will be the main ingredients – include soft cuttings and discarded plants. Include some twigs in the lower layers.

Pick the right time when you eventually plan to use the compost in the garden. Early summer is best, when all the hibernating animals will have left.

Looking at BIRDS

There is no need to consult surveys to discover that birds are our favourite form of garden wildlife – just ask the neighbours. The birds most likely to visit the bird table are the robin, blackbird, blue tit, great tit, dunnock, chaffinch, greenfinch and collared dove – the best-loved ones are the robin and blue tit.

Nearly 150 species have been seen feeding in gardens, but some of these are infrequent visitors which are rarely seen. Only about a fifth of these species can be properly classed as 'garden' birds which may visit the bird table, and 21 have been chosen for this book. You may see or hear some other birds such as the cuckoo, bullfinch, nuthatch, rook, serin, suskin, swallow, spotted flycatcher, blackcap and mistle thrush. On a rural estate you may see non-garden types such as pheasant, moorhen, barn owl and sparrowhawk.

As you will see on the following pages some are permanent residents which may build their nest in a tree or shrub in your garden. Some like the house martin are summer visitors, and these too may nest in your garden. Less common are the winter visitors such as the redwing, fieldfare and brambling. They are becoming increasingly reliant on being fed by gardeners as their countryside feeding sites continue to decline.

BIRD HEAVEN

The features below will ensure that your garden will become a magnet for a varied collection of birds:

A wide range of flowers, shrubs and trees from the list on page 113 to provide insects, seeds, fruits and nesting sites ● Bird table, nest boxes and bird bath ● Log pile and compost heap to provide insects ● Regular supply of peanuts, mixed seeds and source of fat such as bird cake ● Wild area of unmown grass

Blue tit   Great tit   Coal tit

WHICH TIT? The two commonest garden tits have yellow breasts and blue/grey wings – the *blue tit* has a bright blue crown and a black eye-stripe, the *great tit* has a black and white head and a black stripe down its chest. The *coal tit* is quite different – the body is grey and buff.

Goldfinch   Greenfinch   Chaffinch   Bullfinch

WHICH FINCH? The *goldfinch* has a black, white and red head plus black and yellow wings. The *greenfinch* is olive green with yellow wing-bars and the *chaffinch* has a slate-blue head with a pinkish-brown chest. The *bullfinch* is easy to recognise – powerful beak, black head, red breast and a back of grey, black and white.

Garden Birds A–Z

BLACKBIRD

Description 25 cm. Male all-black with orange beak and yellow eye ring. Female brown with brown bill and spotted/streaked breast.
Habit Present all year. Hops over ground – cocks head. Unfussy diet – insects, worms, fruit, berries.
Breeding Grass/mud nests in shrubs/climbers. Eggs blue with red spots.

BLUE TIT

Description 12 cm. The back is blue/grey or blue green – the breast is all-yellow. Both sexes are alike – young have yellow (not white) faces.
Habit Present all year. Acrobatic antics on the bird table. Unfussy diet – insects, fruit, seeds.
Breeding Nests in tree holes and nest boxes. Eggs white with red spots.

CHAFFINCH

Description 15 cm. The head and breast of the male are described above – the brown wings have white bars. Female has duller colours.
Habit Present all year. One of the friendliest wild birds. Eats seeds, berries, insects.
Breeding Mossy nests in trees and shrubs. Eggs blue with red streaks.

COAL TIT

Description 12 cm. A small tit with a wide white patch on its black head. Wings have white bars. Both sexes are alike.
Habit Present all year. Much more shy than the blue and great tits. Eats insects, seeds.
Breeding Nests in tree holes and nest boxes. Eggs white with brown spots.

COLLARED DOVE

Description 30 cm. The back is greyish-brown, the head and breast are pinkish-grey. Look for the black collar. Both sexes are alike.
Habit Present all year. A post-War immigrant – now seen on bird tables everywhere. Eats seeds, grain.
Breeding Flat nests of twigs high up in trees. Eggs white.

DUNNOCK

Description 15 cm. Brown with dark streaks. Sparrow-like (other name – hedge sparrow) but beak is narrow and pointed. Both sexes are alike.
Habit Present all year. Hops and feeds on the ground. Eats insects, seeds.
Breeding Moss-lined grass nests in hedges and shrubs. Eggs pale blue.

FIELDFARE

Description 25 cm. Grey cap and brown wings above the speckled breast – member of the thrush family. Both sexes are alike.
Habit Winter visitor. Found in parks and large gardens. Eats berries, fruit, insects.
Breeding Raises young in Scandinavia.

GOLDFINCH

Description 12 cm. One of the beauties of the garden bird world – red, white, black, gold, brown and yellow. Both sexes are alike.
Habit Present all year. Now a common sight in gardens. Attractive call. Eats seeds, insects, berries.
Breeding Grass/moss nests in trees. Eggs blue with brown spots.

GREAT TIT

Description 15 cm. Look for its black head and prominent chest stripe. Has a very wide range of calls. Both sexes are alike.
Habit Present all year. A bird table favourite – acrobatic and aggressive. Eats seeds, insects, berries.
Breeding Nests in tree holes and nest boxes. Eggs white with brown spots.

GREEN WOODPECKER

Description 35 cm. Distinctive red cap and green wings. Male 'moustache' red – female black. Rarely drums on trees.
Habit Present all year. Usually seen hopping on lawns looking for insects. Eats ants, grubs.
Breeding Nests in holes made in trees. Eggs white.

GREENFINCH

Description 15 cm. The yellow wings and tail patches are recognition features when in flight. Female is dull brown rather than olive green.
Habit Present all year. Feeds on the ground and bird table. Eats seeds, nuts, berries, insects.
Breeding Nests in hedges and shrubs. Eggs blue with brown spots.

HOUSE SPARROW

Description 15 cm. Known to everyone, but numbers have declined in gardens. Male has a black bib – missing on the duller female.
Habit Present all year. Very friendly – rare in unpopulated areas. Eats seeds, berries, scraps.
Breeding Nests in trees and walls. Eggs grey with brown blotches.

JACKDAW

Description 30 cm. One of the crow family – look for grey area at the back of the neck. Both sexes are alike.
Habit Present all year. Sociable. Unfussy diet – insects, grain, worms, chicks etc.
Breeding Nests in tree holes and chimneys. Eggs blue with dark spots.

MAGPIE

Description 45 cm. Large, black and white, and with a tail held aloft. Both sexes are alike.
Habit Present all year. Becoming more common on garden lawns. Eats carrion, seeds, insects.
Breeding Domed twiggy nests in shrubs and trees. Eggs pale green with brown spots.

PIED WAGTAIL

Description 18 cm. Male has black back, head and chin – female has a dark grey back. Long tail wags up and down when in motion.
Habit Present all year. Moves rapidly over lawns, paths etc. Eats insects.
Breeding Twiggy nests in walls, thatch, Ivy etc. Eggs greyish-white with brown spots.

Animal Friendly

ROBIN

Description 13 cm. Britain's national bird – brown above, red and white below. Both sexes are alike.
Habit Present all year. Not shy, but extremely territorial. Eats insects, seeds, berries.
Breeding Grass/moss nests in tree holes, Ivy and nest boxes. Eggs white with red spots.

SONG THRUSH

Description 22 cm. Brown above, breast streaked with brown. Attractive song – each part repeated several times. Both sexes are alike.
Habit Present all year. Hops over lawn with head on one side. Eats snails, worms, seeds.
Breeding Grass/twig nests in trees and hedges. Eggs pale blue.

SPOTTED WOODPECKER

Description Great spotted woodpecker (25 cm) is the common garden one. Black, white and red – female neck all-black.
Habit Present all year. Drums on trees in spring. Eats seeds, nuts, insects.
Breeding Nests in holes made in trees. Eggs white.

STARLING

Description 22 cm. Blackbird-like, but feathers are metallic greenish-black. Common, but numbers are declining. Both sexes are alike.
Habit Present all year. Not popular – noisy, aggressive and fouls buildings. Eats insects, seeds, berries.
Breeding Grass/straw nests in holes in trees and buildings. Eggs pale blue.

WOOD PIGEON

Description 40 cm. The pigeon with a grey back, green and white neck patch, pink breast, and a 'coo-coo' call. Both sexes are similar.
Habit Present all year. Continues to spread from rural gardens to town plots. Eats seeds and berries.
Breeding Twiggy flat nests in trees and large shrubs. Eggs white.

WREN

Description 10 cm. Small brown bird with a short upturned tail. Wings and tail are barred. Male builds several nests. Both sexes are alike.
Habit Present all year. Hunts for food at or near ground level. Eats insects, seeds.
Breeding Nests in hedges and sheds. Eggs white with brown spots.

Looking at BUTTERFLIES

There are about 70 species of butterflies classed as British, although some travel here for their summer vacation. Some once-common types have become rarities and nobody really knows why. The environment has of course changed, and hedge removal, pesticides and modern farming have all been blamed. One fact is certain – butterflies are sun-lovers and Britain is close to the northern edge of their ability to survive. This means that the major controlling factor is summer weather – cold and damp conditions will mean that few will visit your garden.

The fact that butterflies can be elusive adds to their charm. They are second only to birds as our most-loved types of wildlife, and seeing an unusual butterfly flitting among the flowers is always exciting. The coiled proboscis under the butterfly's head is unwound at feeding time – drinking in nectar from flowers between late winter and late autumn, depending on the species. Flowers are not the only source of nourishment – some types drink the juice from rotting Apples and Pears.

The 'one day of life' legend is untrue – butterflies can be remarkably long-lived. If not killed by birds, mice, wasps, spiders or human collectors they survive for between ten days and ten months, depending on the species. The long-living ones hibernate in sheds and in the garden.

MOTHS

The number of moths which visit your garden greatly exceeds the butterfly population. You can expect to find hundreds of different species, which may come as a surprise. The reason for their low profile is their drab appearance which blends in with the background, and their night-flying habit. Some, however, are brightly coloured – the cinnabar moth, magpie moth and tiger moth are examples.

BUTTERFLY HEAVEN

The features below will ensure that your garden will become a magnet for a varied collection of butterflies:

A wide range of plants bearing nectar-rich flowers from the list on page 113 to feed the adult butterflies – aim to have some blooms from February to November. Butterfly favourites include Buddleia, Lavender, Privet, Michaelmas Daisy, Hebe and Alyssum – with bedding plants choose single rather than double varieties ● Plant in groups – choose sunny protected sites wherever possible ● Provide water in a bird bath, water-filled bowls, pond etc ● Have an area of long grasses and nettles to provide food for the caterpillars of painted lady, red admiral, peacock etc

CATERPILLARS

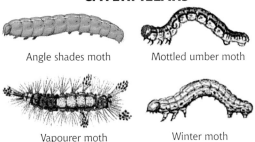

Angle shades moth   Mottled umber moth

Vapourer moth   Winter moth

The green caterpillars on Cabbages turn into cabbage whites, but practically all of the rest of the caterpillars in the garden turn into moths. Butterflies and moths don't just lay their eggs anywhere – they pick specific plants which provide acceptable food for the caterpillars. A wide variety of garden plants are chosen by moths, and the caterpillars can be really destructive. Butterflies, however, pick native plants. Leaving a patch of nettles and unmown grass in the garden can provide a lure as noted above. However, the wild plants growing in the open countryside are the usual choice. The eggs hatch to produce caterpillars, which after eating their fill pupate to produce a chrysalis or pupa. This case is usually hung from the plant or other support by silken threads, and from it the butterfly emerges.

BUTTERFLY or MOTH?

BUTTERFLY

Butterflies and moths are separated from all other insects by having scales on their wings. They have many similarities, especially in their life cycle, but there are enough points of difference to enable you to tell them apart.

MOTH

- Each antenna ends in a small knob
- All fly in the daytime
- Wings are usually brightly coloured
- Wings are nearly always held vertically when at rest

- Each antenna ends in a sharp point or fine 'feathers'
- Nearly all fly at night
- Wings are usually dull
- Wings are nearly always held horizontally when at rest

Garden Butterflies A–Z

Brimstone

Cabbage
White

Comma

Common
Blue

Holly
Blue

Orange Tip

Painted
Lady

Peacock

Red
Admiral

Small Copper

Small
Tortoiseshell

Wall Brown

About a dozen species are commonly seen in gardens, although a much larger number may drift in occasionally from surrounding fields or woodland. The male butterfly is generally the one illustrated for identification purposes, as he usually has the bolder colours and is sometimes the one which gave rise to the common name. For instance, the female of the common blue is brown – it is the male which is shining blue.

The adults of the **brimstone** hibernate in the leaves of evergreens over winter, emerging in the early spring. Eggs are laid on Buckthorn. **Cabbage whites** are the only butterflies which are not welcome in the garden. There are three species, fluttering in the garden in May and August and laying their eggs on members of the Cabbage family in the vegetable patch and Nasturtiums in the flower bed. The **comma** hibernates over winter and appears in the spring. Later broods are seen in June and August, the caterpillars eating Nettles, Elms and Hops.

The **common blue** is a small butterfly which you may see in early or late summer. The **holly blue** is a more frequent visitor to the garden, but you probably won't be able to tell the difference. It lays its eggs on Holly and Ivy. The **orange tip** is a familiar visitor in May, flitting amongst the spring blossoms. The caterpillars feed on weeds belonging to the Cabbage family. The **painted lady** is one of our larger bright butterflies. It arrives from N. Africa in May and lays its eggs on Nettles or Thistles. They are most numerous in August and a Buddleia is the place to see them. The **peacock** is equally showy with its large eye-markings on each wing. It hibernates over winter and emerges in March. Eggs are laid on Nettles.

The **red admiral** is another garden favourite, arriving from S. Europe in May but not becoming abundant until August or September. The **small copper** may not be as big or pretty as some other garden butterflies but it is certainly faster as it races from flower to flower. The **small tortoiseshell** wins the 'early bird' prize – it wakes from hibernation in January if the weather is mild. The **wall brown** is recognised by its eye-markings on each wing. The caterpillars feed on grasses.

Looking at INSECTS

The word 'insect' is used here in its popular sense and not with its scientific meaning. Included is a rag-bag of small animals without backbones, and their number and variety far exceed the sum of all the other groups described in this chapter.

There are the true insects – creatures with six legs, and bodies made up of three parts. Bees, dragonflies, weevils, ladybirds and many more belong here, but the butterflies have been given a section of their own (pages 118–119). In addition there are the creepy-crawlies which are not really insects – the spiders, centipedes, worms, slugs etc. Some 'insects' are the gardeners' friends – for example the ladybirds, worms and flies. Others are enemies – carrot fly, lily beetle, keeled slug and the rest. Most of them, however, are neutral ... but all are a part of the complex ecology of the garden. Birds may gratefully come to your bird table to add to their natural diet, but they rely on the grubs, ants, small beetles etc in your garden to feed their young.

LARGE RED DAMSELFLY

Dragonflies come in a variety of colours and sizes. At the top of the range are the hawker dragonflies with bodies up to 75 mm. The darter and chaser types are smaller – the four-spotted chaser is a frequent visitor to garden ponds. Dragonflies rest with their wings spread out – the smallest varieties are the damselflies which hold their wings vertically when resting. The large red damselfly illustrated above is the commonest species.

Eggs are laid in ponds, streams etc and the carnivorous nymphs hunt for tadpoles, midges etc. After several years they change into adults.

HONEY BEE

The familiar bee, seen flitting from flower to flower gathering nectar and pollen between spring and late autumn. These are the workers which are 12–14 mm long – the drones are less frequently seen and the large queen remains in the nest. Nests are usually located in hollows in trees and may contain many thousands of bees. There are also solitary bees which do not live in colonies – examples are the mining bee and the leaf-cutter bee.

BUMBLE BEE

Bigger and much hairier than honey bees – bumble bees are 16–24 mm long, depending on the species. Only the queens survive the winter, leaving the old nests in spring and founding new ones in underground holes, abandoned bird nests, bird boxes, sheds, long grass etc. 'Bee hotels' provided by gardeners are rarely used. Favourite bee flowers include Bluebell, Rhododendron, Geranium, Foxglove, Honeysuckle, Lavender, Fuchsia and Scabious.

COMMON WASP

This is the yellow and black wasp which attacks fruit and picnic tables in autumn. The nests are built from wood pulp and are located in trees, hedges or buildings. Unlike bees they collect insects such as aphids, caterpillars or spiders to feed the young in the nest. Only the queen survives the winter, waking up in spring to found a new colony. Some wasp species are all-black. The giant wasp is the hornet. Frightening, but stings only when disturbed.

GARDEN SNAIL

The garden snail is the large one (3–4 cm across) which has a yellowish brown shell with dark brown bands. It hides during the day and eats a variety of plants at night. Other plant eaters include the strawberry snail and white-lipped snail, but some snails have a different diet – e.g the door snail eats lichen and mossy growth on paths, and the kentish slug chooses decayed vegetation.

7-SPOT LADYBIRD

A small beetle loved by gardeners for the enormous appetite of both the adult and black larva for aphids. It has red wing cases, black legs and usually (but not always) seven black spots on its back. In addition there are 2-spot, 10-spot and 22-spot ladybirds. Disturbingly the harlequin ladybird has arrived. It is much larger than the native species and eats other ladybirds as well as invading houses in large numbers.

GARDEN SPIDER

The cartwheel webs of the garden spider are a common sight, especially in autumn. The female is about 10 mm long – the male is smaller. The house spider is larger but rather similar, but does not have a white cross on its back. Some species such as the black-and-white zebra spider do not produce webs. The harvestman has a tiny body and long thin legs – it feeds at night. All are harmless.

GROUND BEETLE

This 2–5 cm long blue-black beetle is very common everywhere. It hides during the day and feeds on insects at night. There will be many other types of beetles in your garden – there are more than 4000 species in Britain. There are the broad-backed chafers on your Roses, fearsome-looking stag beetles on rotting wood, long-nosed weevils on various plants, and the devil's coach-horse with its upturned tail. The ladybird is everybody's favourite beetle.

GARDEN ANT

This is the familiar small black ant which nests in walls and paving, and occasionally comes indoors. The 5 mm long wingless workers are the ones you usually see. The winged male and female ants emerge from the nest in summer to mate – the males die after mating, the females seek nesting sites. This ant does not sting, but the red one does. Both types are attracted by sugary substances and they farm aphids which they 'milk' for their honeydew. Wood ants move in long lines.

EARTHWORM

It was Darwin who first revealed the vital role played by this lowly creature in producing crumbly soil. Fallen leaves are dragged down, aeration channels are created. This reddish-brown 10–30 cm long worm has an orange saddle. A sq metre of fertile soil contains more than a hundred, and they will share the garden with other types – the brandling in the compost heap, the cockspur in leaf mould. The turgid worm in the lawn forms casts, and is not an efficient aerator.

Looking at MAMMALS

In a rural area 25–35 different species may be temporary or permanent residents in a large garden – in a small plot in the middle of town there will be just a handful. However, a survey by the RHS/Wildlife Trusts revealed that Britain's favourite garden creature was the hedgehog, and this small mammal is to be found in both large and small gardens.

Some (e.g squirrel and muntjac) can harm our plants, and at the other end of the scale the hedgehog helps by eating insect pests, but most have no effect on our shrubs and flowers. But there is one mammal which does affect the wildlife around our house and may not appear in the garden wildlife textbooks – the common cat. Domestic cats which live in our homes, and feral cats which live in the wild kill about two hundred million birds and other small creatures every year. Always site bird tables away from areas where cats can hide, and place nest boxes out of their reach.

GREY SQUIRREL

Since its introduction from N. America this species has spread rapidly while the native red squirrel has disappeared from most English counties. Eats nuts, bulbs and (unfortunately) bark stripped from trees. Does not hibernate.

WOOD MOUSE

The wood mouse is the basic garden mouse. It lives in underground burrows beneath hedges and buildings. It feeds at night – when disturbed it can jump 1 m in the air. It eats insects, fruit, bulbs and root vegetables.

PIPISTRELLE

The bat you are most likely to see flitting about outside the house at dusk is the pipistrelle. Tiny (3–4 cm long), dark brown above and paler below. You may also see the long-eared bat which is larger and has extremely long ears.

MAMMAL TRACKS

Most mammals feed at night so you might not see them, but you will find their tracks in snow or mud. These impressions are not to scale.

Hedgehog

Wood mouse

Dog

Muntjac

Squirrel

Rabbit

Cat

Fox

Badger

HEDGEHOG

Cars, bonfires, foxes and mowers have put them on the endangered species list. They feed mainly at night – provide tinned pet food and water, not bread and milk. An active little animal – it can swim, climb, burrow underground and walk a mile or two during the night. It hibernates between October and April.

MOLE

Small (15 cm), black and velvety – this underground mammal prefers large gardens, where it can ruin a lawn with its hills. Turf with a high worm population is preferred whereas poor, acid soil is rarely invaded. They are solitary animals – a single mole is usually responsible for the molehills in your garden.

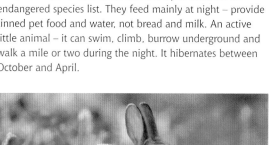

RABBIT

Rabbits scampering over the lawn may be fun to watch but they can wreak havoc in all areas of the garden. Colours range from grey to fawn and occasionally black. They live in large colonies in underground warrens. Under large trees and in grassy banks are the favourite sites. An active dog is the best deterrent.

MUNTJAC

This small deer (50 cm high, 100 cm long) was introduced from China in the 20th century – now a regular visitor to large gardens in rural areas. Shrubs and trees may have to be protected, but they bring a countryside feel to the garden. Roe deer are taller and more graceful, have a black nose and do not bark.

BADGER

Badgers rarely live in average-sized gardens – they are much more likely to pass through your garden at night when they leave their setts to search for food. They are quite unmistakable – large (70–80 cm long), grey fur, black-striped white face. Its varied diet consists of small animals, worms, bulbs, carrion etc.

RED FOX

Foxes feed mainly at night. The rural fox chooses worms, rabbits, mice, birds, carrion etc – the urban fox lives mainly on domestic refuse. Length is usually about 75 cm – colours range from pale fawn to dark reddish brown. Family lives in an underground earth – cubs disperse in autumn.

Looking at AMPHIBIANS & REPTILES

The life cycle of garden amphibians involves both land and water. They develop from eggs to tadpoles and then to young adults in pools and ponds. The adults move to dry land which may be some distance from their birthplace, and with the approach of winter they hibernate in compost heaps, under logs or in mud on the pond bottom. In Britain there are three types of these cold-blooded animals – the frog, toad and newt.

The grass snake and the slow-worm are the only reptiles which are widespread in Britain, although you may occasionally find a common lizard or adder. Unlike amphibians, reptiles bear scales. They do not need water in their life cycle – their prime requirements are a spot where they can bask in the morning sunshine, a cool place to shelter on hot days and a warm spot where they can hibernate in winter.

SLOW-WORM

This snake-like creature is really a tailless lizard. The male has a uniform greyish-brown colour – the female has a line along her back. They reach 30–50 cm and may look frightening, but these reptiles are quite harmless – their diet consists of slugs, worms, grubs etc. Unlike the grass snake the young develop inside the female. The compost heap is their favourite haunt, so try not to harm them when removing material.

COMMON NEWT

Mating takes place in ponds – the eggs are laid singly on the leaves of water plants. During the breeding season the male develops a wavy crest along its back – the underside is yellow with black spots. Its diet of slugs, caterpillars etc also includes the tadpoles of frogs and toads. The mature adult is 8–10 cm long – the great crested newt is larger and showier, but is much less common.

GRASS SNAKE

A true snake which can grow up to 150 cm. An unusual fact is that the females are longer than the males. The colour is greenish-brown with dark stripes on the sides – not to be confused with the zig-zag pattern of the adder. The distinctive feature is the pale collar round its neck. Harmless – it eats mice, frogs, small birds etc. Eggs are laid in summer.

FROG or TOAD?

COMMON FROG

8 cm long. Various skin colours, marbled black or brown

- Smooth, moist skin, angular body
- Dark marking behind the eye
- Moves in a series of leaps, up to 50 cm in length
- Tadpoles have a pointed tip, long and powerful hind legs

- Warty, dry skin, squat, rounded body
- No dark marking behind the eye
- Moves with a clumsy, ambling gait. Hops are very feeble
- Tadpoles have a rounded tip, hind legs shorter and less powerful

COMMON TOAD

10 cm long. Skin colour brown, olive or grey

In early spring frogs and toads move to ponds where mating takes place. In May–June tadpoles emerge from the spawn. In July the tiny frogs and toads move on to the land – in October they hibernate.

Chapter 8

CARING FOR THE ENVIRONMENT

What you do on your own plot can have no measurable effect on the general environment, but the effect of gardening on a national scale certainly does. Gardens cover about 3 per cent of the country, and their role in helping to preserve wildlife is becoming increasingly important. With the changes in the way we use our landscape the garden pond has become one of the main habitats for amphibians such as frogs and toads. Intensive farming with the removal of hedges has resulted in some birds such as the song thrush and blackbird increasingly turning to garden shrubs and trees for nesting sites.

However, we should be doing more. According to Graham Madge of the Royal Society for the Protection of Birds 'Wildlife is ebbing away … it's up to everyone who owns land to make a difference. The problem is that for so many years the UK landscape has been under such pressure. Look at our rivers and how our hedgerows are being pulled up, and our gardens are now so manicured.'

The final point in this statement means that we should be introducing wildlife-promoting features such as areas of unmown grass, log piles, bird tables and other projects outlined on pages 109–114. We can make a difference. Thirty years ago the goldfinch was a rarity in our gardens – now it is found in more than 80 per cent of them. The reason is that many more people are providing food for birds and are offering a wide range of seed etc rather than just the household scraps of former years.

There is an atmospheric role to play as well as a wildlife one. If you feel that driving your car and your aeroplane trip to Spain are adding to the climate change problem then compensate for the effect by planting more shrubs, trees and hedges. Do not get involved with any design fads which replace living plants with wood or stone.

Finally we should not forget the impact we can have on the local environment – the living space of our neighbours. We can spoil this environment with both smoke and noise, and these nuisances are dealt with in this chapter.

YOU and the WORLD

GREEN CORRIDOR

Much has been written about the world-wide Green Corridor concept – the creation of green zones across urban areas. These schemes involve tree planting, cycleways, noise screens and so on for the benefit of residents, but often offer little benefit to the wildlife of the nation.

We must look to gardens to provide a national green corridor for our wildlife. Gardens vary widely in style and planting, which means that the wildlife population of each one differs from its neighbours. We should do as much as we can to increase the number and variety of creatures which visit us by providing both food and shelter. In this way gardens create a network of green corridors through the ever-expanding urban areas and the ever-decreasing areas of animal-friendly countryside. Regard your garden as a staging post on the national green corridor by providing nest sites, food, water, log piles, areas of rough grass, compost heaps and a wide range of trees and shrubs.

PRESERVING HARDWOOD

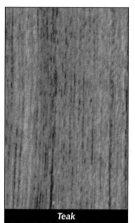

Teak

Iroko

Much of the garden furniture sold today is made of plastic or metal – hard-wearing, easy to maintain and often inexpensive. But for some there is nothing to take the place of hardwood benches, chairs and tables. Teak has long been the favourite type – it is resistant to water, rot and fire. But it is costly, and cheaper items of furniture are made from W. African Iroko or red-coloured Meranti from Malaysia.

It is sometimes stated that it is environmentally damaging to buy furniture made from tropical hardwood. Equatorial forests are being felled for this purpose, and this loss of leaf cover may be a factor in global warming. Felling of wild forests is indeed taking place on a large scale in Brazil, but this is for land clearance rather than for commercial timber – it would go on if the wood was sold or not. Less than one tenth of the tropical hardwood used by manufacturers in Britain comes from Brazil – much more comes from China and the Far East.

Wherever it has been sourced, it is crucial to try to ensure the wood we buy comes from managed forests. In this way we can actually help the environment. If hardwoods were no longer bought then the managed forests would be of no value. The sites would then be cleared and planted with cash-yielding but environmentally-useless crops.

PRESERVING PEAT

Sphagnum Peat

Sedge Peat

There is concern these days that the peat resources of the world are being steadily depleted. Sedge peat is the dark and rather heavy type dug from English heaths and moors. It is made up of the remains of sedges, rushes and heather, and removal has scarred the landscape and cannot be justified.

Spagnum (or moss) peat is quite different. Vast deposits occur in Iceland, Canada, Norway, Finland and Russia. It consists of the undecayed remains of sphagnum moss – the spongy material is light, more acidic and much more absorbent than sedge peat. Here the situation is more complex. Like sedge peat it has been regarded as a non-renewable biomass which should not be harvested for horticultural use. However, the Intergovernmental Panel on Climate Change, a UN advisory body, has reclassified sphagnum peat from a 'fossil fuel' to a 'renewable biomass' resource.

Harvesting these out-of-the-way deposits and transporting them long distances involves a carbon emission problem, so the recommendations remain unaltered. Don't use peat for overall soil improvement – it is not efficient, and garden compost or manure will do a much better job. The non-orthodox green gardener may use it in composts and planting mixtures where there are no substitutes of equal merit.

YOU and your NEIGHBOURS

SMOKE

Bonfires are distinctly non-green. Neighbours are annoyed and valuable organic matter is often needlessly destroyed. Compost or dump rubbish whenever you can rather than burn it. The problem is that bonfires are more dangerous than you realise. Of course there is a risk of a fire getting out of control, and breathing smoke is obviously unpleasant for people with asthma or bronchitis.

But there are hidden dangers. Burning foam, old cushions or ceiling tiles can release lethal vapours, and burning green material releases smoke which contains 350 times more cancer-causing chemical than cigarette smoke. Burning preserved timber may release dioxins.

If you *must* have a bonfire then follow the rules. Site it well away from buildings, trees, fences etc and choose a still day. If possible use an incinerator. Never use paraffin or petrol to start the fire or to liven up a dying one. Burn dry material so that there are flames rather than smoke. Keep a bucket of water close by – keep children and pets far away. Never leave a fire unattended and avoid breathing in the smoke.

It is an offence (maximum fine £5,000) to allow dense smoke to drift across a road. Recurrent bonfires which cause a nuisance to neighbours can lead to legal action by the council – maximum fine £5,000.

OVER THE FENCE

Millions of Americans and Scandinavians live quite happily without fences, but in Britain we feel that the fence, wall or hedge around our property is sacred – any trespass across it spoils our environment. Overhanging trees should not be a problem – you can cut down growth on your side, but it is sometimes wise to discuss your proposed action with your neighbour. Ask your council for help if oversized boundary hedges or trees are causing light problems.

Your neighbour may share your concern for wildlife and is therefore quite happy for you to have a patch of rough grassland and its weed population next to his fence. But if he or she has one of the manicured gardens so criticised by environmentalists, it is wise to site your wilder areas well away from the fence.

NOISE

A householder who enjoys a regular Sunday afternoon nap and a neighbour who always chooses that time to cut the lawn with his motor mower are set on a collision course. Disputes over noise are all too frequent and lead to a great deal of ill-will – avoid trouble if you can. Discuss mowing times if this has become a problem – tell your neighbour if you are going to create a temporary disturbance such as using a noisy power tool or erecting a fence.

You may be the one who suffers noise disturbance from your neighbour. If this is excessive and occurs regularly you can complain to the council. If they think that your complaint is reasonable (persistent loud music, all-night dog barking etc) they may suggest Mediation UK or may take legal action. If the action is successful an abatement notice is served. The fine for non-compliance is £5,000.

Even if the world were
to end tomorrow
I would still
plant an
apple
tree
today

Martin Luther

ACKNOWLEDGEMENTS

The author wishes to acknowledge the painstaking work of Gill Jackson and Susanna Wadeson.

Grateful acknowledgement is also made for the help received from Barry Highland and Ian Harris (Spot On Digital Imaging Ltd), Roger Vincent (RoSPA), Robert Updegraff, Sheila Lee, Manpreet Grewal, Gareth Pottle and Eliza Walsh.

The author is also grateful for the photographs or artworks received from John Stratford (Gardman Ltd), Garden World Images, Garden Picture Library, David Guthrie (Bluebridge Farm Studio) and Christine Wilson.

Additional photographs: 3 top left: Alamy, top right © A. Green/zefa/Corbis, bottom left Getty Images/Sozaijiten, bottom right Alamy; 6 Getty Images; 7 (top) © Nik Keevil; (bottom) Geoff Kidd/Science Photo Library; 20 Photostock, Deiter Heinemann/Alamy; 51 Getty Images/Photolibrary RM; 106 Picture Partners/Alamy; 107: Sue Tranter (rspb-images.com) (woodpecker); 112: William Leaman/Alamy (Monarch butterfly); 113 Chris A Crumley / Alamy (bee); 116:Nature Photographers Ltd /Alamy (greenfinch); Philip Mugridge / Alamy (green woodpecker); Sean Bolton / Alamy (collared dove); Juniors Bildarchiv / Alamy (house sparrow); 117: Arco Images / Alamy (pied wagtail); David Cole / Alamy (wood pigeon): David Tipling / Alamy (jackdaw); Martin Harvey / Alamy (Madagascar magpie); Daniel Dempster Photography / Alamy (wren); imagebroker / Alamy (starling); 120: Chris Gomersall / Alamy (bumble bee): David J. Slater / Alamy (honey bee); Juniors Bildarchiv / Alamy (wasp); Pat Bennett / Alamy (damselfly); 121:WildPictures / Alamy(ladybird); David Boag / Alamy (beetle): Papilio / Alamy (ants); David Chapman / Alamy (earthworm); Juniors Bildarchiv / Alamy (spider); Nic Hamilton / Alamy (snail); 122: David Cole / Alamy (pipistrelle); Pat Bennett / Alamy (grey squirrel); imagebroker / Alamy (wood mouse); 123: Hugh Lansdown / Alamy (muntjac); David Chapman / Alamy (mole); Pat Bennett / Alamy (fox); ImageState / Alamy (hedgehog); Mike Lane / Alamy (badger); David Norton / Alamy (rabbit); 124: John Cancalosi / Alamy (slow worm); © DK Limited/Corbis (newt); © Tony Hamblin; Frank Lane Picture Agency/CORBIS (grass snake); 128: archivberlin Fotoagentur GmbH / Alamy (apple tree).